Helmut Graupner, JD
Phillip Tahmindjis, JS
Editors

Sexuality and Human Rights: A Global Overview

Sexuality and Human Rights: A Global Overview has been co-published simultaneously as *Journal of Homosexuality*, Volume 48, Numbers 3/4 2005.

Pre-publication REVIEWS, COMMENTARIES, EVALUATIONS . . .

"An important resource for anybody concerned about the status of legal protection for the human rights of sexual minorities, especially for those concerned with attaining a comparative perspective. The chapters are all of high quality and are written in a straightforward manner that will be accessible to the non-specialist while containing much detail of interest to specialists in the area."

Arthur S. Leonard, JD
Professor of Law
New York Law School

More pre-publication
REVIEWS, COMMENTARIES, EVALUATIONS . . .

"THIS BOOK LAYS A MOST VALUABLE GROUNDWORK not only for the legal and political professions but also for the minorities concerned. . . . Covers the organizational background of bottom-up GLBT human rights activities, the development and contradictions of human rights declarations, and national legislation and judicial practice in different hemispheres of the world."

Lorenz Boellinger, Dr. Jur
*Professor of Criminal Law
and Criminology
University of Bremen Law School
Germany*

Harrington Park Press

Sexuality and Human Rights: A Global Overview

Sexuality and Human Rights: A Global Overview has been co-published simultaneously as *Journal of Homosexuality*, Volume 48, Numbers 3/4 2005.

The *Journal of Homosexuality* Monographic "Separates"

Below is a list of "separates," which in serials librarianship means a special issue simultaneously published as a special journal issue or double-issue *and* as a "separate" hardbound monograph. (This is a format which we also call a "DocuSerial.")

"Separates" are published because specialized libraries or professionals may wish to purchase a specific thematic issue by itself in a format which can be separately cataloged and shelved, as opposed to purchasing the journal on an on-going basis. Faculty members may also more easily consider a "separate" for classroom adoption.

"Separates" are carefully classified separately with the major book jobbers so that the journal tie-in can be noted on new book order slips to avoid duplicate purchasing.

You may wish to visit Haworth's website at . . .

http://www.HaworthPress.com

. . . to search our online catalog for complete tables of contents of these separates and related publications.

You may also call 1-800-HAWORTH (outside US/Canada: 607-722-5857), or Fax 1-800-895-0582 (outside US/Canada: 607-771-0012), or e-mail at:

docdelivery@haworthpress.com

Sexuality and Human Rights: A Global Overview, edited by Helmut Graupner and Phillip Tahmindjis (Vol. 48, No. 3/4, 2005). *"An important resource for anybody concerned about the status of legal protection for the human rights of sexual minorities, especially for those concerned with attaining a comparative perspective. The chapters are all of high quality and are written in a straightforward manner that will be accessible to the non-specialist while containing much detail of interest to specialists in the area." (Arthur S. Leonard, JD, Professor of Law, New York Law School)*

Eclectic Views on Gay Male Pornography: Pornucopia, edited by Todd G. Morrison, PhD (Vol. 47, No. 3/4, 2004). "An instant classic. . . . Lively and readable." *(Jerry Zientara, EdD, Librarian, Institute for Advanced Study of Human Sexuality)*

The Drag Queen Anthology: The Absolutely Fabulous but Flawlessly Customary World of Female Impersonators, edited by Steven P. Schacht, PhD, with Lisa Underwood (Vol. 46, No. 3/4, 2004). *"Indispensable. . . . For more than a decade, Steven P. Schacht has been one of the social sciences' most reliable guides to the world of drag queens and female impersonators. . . . This book assembles an impressive cast of scholars who are as theoretically astute, methodologically careful, and conceptually playful as the drag queens themselves." (Michael Kimmel, author of* The Gendered Society; *Professor of Sociology, SUNY Stony Brook)*

Queer Theory and Communication: From Disciplining Queers to Queering the Discipline(s), edited by Gust A. Yep, PhD, Karen E. Lovaas, PhD, and John P. Elia, PhD (Vol. 45, Nov. 2/3/4, 2003). *"Sheds light on how sexual orientation and identity are socially produced–and how they can be challenged and changed–through everyday practices and institutional activities, as well as academic research and teaching. . . . Illuminates the theoretical and practical significance of queer theory–not only as a specific area of inquiry, but also as a productive challenge to the heteronormativity of mainstream communication theory, research, and pedagogy." (Julia T. Wood, PhD, Lineberger Professor of Humanities, Professor of Communication Studies, The University of North Carolina at Chapel Hill)*

Gay Bathhouses and Public Health Policy, edited by William J. Woods, PhD, and Diane Binson, PhD (Vol. 44, No. 3/4, 2003). *"Important. . . . Long overdue. . . . A unique and valuable contribution to the social science and public health literature. The inclusion of detailed historical descriptions of public policy debates about the place of bathhouses in urban gay communities, together with summaries of the legal controversies about bathhouses, insightful examinations of patrons' behaviors and reviews of successful programs for HIV/STD education and testing programs in bathhouses provides. A well rounded and informative overview." (Richard Tewksbury, PhD, Professor of Justice Administration, University of Louisville)*

Icelandic Lives: The Queer Experience, edited by Voon Chin Phua (Vol. 44, No. 2, 2002). *"The first of its kind, this book shows the emergence of gay and lesbian visibility through the biographical narratives of a dozen Icelanders. Through their lives can be seen a small nation's transition, in just a few decades, from a pervasive silence concealing its queer citizens to widespread acknowledgment char-*

acterized by some of the most progressive laws in the world." (Barry D. Adam, PhD, University Professor, Department of Sociology & Anthropology, University of Windsor, Ontario, Canada)

The Drag King Anthology, edited by Donna Jean Troka, PhD (cand.), Kathleen LeBesco, PhD, and Jean Bobby Noble, PhD (Vol. 43, No. 3/4, 2002). *"All university courses on masculinity should use this book . . . challenges preconceptions through the empirical richness of direct experience. The contributors and editors have worked together to produce cultural analysis that enhances our perception of the dynamic uncertainty of gendered experience."* (Sally R. Munt, DPhil, Subject Chair, Media Studies, University of Sussex)

Homosexuality in French History and Culture, edited by Jeffrey Merrick and Michael Sibalis (Vol. 41, No. 3/4, 2001). *"Fascinating. . . . Merrick and Sibalis bring together historians, literary scholars, and political activists from both sides of the Atlantic to examine same-sex sexuality in the past and present."* (Bryant T. Ragan, PhD, Associate Professor of History, Fordham University, New York City)

Gay and Lesbian Asia: Culture, Identity, Community, edited by Gerard Sullivan, PhD, and Peter A. Jackson, PhD (Vol. 40, No. 3/4, 2001). *"Superb. . . . Covers a happily wide range of styles . . . will appeal to both students and educated fans."* (Gary Morris, Editor/Publisher, Bright Lights Film Journal)

Queer Asian Cinema: Shadows in the Shade, edited by Andrew Grossman, MA (Vol. 39, No. 3/4, 2000). *"An extremely rich tapestry of detailed ethnographies and state-of-the-art theorizing. . . . Not only is this a landmark record of queer Asia, but it will certainly also be a seminal, contributive challenge to gender and sexuality studies in general."* (Dédé Oetomo, PhD, Coordinator of the Indonesian organization GAYa NUSANTARA; Adjunct Reader in Linguistics and Anthropology, School of Social Sciences, Universitas Airlangga, Surabaya, Indonesia)

Gay Community Survival in the New Millennium, edited by Michael R. Botnick, PhD (cand.) (Vol. 38, No. 4, 2000). *Examines the notion of community from several different perspectives focusing on the imagined, the structural, and the emotive. You will explore a theoretical overview and you will peek into the moral discourses that frame "gay community," the rift between HIV-positive and HIV-negative gay men, and how Israeli gays seek their place in the public sphere.*

The Ideal Gay Man: The Story of Der Kreis, by Hubert Kennedy, PhD (Vol. 38, No. 1/2, 1999). *"Very profound. . . . Excellent insight into the problems of the early fight for homosexual emancipation in Europe and in the USA. . . . The ideal gay man (high-mindedness, purity, cleanness), as he was imagined by the editor of 'Der Kreis,' is delineated by the fascinating quotations out of the published erotic stories."* (Wolfgang Breidert, PhD, Academic Director, Institute of Philosophy, University Karlsruhe, Germany)

Multicultural Queer: Australian Narratives, edited by Peter A. Jackson, PhD, and Gerard Sullivan, PhD (Vol. 36, No. 3/4, 1999). *Shares the way that people from ethnic minorities in Australia (those who are not of Anglo-Celtic background) view homosexuality, their experiences as homosexual men and women, and their feelings about the lesbian and gay community.*

Scandinavian Homosexualities: Essays on Gay and Lesbian Studies, edited by Jan Löfström, PhD (Vol. 35, No. 3/4, 1998). *"Everybody interested in the formation of lesbian and gay identities and their interaction with the sociopolitical can find something to suit their taste in this volume."* (Judith Schuyf, PhD, Assistant Professor of Lesbian and Gay Studies, Center for Gay and Lesbian Studies, Utrecht University, The Netherlands)

Gay and Lesbian Literature Since World War II: History and Memory, edited by Sonya L. Jones, PhD (Vol. 34, No. 3/4, 1998). *"The authors of these essays manage to gracefully incorporate the latest insights of feminist, postmodernist, and queer theory into solidly grounded readings . . . challenging and moving, informed by the passion that prompts both readers and critics into deeper inquiry."* (Diane Griffin Growder, PhD, Professor of French and Women's Studies, Cornell College, Mt. Vernon, Iowa)

Reclaiming the Sacred: The Bible in Gay and Lesbian Culture, edited by Raymond-Jean Frontain, PhD (Vol. 33, No. 3/4, 1997). *"Finely wrought, sharply focused, daring, and always dignified. . . . In chapter after chapter, the Bible is shown to be a more sympathetic and humane book in its attitudes toward homosexuality than usually thought and a challenge equally to the straight and gay moral imagination."* (Joseph Wittreich, PhD, Distinguished Professor of English, The Graduate School, The City University of New York)

Activism and Marginalization in the AIDS Crisis, edited by Michael A. Hallett, PhD (Vol. 32, No. 3/4, 1997). *Shows readers how the advent of HIV-disease has brought into question the utility of certain forms of "activism" as they relate to understanding and fighting the social impacts of disease.*

Gays, Lesbians, and Consumer Behavior: Theory, Practice, and Research Issues in Marketing, edited by Daniel L. Wardlow, PhD (Vol. 31, No. 1/2, 1996). *"For those scholars, market researchers, and marketing managers who are considering marketing to the gay and lesbian community, this book should be on their required reading list."* (Mississippi Voice)

Gay Men and the Sexual History of the Political Left, edited by Gert Hekma, PhD, Harry Oosterhuis, PhD, and James Steakley, PhD (Vol. 29, No. 2/3/4, 1995). *"Contributors delve into the contours of a long-forgotten history, bringing to light new historical data and fresh insight.... An excellent account of the tense historical relationship between the political left and gay liberation." (People's Voice)*

Sex, Cells, and Same-Sex Desire: The Biology of Sexual Preference, edited by John P. De Cecco, PhD, and David Allen Parker, MA (Vol. 28, No. 1/2/3/4, 1995). *"A stellar compilation of chapters examining the most important evidence underlying theories on the biological basis of human sexual orientation." (MGW)*

Gay Ethics: Controversies in Outing, Civil Rights, and Sexual Science, edited by Timothy F. Murphy, PhD (Vol. 27, No. 3/4, 1994). *"The contributors bring the traditional tools of ethics and political philosophy to bear in a clear and forceful way on issues surrounding the rights of homosexuals." (David L. Hull, Dressler Professor in the Humanities, Department of Philosophy, Northwestern University)*

Gay and Lesbian Studies in Art History, edited by Whitney Davis, PhD (Vol. 27, No. 1/2, 1994). *"Informed, challenging ... never dull.... Contributors take risks and, within the restrictions of scholarly publishing, find new ways to use materials already available or examine topics never previously explored." (Lambda Book Report)*

Critical Essays: Gay and Lesbian Writers of Color, edited by Emmanuel S. Nelson, PhD (Vol. 26, No. 2/3, 1993). *"A much-needed book, sparkling with stirring perceptions and resonating with depth.... The anthology not only breaks new ground, it also attempts to heal wounds inflicted by our oppressed pasts." (Lambda)*

Gay Studies from the French Cultures: Voices from France, Belgium, Brazil, Canada, and The Netherlands, edited by Rommel Mendès-Leite, PhD, and Pierre-Olivier de Busscher, PhD (Vol. 25, No. 1/2/3, 1993). *"The first book that allows an English-speaking world to have a comprehensive look at the principal trends in gay studies in France and French-speaking countries." (André Bèjin, PhD, Directeur, de Recherche au Centre National de la Recherche Scientifique [CNRS], Paris)*

If You Seduce a Straight Person, Can You Make Them Gay? Issues in Biological Essentialism versus Social Constructionism in Gay and Lesbian Identities, edited by John P. De Cecco, PhD, and John P. Elia, PhD (cand.) (Vol. 24, No. 3/4, 1993). *"You'll find this alternative view of the age old question to be one that will become the subject of many conversations to come. Thought-provoking to say the least!" (Prime Timers)*

Gay and Lesbian Studies: The Emergence of a Discipline, edited by Henry L. Minton, PhD (Vol. 24, No. 1/2, 1993). *"The volume's essays provide insight into the field's remarkable accomplishments and future goals." (Lambda Book Report)*

Homosexuality in Renaissance and Enlightenment England: Literary Representations in Historical Context, edited by Claude J. Summers, PhD (Vol. 23, No. 1/2, 1992). *"It is remarkable among studies in this field in its depth of scholarship and variety of approaches and is accessible." (Chronique)*

Coming Out of the Classroom Closet: Gay and Lesbian Students, Teachers, and Curricula, edited by Karen M. Harbeck, PhD, JD, Recipient of Lesbian and Gay Educators Award by the American Educational Research Association's Lesbian and Gay Studies Special Interest Group (AREA) (Vol. 22, No. 3/4, 1992). *"Presents recent research about gay and lesbian students and teachers and the school system in which they function." (Contemporary Psychology)*

Homosexuality and Male Bonding in Pre-Nazi Germany: The Youth Movement, the Gay Movement, and Male Bonding Before Hitler's Rise: Original Transcripts from Der Eigene, the First Gay Journal in the World, edited by Harry Oosterhuis, PhD, and Hubert Kennedy, PhD (Vol. 22, No. 1/2, 1992). *"Provide[s] insight into the early gay movement, particularly in its relation to the various political currents in pre-World War II Germany." (Lambda Book Report)*

Gay People, Sex, and the Media, edited by Michelle A. Wolf, PhD, and Alfred P. Kielwasser, MA (Vol. 21, No. 1/2, 1991). *"Altogether, the kind of research anthology which is useful to many disciplines in gay studies. Good stuff!" (Communique)*

Gay Midlife and Maturity: Crises, Opportunities, and Fulfillment, edited by John Alan Lee, PhD (Vol. 20, No. 3/4, 1991). *"The insight into gay aging is amazing, accurate, and much-needed.... A real contribution to the older gay community." (Prime Timers)*

Monographs "Separates" list continued at the back

Sexuality and Human Rights: A Global Overview

Helmut Graupner
Phillip Tahmindjis
Editors

Sexuality and Human Rights: A Global Overview has been co-published simultaneously as *Journal of Homosexuality*, Volume 48, Numbers 3/4 2005.

HPP

Harrington Park Press®
An Imprint of The Haworth Press, Inc.

New York • London • Victoria (AU)
www.HaworthPress.com

Published by

Harrington Park Press®, 10 Alice Street, Binghamton, NY 13904-1580 USA

Harrington Park Press® is an imprint of The Haworth Press, Inc., 10 Alice Street, Binghamton, NY 13904-1580 USA.

Sexuality and Human Rights: A Global Overview has been co-published simultaneously as *Journal of Homosexuality*, Volume 48, Numbers 3/4 2005.

© 2005 by The Haworth Press, Inc. All rights reserved. No part of this work may be reproduced or utilized in any form or by any means, electronic or mechanical, including photocopying, microfilm and recording, or by any information storage and retrieval system, without permission in writing from the publisher. Printed in the United States of America.

The development, preparation, and publication of this work has been undertaken with great care. However, the publisher, employees, editors, and agents of The Haworth Press and all imprints of The Haworth Press, Inc., including The Haworth Medical Press® and Pharmaceutical Products Press®, are not responsible for any errors contained herein or for consequences that may ensue from use of materials or information contained in this work. Opinions expressed by the author(s) are not necessarily those of The Haworth Press, Inc. With regard to case studies, identities and circumstances of individuals discussed herein have been changed to protect confidentiality. Any resemblance to actual persons, living or dead, is entirely coincidental.

Cover design by Jennifer M. Gaska

Library of Congress Cataloging-in-Publication Data

International Bar Association. Conference (2000 : Amsterdam, Netherlands)
    Sexuality and human rights : a global overview / Helmut Graupner, Phillip Tahmindjis, editors.
       p. cm.
    "Co-published simultaneously as Journal of homosexuality, volume 48, numbers 3/4 2005."
    "Updated versions of papers delivered to the biennial conference of the International Bar Association held in 2000 in Amsterdam"–Frwd.
    Includes bibliographical references and index.
    ISBN 1-56023-554-3 (hard cover : alk. paper)–ISBN 1-56023-555-1 (soft cover : alk. paper)
    1. Gay rights–Congresses. 2. Gays–Legal status, laws, etc.–Congresses. 3. Homosexuality–Law and legislation–Congresses. 4. Sex and law–Congresses. 5. Human rights–Congresses. I. Graupner, Helmut, 1965- II. Tahmindjis, Phillip. III. Journal of homosexuality. IV. Title.
HQ76.5.I57 2000
306.76'6–dc22
                                                                                 2004022790

Indexing, Abstracting & Website/Internet Coverage

Journal of Homosexuality

This section provides you with a list of major indexing & abstracting services and other tools for bibliographic access. That is to say, each service began covering this periodical during the year noted in the right column. Most Websites which are listed below have indicated that they will either post, disseminate, compile, archive, cite or alert their own Website users with research-based content from this work. (This list is as current as the copyright date of this publication.)

Abstracting, Website/Indexing Coverage . . . . Year When Coverage Began

- *Abstracts in Anthropology* 1982
- *Academic Abstracts/CD-ROM* 1989
- *Academic ASAP <http://www.galegroup.com>* 2000
- *Academic Search: database of 2,000 selected academic serials, updated monthly: EBSCO Publishing* 1995
- *Applied Social Sciences Index & Abstracts (ASSIA) (Online: ASSI via Data-Star) (CD-Rom: ASSIA Plus) <http://www.csa.com>* 1987
- *ATLA Religion Database. This periodical is indexed in ATLA Religion Database, published by the American Theological Library Association <http://www.atla.com>* 1983
- *ATLA Religion Database with ATLASerials. This periodical is indexed in ATLA Religion Database with ATLASerials, published by the American Theological Library Association <http://www.atla.com>* 1983
- *Book Review Index* 1996
- *Business Source Corporate: coverage of nearly 3,350 quality magazines and journals; designed to meet the diverse information needs of corporations; EBSCO Publishing <http://www.epnet.com/corporate/bsource.asp>* 1974

(continued)

- *Cambridge Scientific Abstracts is a leading publisher of scientific information in print journals, online databases, CD-ROM and via the Internet <http://www.csa.com>* 1993
- *Contemporary Women's Issues* 1998
- *Criminal Justice Abstracts* 1982
- *Current Contents/Social & Behavioral Sciences <http://www.isinet.com>* 1985
- *EBSCOhost Electronic Journals Service (EJS) <http://ejournals.ebsco.com>* 2001
- *EMBASE/Excerpta Medica Secondary Publishing Division. Included in newsletters, review journals, major reference works, magazines & abstract journals <http://www.elsevier.nl>* 1974
- *e-psyche, LLC <http://www.e-psyche.net>* 2001
- *Expanded Academic ASAP <http://www.galegroup.com>* 1989
- *Expanded Academic Index* 1992
- *Family & Society Studies Worldwide <http://www.nisc.com>* 1996
- *Family Index Database <http://www.familyscholar.com>* 2002
- *Family Violence & Sexual Assault Bulletin* 1992
- *GenderWatch <http://www.slinfo.com>* 1999
- *GLBT Life, EBSCO Publishing <http://www.epnet.com/academic/glbt.asp>* 2004
- *Google <http://www.google.com>* 2004
- *Google Scholar <http://www.scholar.google.com>* 2004
- *Haworth Document Delivery Center* 1974
- *Health & Psychosocial Instruments (HaPI) Database (available through online and as a CD-ROM from OVID Technologies)* 1986
- *Higher Education Abstracts, providing the latest in research and theory in more than 140 major topics* 1997
- *HOMODOK/"Relevant" Bibliographic Database, Documentation Centre for Gay & Lesbian Studies, University of Amsterdam (selective printed abstracts in "Homologie" and bibliographic computer databases covering cultural, historical, social & political aspects) <http://www.ihlia.nl/>* 1995

(continued)

- *IBZ International Bibliography of Periodical Literature*
  <http://www.saur.de> 1996
- *IGLSS Abstracts* <http://www.iglss.org>...................... 2000
- *Index Guide to College Journals (core list compiled by integrating 48 indexes frequently used to support undergraduate programs in small to medium sized libraries)* 1999
- *Index Medicus (National Library of Medicine) (print edition ceased ... see instead MEDLINE)* <http://www.nlm.nih.gov> 1992
- *Index to Periodical Articles Related to Law* <http://www.law.utexas.edu> 1986
- *InfoTrac Custom* <http://www.galegroup.com> 1996
- *InfoTrac OneFile* <http://www.galegroup.com> 1996
- *International Bibliography of the Social Sciences*
  <http://www.ibss.ac.uk> 2003
- *Internationale Bibliographie der geistes- und sozialwissenschaftlichen Zeitschriftenliteratur ... See IBZ* <http://www.saur.de> 1996
- *ISI Web of Science* <http://www.isinet.com> 2003
- *ITER–Gateway to the Middle Ages & Renaissance*
  <http://iter.utoronto.ca> 1974
- *LegalTrac on InfoTrac Web*
  <http://www.galegroup.com> 1990
- *Lesbian Information Service*
  <http://www.lesbianinformationservice.org> 1991
- *Magazines for Libraries (Katz) ... (see 2003 edition)* 2003
- *MasterFILE: Updated database from EBSCO Publishing* 1995
- *MEDLINE (National Library of Medicine)*
  <http://www.nlm.nih.gov> 1992
- *MLA International Bibliography provides a classified listing & subject index for books & articles published on modern languages, literatures, folklore, & linguistics. Available in print and in several electronic versions. Indexes over 50,000 publications* <http://www.mla.org> 1995
- *National Child Support Research Clearinghouse* <http://www.spea.indiana.edu/ncsea/> 1998
- *OCLC Public Affairs Information Service* <http://www.pais.org> ... 1982

(continued)

- *PASCAL, c/o Institut de L'Information Scientifique et Technique. Cross-disciplinary electronic database covering the fields of science, technology & medicine. Also available on CD-ROM, and can generate customized retrospective searches* <http://www.inist.fr> 1986
- *PlanetOut "Internet site for key Gay/Lesbian Information"* <http://www.planetout.com/> 1999
- *ProQuest 5000. Contents of this publication are indexed and abstracted in the ProQuest 5000 database (includes only abstracts ... not full-text), available on ProQuest Information & Learning* <http://www.proquest.com> 1974
- *Psychological Abstracts (PsycINFO)* <http://www.apa.org> 1995
- *Psychology Today* 1999
- *PubMed* <http://www.ncbi.nlm.nih.gov/pubmed/> 2003
- *RESEARCH ALERT/ISI Alerting Services* <http://www.isinet.com> 1985
- *Sage Family Studies Abstracts (SFSA)* 1986
- *Sexual Diversity Studies: Gay, Lesbian, Bisexual & Transgender Abstracts (formerly Gay & Lesbian Abstracts) provides comprehensive & in-depth coverage of the world's GLBT literature compiled by NISC & published on the Internet & CD-ROM* <http://www.nisc.com> 1999
- *Social Science Source: coverage of 400 journals in the social sciences area: updated monthly; EBSCO Publishing* 1995
- *Social Sciences Abstracts indexes & abstracts more than 460 publications, specifically selected by librarians & library patrons. Wilson's databases comprise the peer-reviewed & peer-selected core journals in each field* <http://www.hwwilson.com> 1999
- *Social Sciences Citation Index (ISI)* <http://www.isinet.com> 1985
- *Social Sciences Full Text (available only electronically)* <http://www.hwwilson.com> 1991
- *Social Sciences Index (from Volume 1 and continuing)* <http://www.hwwilson.com> 1991
- *Social Scisearch* <http://www.isinet.com> 1985
- *Social Services Abstracts* <http://www.csa.com> 1982
- *Social Work Abstracts* <http://www.silverplatter.com/catalog/swab.htm> 1994
- *Sociological Abstracts (SA)* <http://www.csa.com> 1982
- *Studies on Women and Gender Abstracts* <http://www.tandf.co.uk/swa> . 1987

(continued)

- *SwetsWise* <http://www.swets.com> 2001
- *Violence and Abuse Abstracts: A Review of Current Literature on Interpersonal Violence (VAA)* 1995
- *Wilson OmniFile Full Text: Mega Edition (available only electronically)* <http://www.hwwilson.com> 1987
- *zetoc* <http://zetoc.mimas.ac.uk> 2004

Special Bibliographic Notes related to special journal issues (separates) and indexing/abstracting:

- indexing/abstracting services in this list will also cover material in any "separate" that is co-published simultaneously with Haworth's special thematic journal issue or DocuSerial. Indexing/abstracting usually covers material at the article/chapter level.
- monographic co-editions are intended for either non-subscribers or libraries which intend to purchase a second copy for their circulating collections.
- monographic co-editions are reported to all jobbers/wholesalers/approval plans. The source journal is listed as the "series" to assist the prevention of duplicate purchasing in the same manner utilized for books-in-series.
- to facilitate user/access services all indexing/abstracting services are encouraged to utilize the co-indexing entry note indicated at the bottom of the first page of each article/chapter/contribution.
- this is intended to assist a library user of any reference tool (whether print, electronic, online, or CD-ROM) to locate the monographic version if the library has purchased this version but not a subscription to the source journal.
- individual articles/chapters in any Haworth publication are also available through the Haworth Document Delivery Service (HDDS).

∞ ALL HARRINGTON PARK PRESS BOOKS AND JOURNALS ARE PRINTED ON CERTIFIED ACID-FREE PAPER

ABOUT THE EDITORS

Helmut Graupner (www.graupner.at), Doctor in Law (University of Vienna), is *Rechtsanwalt* (attorney-at-law), admitted to the bar in Austria and in the Czech Republic. He is Vice President of the Austrian Society for Sex Research (ÖGS); President of the Austrian lesbian and gay rights organisation Rechtskomitee LAMBDA (RKL); Vice President for Europe, International Lesbian and Gay Law Association (ILGLaw); and Austrian member, European Group of Experts on Combating Sexual Orientation Discrimination working for the Commission of the European Union. He is also a member of the Scientific Committee of the Center for Research and Comparative Legal Studies on Sexual Orientation and Gender Identity (CERSGOSIG), Turin; a member of the Editorial Board of the *Journal of Homosexuality*; and a member of the World Association for Sexology (WAS). He has supplied repeated expertise to the Austrian Minister of Justice and to the Austrian Federal Parliament on issues of sexual offences and antidiscrimination legislation. In 2002 and 2004, he was a lecturer at the University of Innsbruck ("Sexuality and the Law"). In 2001, he received the Gay and Lesbian Award (G.A.L.A.) of the Austrian Lesbian and Gay Movement.

Phillip Tahmindjis, BA, LLB (Sydney), LLM (London), JSD (Dalhousie), is Program Lawyer, International Bar Association, London. Dr. Tahmindjis was for over 20 years an academic teaching in Australia, North America and Hong Kong, and was active in the struggle for gay law reform in his home state of Queensland. A consultant on discrimination and human rights to government agencies and private industry, he was also a member of the Queensland Anti-Discrimination Tribunal.

Sexuality and Human Rights: A Global Overview

CONTENTS

Foreword	xvii
International Lesbian and Gay Law Association *R. Douglas Elliott*	1

CERSGOSIG: Perspectives and Objectives
    to Challenge Discrimination. A Network on Global Scale
    Stefano Fabeni
	3

Sexuality and International Human Rights Law *Phillip Tahmindjis, BA, LLB, LLM, JSD*	9
Sexuality and Australian Law *The Hon. Justice Michael Kirby, AC, CMG*	31
Transsexuals and European Human Rights Law *The Hon. Lord Robert Reed*	49

Sexual Orientation and Gender Identity in North America:
    Legal Trends, Legal Contrasts
    R. Douglas Elliott
    Mary Bonauto
	91

Sexuality and Human Rights in Europe *Helmut Graupner, JD*	107

Advancing Human Rights Through Constitutional Protection
    for Gays and Lesbians in South Africa
    Ronald Louw, B Proc, BA(Hons), LLM
	141

Sexuality and Human Rights: An Asian Perspective *Erick Laurent, PhD*	163
Laws and Sexual Identities: Closing or Opening the Circle? *Phillip Tahmindjis, BA, LLB, LLM, JSD*	227
Index	233

Foreword

The essays in this special volume are, with one exception,[1] amended and updated versions of papers delivered to the biennial conference of the International Bar Association held in 2000 in Amsterdam. They were delivered at a session of the IBA's Human Rights Law Committee entitled: "Human Rights: Help or Hindrance." This session was significant for a number of reasons. It was the first time that the IBA, an organisation of over 16,000 individual lawyers and bar associations representing 2,000,000 lawyers around the world, had tackled the issue of the law and sexuality at its conference. It was also the occasion for the establishment of a new international organisation dedicated to this issue: the International Lesbian and Gay Law Association (ILGLaw). At the same time CERSGOSIG (Centro di Ricerca e di Studi Giuridici Comparati Sull'Orientamento Sessuale e l'Identita di Genere–the Centre for Research and Comparative Legal Studies on Sexual Orientation and Gender Identity) opened and expanded its searchable database on legal materials relating to sexuality and gender identity.

The times were also significant for GLBT communities: the Netherlands was on the cusp of introducing its historic same-sex marriage legislation. Since then, much has happened, with other countries following suit with legislation[2] or through court-mandated action.[3] But much still needs to be done. The essays in this volume analyse the situation in North America, South Africa, Australia, Europe and Asia, and indicate how the further necessary advances might be achieved.

The editors sincerely thank the authors for their efforts in writing and revising their papers and for giving us permission to publish them.

Dr. Helmut Graupner, Vienna
Dr. Phillip Tahmindjis, London

[Haworth co-indexing entry note]: "Foreword." Graupner, Helmut, and Phillip Tahmindjis. Co-published simultaneously in *Journal of Homosexuality* (Harrington Park Press, an imprint of The Haworth Press, Inc.) Vol. 48, No. 3/4, 2005, pp. xxiii-xxiv; and: *Sexuality and Human Rights: A Global Overview* (ed: Helmut Graupner, and Phillip Tahmindjis) Harrington Park Press, an imprint of The Haworth Press, Inc., 2005, pp. xvii-xviii. Single or multiple copies of this article are available for a fee from The Haworth Document Delivery Service [1-800-HAWORTH, 9:00 a.m. - 5:00 p.m. (EST). E-mail address: docdelivery@haworthpress.com].

http://www.haworthpress.com/web/JH
© 2005 by The Haworth Press, Inc. All rights reserved.

NOTES

1. The article by Erick Laurent.
2. Belgium
3. *Halpern & MCCT v Canada (A.G.)* [2003] O.J. No.2268 (C.A.)

International Lesbian and Gay Law Association

R. Douglas Elliott

ILGLaw

KEYWORDS. IGLAW, equality, homosexuality, LGBT, human rights, gay rights, sexual orientation, gender identity, international, organization, association, network, lawyer, conference, community, director, Canada, Toronto, Turin, London

During the historic conference held at King's College, London, in 1999,[1] a small group of lawyers from three different continents gathered at the Admiral Duncan. This popular pub had just recovered from of one of the most infamous hate crimes against the lesbian and gay community in modern times. It was emblematic of our community's spirit of courage and determination that this place of tragedy became the birthplace of of one of the newest organizations dedicated to the cause of equality for lesbian, gay, bisexual and transgendered people: the International Lesbian and Gay Law Association (ILGLaw).

From these humble beginnings, ILGLaw has grown and flourished. A further organizational meeting was held in 2000 in Amsterdam, and a Board of Directors began to take shape. That process was completed in Turin, Italy, in June of 2002. ILGLaw now enjoys a Board that is gender balanced and represents all of the regions of the world. It has also devel-

---

R. Douglas Elliott is President, International Lesbian and Gay Law Association (ILGLaw).

[Haworth co-indexing entry note]: "International Lesbian and Gay Law Association." Elliott, R. Douglas. Co-published simultaneously in *Journal of Homosexuality* (Harrington Park Press, an imprint of The Haworth Press, Inc.) Vol. 48, No. 3/4, 2005, pp. 1-2; and: *Sexuality and Human Rights: A Global Overview* (ed: Helmut Graupner, and Phillip Tahmindjis) Harrington Park Press, an imprint of The Haworth Press, Inc., 2005, pp. 1-2. Single or multiple copies of this article are available for a fee from The Haworth Document Delivery Service [1-800-HAWORTH, 9:00 a.m. - 5:00 p.m. (EST). E-mail address: docdelivery@haworthpress.com].

http://www.haworthpress.com/web/JH
© 2005 by The Haworth Press, Inc. All rights reserved.
Digital Object Identifier: 10.1300/J082v48n03_01

oped a Website to inform others about the association and its activities, which can be found at <www.ILGLaw.org>.

ILGLaw is committed to promoting equality for all, regardless of sexual orientation or gender identity. It does so by providing a network for persons working on these issues internationally, and through lobbying of governments and international bodies. ILGLaw is also supportive of the efforts of CERSGOSIG to develop an international databank of resources for those working on issues of equality for lesbian, gay, bisexual and transgendered persons.

ILGLaw is committed to continuing the excellent work that was begun at the first international conference in 1999. A second highly successful conference was held in conjunction with Informagay and CERSGOSIG[2] in Turin, Italy, in June of 2002.[3] Delegates from all over the world gathered to learn about the most recent developments, to offer mutual support and encouragement and to share strategies. Outstanding speakers from around the globe presented at the conference, including a distinguished panel of judges featuring Justice Edwin Cameron of South Africa and Justice Wilhelmina Thomassen of the European Court of Human Rights.

ILGLaw will be participating in many regional events over the coming years, including the Lavender Law Conference to be held in New York City in October of 2003. Plans are under way for the third triennial international conference, "Right to Life–Right to Sex–Right to Love," to be held in conjunction with the University of Toronto Faculty of Law in Toronto, Canada, in June of 2005.[4]

Membership in ILGLaw is open to both lawyers and non-lawyers alike who are committed to the association's objectives. For more information, please contact ILGLaw at <ilglaw@ilglaw.org>.

NOTES

1. Recognition of Same-Sex Partnerships: A Conference on National, European and International Law, Centre of European Law, School of Law, King's College, University of London (1-3 July 1999)

2. www.cersgosig.informagay.it

3. "Marriage, Partnerships and Parenting in the 21st Century–The current international situation and new perspectives for gay, lesbian, bisexual and transgendered people and their families–a comparative approach," Congress Center–Torino Incontra (5-8 June 2002)

4. Information at www.ILGLaw.org

CERSGOSIG:
Perspectives and Objectives to Challenge Discrimination.
A Network on Global Scale

Stefano Fabeni

CERSGOSIG

KEYWORDS. CERSGOSIG, legal information, legal research, comparative research, antidiscriminatory strategies, (comparative) studies on sexual orientation, (comparative) studies on gender identity, international networks, database

When I was a law student I found in a bookstore in Turin and bought a book, one of the first I entirely read in English, whose author is an important jounalist. At a certain point, the author was asking to himself what he could do in order to support equality. I made the same question

---

Stefano Fabeni is Director, Center of Research and Legal Comparative Studies on Sexual Orientation and Gender Identity (CERSGOSIG). For any information visit the CERSGOSIG Website at <www.cersgosig.informagay.it>; in order to receive the application form to join the CERSGOSIG network (which is open to lawyers who are experts in the field of interest of the data bank and support equality under the law for gay men, lesbians, bisexuals and transgendered people), please contact Mr. Fabeni at <cersgosig@informagay.it>.

[Haworth co-indexing entry note]: "CERSGOSIG: Perspectives and Objectives to Challenge Discrimination. A Network on Global Scale." Fabeni, Stefano. Co-published simultaneously in *Journal of Homosexuality* (Harrington Park Press, an imprint of The Haworth Press, Inc.) Vol. 48, No. 3/4, 2005, pp. 3-7; and: *Sexuality and Human Rights: A Global Overview* (ed: Helmut Graupner, and Phillip Tahmindjis) Harrington Park Press, an imprint of The Haworth Press, Inc., 2005, pp. 3-7. Single or multiple copies of this article are available for a fee from The Haworth Document Delivery Service [1-800-HAWORTH, 9:00 a.m. - 5:00 p.m. (EST). E-mail address: docdelivery@haworthpress.com].

http://www.haworthpress.com/web/JH
© 2005 by The Haworth Press, Inc. All rights reserved.
Digital Object Identifier: 10.1300/J082v48n03_02

to myself, and decided that, first of all, I could have begun my legal research on sexual orientation and the law by writing on this subject my graduation thesis. The research of material has not been so easy in a country like Italy, where legal research on this issue is extremely poor. I understood very soon that in countries where the legal debate is not developed, and the legislative reforms are weak or nonexistent, the circulation of legal information, the promotion of legal events and the exchange of experiences among experts on an international scale are central points for combating discrimination based on sexual orientation and gender identity, and promoting the legal recognition of same-sex couples. The poor attention by the lawyers has a relevant consequence, to some extent, on the lack of consideration by the lawmakers. And, of course, the legislative process always has a strong impact on the social level. I believed, therefore, that the promotion of the legal debate could have contributed not only to the improvement of the scientific debate, but also to social-political change. The circulation of information was, on this purpose, a central aspect of the whole "architecture."

Therefore, I begun to conceive a project having those aims. I contacted some of the most distinguished legal experts in Europe, proposing my ideas, and I found a lot of interest and availability.

The project was called CERSGOSIG, a very strange and not easily pronounceable (for any language in the world!) acronym standing for Center of Research and Legal Comparative Studies on Sexual Orientation and Gender Identity. I was the coordinator of the project (now the director and responsible of the permanent scientific committee).

The CERSGOSIG project was submitted by the local NGO InformaGay, approved and funded (until June 2002) by the Commission of the European Union and the local government of the Province of Turin. It originally had four objectives.

1. The creation of a legal archive, on paper and, in part, on electronic support, available in Turin and formed by legal literature, pieces of legislation, case law and other legally relevant material.
2. The setting up of a Website, whose purpose is the circulation of legal information. The CERSGOSIG Website not only contains general information, but gives hospitality to the world databank and has "spaces" for debates among legal experts and interested people, such as activists, representatives of the institutions, journalists.
3. The most important and innovative result of the CERSGOSIG project is represented without any doubt by the legal databank

containing bibliographical resources concerning sexual orientation, gender identity and the law. The databank is formed by five sections, devoted to the collection of specific material: legal literature (articles and books); international, national, local and administrative written law; case law and, more generally, decisions binding to the parties; decisions not binding to the parties, such as those issued by governative or independent enforcement bodies (ombudsman, agencies, commissions); other legally relevant material (such as models of contract, deontological codes, codes of conduct, opinion briefs).

The databank works as a global network: each legal expert who is a member of the network is authorized to enter data, which are elaborated according to uniform criteria, collected and filed by the central administrator into the databank. In this way, the resources of each one can be shared by means of a central instrument which is a global source of information. An important result of the "European phase" of the project has been, among others, the elaboration of a list of areas, subareas, topics which represent a uniform conventional classification code for all the entered data: the list has been formulated by the scientific committee, taking into account the legal issues concerning sexual orientation and gender identity, but also the different legal traditions and approaches in the various legal systems worldwide, at national or supranational level. Furthermore, the databank works as a sort of online and interactive archive since, whenever possible, the full text of the documents is available for download or for consultation on the Internet (by means of an hyperlink connection).

Even though the databank with its current 700 data is still far from being an exhaustive source and from working at full extent, it is clear that it represents right now one of the most important and innovative global legal instruments on sexual orientation and gender identity: by developing the network and promoting the participation of legal experts worldwide, it could easily and quite soon put at the disposal of its users thousands of data.

4. As I wrote above, the original project had four objectives; the fourth one, which was also particularly relevant in my original idea, was the creation of the Center itself, which could coordinate the various activities and, in particular, the databank, and manage the network of experts. I think, more than ever, that this is a central point.

The "European phase" of the CERSGOSIG, namely the CERSGOSIG project, came to its natural end in June 2002. Together with the International Lesbian and Gay Law Association (ILGLaw), the world legal conference "Marriage, partnership and parenting in the 21st century. The current international situation and new perspectives for gay, lesbian, bisexual and transgendered people and their families–a comparative approach" has been organised in Turin, Italy, on that occasion. About eighty legal experts, academicians, lawyers, judges coming from more than twenty countries of all the continents joined the four-day event which became, with its seventeen sessions, one of the major events on sexual orientation, gender identity and the law ever organized on global scale.

The important results of the project came to the attention of the Council of Europe and were presented in a joint press conference held in Strasbourg, France, with the President of the Parliamentary Assembly of the Council of Europe, Mr. Peter Schieder.

Also, the CERSGOSIG databank has become an official working instrument of the European Group of Experts on Combating Sexual Orientation Discrimination, an independent group of legal experts working for the European Commission, coordinated by Kees Waaldijk.[1]

Immediately after the conference it has been clear that the project had worked and it was the best moment to extend the network and, in particular, to make the databank an effective global resource, a tool, an interactive tool for legal experts supporting equality under the law for LGBT people. A permanent scientific committee was formed: Susanne Baer, Mark Bell, Daniel Borrillo, Eleonora Ceccherini, Nicola Coco, Douglas Elliott, Helmut Graupner, Andrea Loux, Yuval Merin, Paul Skidmore, Phillip Tahmindjis, Maria Gigliola Toniollo, Kees Waaldijk, Anne Weyembergh, Robert Wintemute, and Hans Ytterberg are the members, and I am honored to coordinate it.

I strongly believe that the committee needs to be enlarged in order to better represent all the areas of the world. Not only. An essential task is the enlargement of the network so that more and more legal experts will share their resources by means of the databank (and the other instruments the Website provides for its members). I think, once again, that this process must involve all the areas of the world, with different purposes.

On the one hand, it is extremely important to focus on those areas, in particular Western Europe, North America, Australia and New Zealand, South Africa and Israel, where the legal and political debate is developed, and the legislative, academic and judicial production provide a relevant contribution to the development of the legal theory and juridical and legislative models. At the same time, we must pay special attention to those areas where the human rights of sexual minorities are violated and equality is far from being granted. The circulation of models, ideas and experiences is a fundamental step in order to support the formation of legal conscience and strategies to combat discrimination under the law and within society.

The first result of the global promotion of the CERSGOSIG has been the enlargement of the network itself, which counts now more than sixty members, academicians, lawyers, judges, MPs, legal experts, from twenty countries of the world. In this context, we intend to develop projects at regional or international level, and, by means of our tools, cooperation with organizations. These are the new objectives of the CERSGOSIG network, a new perspective to challenge inequality under the law.

NOTE

1. http://www.meijers.leidenuniv.nl/index.php3?m=10&c=98

Sexuality and International Human Rights Law

Phillip Tahmindjis, BA, LLB, LLM, JSD

International Bar Association

SUMMARY. This essay considers the extent to which international human rights now protect, or might protect, GLBT communities. The counterpoint between the potential width of application of international human rights instruments and their silence on sexuality has become the *leitmotif* of sexuality and gender identity within the international human rights framework. In addition, there is a symbiotic relationship between the international norms and domestic legal systems which directly affects the meaning of those norms. Domestic laws are not only needed to implement international norms, but are essential in overcoming the equivocations and silences of international human rights law as it has traditionally applied to GLBT communities. A fusion of the interna-

---

Phillip Tahmindjis is Program Lawyer, International Bar Association, London. Dr. Tahmindjis was for over 20 years an academic teaching in Australia, North America and Hong Kong, and was active in the struggle for gay law reform in his home state of Queensland. A consultant on discrimination and human rights to government agencies and private industry, he was also a member of the Queensland Anti-Discrimination Tribunal. The views expressed in this paper are his own and do not necessarily represent the views of the International Bar Association. Correspondence may be addressed: International Bar Association, 10th Floor, 1 Stephen Street, London, W1T 1AT, United Kingdom (E-mail: Phillip. Tahmindjis@int-bar.org).

[Haworth co-indexing entry note]: "Sexuality and International Human Rights Law." Tahmindjis, Phillip. Co-published simultaneously in *Journal of Homosexuality* (Harrington Park Press, an imprint of The Haworth Press, Inc.) Vol. 48, No. 3/4, 2005, pp. 9-29; and: *Sexuality and Human Rights: A Global Overview* (ed: Helmut Graupner, and Phillip Tahmindjis) Harrington Park Press, an imprint of The Haworth Press, Inc., 2005, pp. 9-29. Single or multiple copies of this article are available for a fee from The Haworth Document Delivery Service [1-800-HAWORTH, 9:00 a.m. - 5:00 p.m. (EST). E-mail address: docdelivery@haworthpress.com].

http://www.haworthpress.com/web/JH
© 2005 by The Haworth Press, Inc. All rights reserved.
Digital Object Identifier: 10.1300/J082v48n03_03

tional norms with domestic legal systems through the principle of diversity, rather than the principle of equality, is needed. *[Article copies available for a fee from The Haworth Document Delivery Service: 1-800-HAWORTH. E-mail address: <docdelivery@haworthpress.com> Website: <http://www.HaworthPress.com> © 2005 by The Haworth Press, Inc. All rights reserved.]*

KEYWORDS. Human rights, international law, right to marriage, inherent rights, symbiotic relationships, principle of diversity, gay rights, lesbian rights, transgender rights

INTRODUCTION

International human rights norms are, in general, silent on issues of sexuality. The application of these norms to the gay, lesbian, bisexual and transgender (GLBT) communities has to be gleaned by inferences drawn from language addressed to issues of non-discrimination in the way they are implemented. This essay considers the extent to which international human rights now protect, or might protect, our communities and argues that domestic laws are not only needed to implement international norms, but are essential in overcoming the equivocations and silences of international human rights law as it has traditionally applied to GLBT communities. As such, this essay introduces and provides a background to the papers in this volume which deal with the reception and application of international human rights standards in domestic contexts.

INTERNATIONAL HUMAN RIGHTS STANDARDS

An indication of the potential breadth of the application of human rights norms can be found in Article 2 of the *Universal Declaration of Human Rights*[1] which provides:

> Everyone is entitled to all the rights and freedoms set forth in this Declaration, without distinction of any kind, such as race, colour, sex, language, religion, political or other opinion, national or social origin, property, birth or other status.

Article 2 of the *International Covenant on Civil and Political Rights*[2] (ICCPR) is similarly worded and provides that States must ensure these rights to all individuals within their territory. However, it is significant to note that despite the width of application ("everyone is entitled . . .") there is no specific mention of sexuality in the enumerated categories. Article 1 of the *Universal Declaration* provides: "All human beings are born free and equal in dignity and rights." However, this is an *a priori* presumption. While members of the GLBT communities would obviously fall within the concept of "all human beings," what the Article actually means for us in practice remains a crucial question. The *Universal Declaration*, a resolution of the United Nations General Assembly (and not a treaty as is sometimes mistakenly believed) was passed by vote in 1948. It is the seminal international human rights instrument, emerging after the Second World War when the atrocities of the Nazis were still fresh in the world's collective conscience. The conceptualisation of human rights was thus subject to and reflected the intellectual, political and social currents of the time when these instruments were drafted. Nazi atrocities included the extermination of minorities, which included gay men (of whom 34,000 died at Sachsenhausen concentration camp in Orianenberg). Yet sexuality is nowhere mentioned in the *Declaration*. The counterpoint between the potential width of application of human rights instruments and their silence on sexuality was to become the *leitmotif* of sexuality and gender identity within the international human rights framework.

In the later instruments elaborating upon the *Declaration*, such as the ICCPR, it is stated that everyone has the right to life,[3] the right not to be subjected to torture or cruel, inhuman or degrading treatment,[4] the right to liberty and security of the person,[5] the right to privacy,[6] the right to freedom of thought, conscience and religion,[7] the right to hold opinions,[8] the right to peaceful assembly,[9] freedom of association,[10] the right to marry,[11] and equality before the law and equal protection of the law.[12] The *International Covenant on Economic, Social and Cultural Rights*[13] includes the right to work,[14] the right to social security,[15] the right to an adequate standard of living,[16] the right to the highest attainable standard of physical and mental health,[17] and the right to education.[18] The *Convention Relating to the Status of Refugees*[19] gives to people who cannot return to their country of nationality because of a well-founded fear of persecution, *inter alia* because of the social group to which they belong, the right to refugee status.[20] All of these rights are significant and can apply to issues of importance to GLBT communities, but they are not specifically expressed to so apply. Instances of their breach with respect to GLBT communities have been, and in many places continue to be, commonplace.

THE DISTANCE BETWEEN THE DREAM AND THE REALITY

International human rights as expressed in the Preamble to the *Universal Declaration* are characterised as being "inherent," "inalienable," and "universal." As such they have been classed as a form of natural rights[21] and as being fundamental not only in just societies but also in the context of globalisation.[22] Yet, they are not necessarily absolute (they may clash with each other and derogations are sometimes allowed);[23] they are essentially a legal construction.[24] The final agreement on the wording of the principal instruments was the result of political compromise[25] which created an ambiguous text of indeterminate, contextual, but ultimately universalisable norms.

Enforcement of the norms is a major problem, from several points of view. First, human rights obligations found in international instruments are non-synallagmatic. The parties to these international instruments are States, not human beings. Yet the obligations in the instruments are effectively owed to human beings, not specifically to the other parties, because it is the entitlements of humans which are their subject. Hence, while it is possible for a party to complain of a breach of such an obligation by another (State) party, there is little incentive to do so. Thus, for a person to have the ability to enforce their own human rights effectively at international level, this must be expressly included in the instrument. The United Nations instruments attempt to remedy this situation through Optional Protocols which apply to some treaties[26] but not to most of them. States Parties must expressly agree to be bound by this procedure, which does not apply to breaches occurring before the Protocol is binding on that party. In addition, all local remedies must have first been exhausted, and decisions made under this procedure are only recommendations and are not legally binding.[27] Despite the expressed inalienability and universality of human rights for all people, this procedure of enforcement is hamstrung in the way in which it privileges States over humans. Nevertheless, a significant advance has been made under it.

The complainant in *Nicholas Toonen v Australia*[28] was a gay man who argued that the Tasmanian Criminal Code, under which consenting sexual contact between adult men in private was an offence, breached the *International Covenant on Civil and Political Rights* with respect to

Article 2 (the enjoyment of rights under the Covenant without discrimination), Article 17 (the right to privacy) and Article 26 (the right to equality before, and equal protection of, the law). The complaint was held to be admissible with respect to the exhaustion of local remedies because, even though Toonen had taken no other domestic action, it was the law itself which was the problem and no effective remedies were therefore available. With respect to the merits of the complaint, Australia argued that this was a moral issue best determined domestically, as well as a health issue in that it helped combat the spread of HIV/AIDS. Also, it was argued that this law posed no human rights violations because it had not been enforced for over a decade (Toonen himself had never been arrested or charged under it, even though he and his lover presented themselves at a police station to confess to 1,000 breaches of it!). These arguments were rejected. It was held that even if laws are not enforced, they might be enforced and their very existence thus has a pervasive impact leading to various forms of discrimination and stigmatisation. The argument based on public health was rejected because the law was neither reasonable nor proportionate to the threat it was alleged to address. It was also found that arguments with respect to morals are never exclusively a matter of domestic concern and may be influenced by international human rights norms (something of a shift from the Human Rights Committee's earlier view in *Hertzberg v Finland*[29] in 1982 when it held that moral issues attracted to the national authorities a margin of discretion thus allowing, in that instance, the banning of radio and television programs dealing with homosexuality). It was held that Toonen's right to privacy under Article 17 had been violated. Because of this finding, the Human Rights Committee unfortunately decided that it was unnecessary to make any pronouncements on the possibility of a breach of the other Articles. However, in a remarkable statement with potentially wide ramifications, the Committee held that the reference to "sex" in Article 2(1) of the Covenant (which provides that the rights in the Covenant will be ensured to everyone without distinction of any kind such as race, sex, religion . . .) must be read as including sexual orientation.

This process thus produced a result sensitive to the core issues of discrimination and stigmatisation that members of GLBT communities face daily, and which was of a potentially wide application.

The decision in *Toonen* received considerable media coverage in Australia, but the Tasmanian government nevertheless remained obdurate and refused to amend its laws. Indeed, in the 1996 state elections the Tasmanian government promised to increase the penalty for homosexual behaviour under the Criminal Code (and won the election). Because in the federation of Australia criminal law is a matter of state rather than commonwealth jurisdiction, the federal government could not directly amend Tasmania's law (although it did attempt to do so in a more indirect fashion).[30] Some years later, in the face of national derision, Tasmania finally relented and amended its law. Part of the pressure to do so must have come from, or was supported by, such a strong international pronouncement. This case demonstrates the advances, but distinct limitations, of international human rights norms for the GLBT communities in a domestic situation. It illustrates that international norms can be very influential within, but are only weak antidotes to, domestic legal systems where the local legal, social and political paradigms prevail.

Another way to address the problem of effective enforcement of international human rights norms is to allow individual complaints within the relevant treaty itself. This is the approach taken in the European *Convention for the Protection of Human Rights and Fundamental Freedoms*.[31] In *Dudgeon v United Kingdom*[32] the complainant was an activist with the Northern Ireland Gay Rights Association. The United Kingdom had decriminalised gay male sexual activity in England and Wales, but prohibitions were still in place in Northern Ireland. Unlike the ICCPR, the European Convention does not have a general equality provision. The European Court of Human Rights found that Dudgeon's right to respect for his private life had been violated, rejecting (as the Human Rights Committee later did in *Toonen*) the assertion that the law was necessary for the protection of health or morals. The European Court ruled against similar laws in *Norris v Ireland*[33] and *Modinos v Cyprus*.[34] In 1997 the European Commission of Human Rights applied similar reasoning to strike down the unequal age of consent for homosexual and heterosexual acts in the United Kingdom[35] (as the European Court of Human Rights has recently done with respect to Austria's laws)[36] and the UK's ban on gays and lesbians in the military was successfully challenged in the European Court of Human Rights in 1999.[37] After many years of the European Commission not recognising lesbian and gay families,[38] the Court upheld the right of a gay father to have access to his daughter[39] and there has been some accommodation of transsexual/transgender rights[40] but this has not been consistent.[41] Related property rights (such as survivor rights for same-sex couples) have recently been successfully litigated,[42] and issues of refugee status and discrimination generally are being considered.[43]

On December 7, 2000, the European Union *Charter of Fundamental Rights*[44] was proclaimed by the Parliament, Council and Commission. Its explicit purpose, as set out in the Preamble, is to strengthen fundamental rights. While Article 21 does expressly prohibit discrimination on the ground of sexual orientation, the Charter is not a part of the *Treaty of Nice* and so is not legally binding. Furthermore, unlike the *European Convention on Human Rights*, it only applies to European institutions and to member States in their actions within the scope of European Union law, and not to domestic law. Nevertheless, the European system has been the most proactive with respect to GLBT rights when compared to the UN instruments. The motivation for this must at least in part be due to the generally stronger enforcement procedures in that system.

The institutions of the Inter-American system have not been as proactive as those elsewhere, but treatment of homosexuals has been raised as a concern by the Inter-American Commission on Human Rights in its Annual Report in 1999 with respect to the arrest of 40 homosexuals in Ecuador during a state of emergency,[45] and it has also declared admissible a claim by a lesbian prisoner in Colombia that her privacy rights had been violated because of the refusal to allow conjugal visits from her same-sex partner in circumstances where heterosexual contact visits were allowed.[46]

There is thus no consistency of enforcement (and hence of application) of human rights norms when one compares the instruments of the UN system with those of the regional systems, and also when one compares the instruments within each system.

PROBLEMS OF MEANING AS WELL AS OF STRUCTURE

In addition to the resolution processes privileging State entities over individuals where the latter are not usually accorded legal personality to sue,[47] as well as the effect of the non-synallagmatic structure of the obligations actually owed, as well as the problems of motivation and standing when a State may wish to invoke a State-to-State breach of an international human rights obligation,[48] international standards also carry with them endemic problems of implementation.

The use of reservations, despite the non-derogable nature of some of the rights,[49] circumscribes the substantive reach of the norms. But in addition, and perhaps more significantly, structural issues in the language used to express the obligations can modify the effective implementation of the norms due to the symbiotic relationship between international human rights norms and domestic legal systems. This symbiosis can be seen to be of three types. *Explicit* symbiosis occurs where phrases such as "according to law" or "prescribed by law" are used. For example, the right to freedom of association in Article 22 of the ICCPR is specifically made subject to ". . . restrictions . . . which are prescribed by law and which are necessary in a democratic society in the interests of national security or public safety, public order, the protection of public health or morals. . . ." Similarly, the right to freedom of opinion in Article 19 is expressed to be subject to restrictions "provided by law and are necessary . . . for the respect of the rights and reputations of others . . . [and] for the protection of national security or of public order or of public health or morals." The laws referred to here are the domestic laws of the States parties. The Human Rights Committee has said that the restrictions placed on a right may not put in jeopardy the right itself and must be introduced by law and be based on a criterion of necessity.[50] Nevertheless, it is the relevant State which has the advantage of the first call on whether that necessity arises. As the Committee itself concedes,[51] it is the interplay between the norm and any introduced restrictions which actually determines the precise scope of application of the right for and by an individual.

The second type of symbiosis can be described as *implied* symbiosis. This arises when terms such as "family" and "marriage" are used. These terms, while they have a generalised denotation, may have distinctly and in some cases significantly different legal meanings. Thus, the expression of the right of "men and women of marriageable age to marry and to found a family"[52] does not tell us what marriageable age is, what type of ceremony is necessary for the proper solemnisation of the union, and whether the family is nuclear, extended, single-parent, or comprised of two parents of the same sex–nor, indeed, whether there need be children at all. It is domestic laws, which differ from jurisdiction to jurisdiction, which supply the necessary detail. The Human Rights Committee has recognised that the precise form of the "family" may differ between countries, but has stipulated that "when a group of persons is regarded as a family under the legislation and practice of a State, it must be given the protection referred to in Article 23."[53] This remark clearly leaves it to the laws and customs of any particular State to determine whether unions such as same-sex unions will be tolerated: it is only once that decision has been made at the domestic level that the international rights attaching to the status apply.

This is illustrated by the decision of the European Court of Human Rights in *X, Y & Z v United Kingdom*[54] where it was held that a family consisting of X (a female-to-male transsexual), Y (a woman with whom X had enjoyed a permanent and stable relationship for 18 years), and Z (a child born to Y as a result of artificial insemination by a donor) were not legally a "family" for the purposes of Article 8 of the European Human Rights Convention. Under British law, X and Y could not marry as X is not regarded as a male. This aspect of the case is consistent with the court's rulings in *Cossey v United Kingdom*[55] and *Sheffield and Horsham v United Kingdom*[56] which involved British law under which a person who has undergone gender reassignment surgery retains their pre-operative gender for the purposes of contracting a valid marriage. In both cases, the court found that there was insufficient evidence to outweigh what it considered to be the legitimate concern of the State to regulate marriage. The human right to marry is therefore couched in this context in strictly biological, as well as heterosexist, terms. As Y is therefore an "unmarried" woman giving birth to a child as a result of artificial insemination by a donor, and as she had the consent of her partner to the procedure, the partner (X) might have been treated for legal purposes as being the father of Z. However, because under British law X is not a male, he therefore cannot be a "father." Consequently, Z's birth certificate will not automatically show X as the father, as it might otherwise have done. As a result, Z cannot inherit from X in the event of an intestacy, and she may suffer embarrassment when applying for such things as a passport or an insurance policy, which require the production of a birth certificate, as no one will be shown as the father. The Court of Human Rights held that for X to enjoy "family life" with Z, he would have to be related to her by blood, marriage or adoption. Emotional attachments, commitment and support are treated as being irrelevant in these cases, the court holding that as there is no common European standard in these matters the State may be "justifiably cautious" before changing the law. This approach makes family life more a matter of biology than of love and commitment. Moreover, it is not the approach taken by the same court in cases involving heterosexual de facto relationships.[57]

A topical issue for GLBT communities now is same-sex marriage. Whether the phrase "men and women" in Article 23(2) of the ICCPR dealing with the right to marry can be applied disjunctively to allow unions other than those strictly and clearly between people of the opposite sex has been answered in the negative by the Human Rights Committee. In *Joslin et al. v New Zealand*[58] two lesbian couples applied for marriage licences and were refused. They claimed a breach of their rights under Articles 16 (recognition as a person before the law), 17 (family and privacy), 23 (marriage) and 26 (equality before the law and equal protection of the law). They argued that the New Zealand *Marriage Act* discriminated against them directly because of their sex and indirectly because of their sexual orientation, and that it deprived them of their essential dignity in not recognising them as subjects of the Act. In addition they argued that New Zealand had failed in its obligation to protect their family life, and that the term "men and women" in Article 23 does not mean that only men may marry women, and vice versa, but that men as a group and women as a group may marry. The New Zealand counter-argument was that the approaches to this issue proposed by the applicants would require a redefinition of a legal institution reflective of social and cultural values and that the inability of men and women to marry people of their own sex was not discrimination but arose from the "inherent" nature of marriage itself and hence was objectively and reasonably justified. Claiming the clear and historically objective criteria of the institution of marriage as being heterosexual (and ignoring evidence brought by the complainants to the contrary)[59] New Zealand contended that it is the nature of the couple rather than the nature of the individuals which is determinative. In other words, it is a human right for all gay men and women of sufficient age to marry, as long as they marry someone of the opposite sex. This argument misses the real point which is that marriage, in essence, is about caring rather than biology. It makes the "inherent" nature of marriage relevant to little more than genitalia.

After finding the claim admissible,[60] the Committee dealt with the merits of the complaint in only seven sentences. It noted that Article 23(2) dealing with the right to marry is the only substantive provision in the ICCPR to use the term "men and women" rather than more general terms, such as "everyone," which are used elsewhere in the Covenant. It concluded from this that the provision has been "consistently and uniformly understood"[61] as obliging States only to recognise marriages between men and women. It gives no authority for this sweeping statement, attempts not even a modicum of interpretation,[62] ignores any possibility of evolving social constructions of marriage, and leaves the notion of fundamental meanings of concepts in the Covenant in the care of the States. This approach is also now clearly contrary to that of the European Court of Human Rights in the *Karner* case[63] where it was held that the so-called legislative intention at the time an instrument was concluded is not definitive as to current interpretation and application. The decision is uninformed of, and does not appear to care about, the legitimate expectations of approximately one-tenth of the world's population. Treating such a concern as an irrelevance makes the decision morally questionable, in addition to the intellectual laziness which permeates it. States are allowed to avoid even the consideration of law reform through reliance on a deep-seated heterosexism. This flies in the face of the Committee's decision in *Toonen* which was so alive to the influences international human rights should have on domestic conceptions of morality. Two members of the Committee,[64] in an individual opinion appended to the main view, pointed out that the ICCPR does not prevent States introducing same-sex marriage if they want to, and that discriminatory treatment between married couples and same-sex couples may be a breach of the right to equal protection of the law under Article 26, reiterating the view in *Toonen* that the prohibition of discrimination on the ground of "sex" includes discrimination on the ground of sexual orientation. Nevertheless, "marriage" in the ICCPR is not a human right for same-sex couples: it is a privilege conferred by the State of solemnisation. (The situation in North America is discussed by Elliott and Bonauto in this volume.) Thus, the decision has effectively turned the positive obligation of non-discrimination and equal protection of the law in Article 26 into a negative obligation of non-interference in GLBT concerns.

In Australia, the Family Court has upheld the validity of a marriage involving a female-to-male transsexual,[65] although this is under appeal to the High Court. Courts in the United Kingdom have not yet gone this far, but have expressed their disquiet at the current state of legal affairs.[66] The European Court of Human Rights recently upheld a transsexual's rights to legal recognition of her new gender,[67] and said that, in the case of a post-operative transsexual, this might include the right to marry a person of her original sex. However, it is still up to the State to determine "the conditions under which a person claiming recognition as a transsexual establishes that gender re-assignment has been properly effected or under which past marriages cease to be valid and the formalities applicable to future marriages."[68] The determination again is to be made by the State, and, because of the importance attached to the applicant's post-operative situation, the paradigm of marriage remains focused strongly on the heterosexual. Therefore, while this issue is by no means closed, there is overwhelmingly a tendency to rely on a notion of "normalcy" which is grounded in heterosexism. Gender identity, unless a transsexual person is post-operative, remains biologically based. In the European Court of Human Rights this approach to categorisation of normalcy extends to activities as well. In *Laskey, Jaggard and Brown v United Kingdom*[69] there was found to be no violation of the privacy provision of the European Convention when members of a sado-masochistic group were prosecuted for violence. The activities, which were conducted by consenting adult homosexual males in private, and for no apparent purpose other than the achievement of sexual gratification, included the maltreatment of genitalia, ritualistic beatings, branding and the infliction of injuries. The men were prosecuted for assault and sentenced to varying terms of imprisonment. The European Court of Human Rights found that there had been no violation of the privacy provision in Article 8 because the laws in place were necessary in a democratic society. Essentially, these acts were classified by the court as acts of violence rather than as acts of a sexual nature conducted between consenting adults.

The third type of symbiosis can be called *functional* symbiosis. This arises when words such as "arbitrary" are used in the description of the norm. For example, the right to privacy in Article 17 of the ICCPR states that "no one shall be subjected to arbitrary or unlawful interference with his privacy. . . ." The concept of arbitrariness relates to the manner in which a restriction on a right is introduced. It is thus linked to the notion of unlawfulness, but, according to the Human Rights Committee, it goes beyond this because the law itself might be arbitrary or implemented in an arbitrary fashion[70] (as was held to have occurred in the *Toonen Case* discussed above). Nevertheless, the notion of arbitrariness is necessarily linked to the domestic processes which remain the touchstone of permissible restrictions on the right.

These symbiotic relationships thus can affect–and effect–the meaning and implementation of the international norms. This means that effective implementation is domestically contextual, with relatively weak international supervision. Indeed, it may be said that this can be, in the long run, more significant than the reservations made to the international instruments. Domestic social values are thus crucial and domestic legal systems provide the framework within which, in practice, human rights operate. Human rights norms are thus constructed by law, including domestic laws, as well as being constructed of laws. These problems are potentially magnified in federations where legal systems compete internally for primacy.

ARE GLBT RIGHTS NOW PART OF THE INTERNATIONAL HUMAN RIGHTS AGENDA?

While it cannot yet be said that GLBT rights have been expressly accepted as a specific species of human rights, and while the application of human rights generally to GLBT communities is uneven, there is no question that the GLBT rights movement is developing, although the principal advances to date have been primarily in western countries. The Netherlands has introduced legislation allowing same sex marriages,[71] as has Belgium.[72] Canadian courts have also considered and upheld the validity of same-sex marriages.[73] Other countries have adopted legislation recognising same sex relationships, but not as full marriages.[74] The South African Constitutional Court has struck down a sodomy law and recognised same-sex partner rights in immigration law,[75] and the United States Supreme Court has struck down the sodomy law in Texas.[76]

The more salient question is the extent to which these developments have occurred as a result of, or whether they have arisen despite, the level of support international human rights norms are giving–or can give–to GLBT issues. Membership of the Council of Europe–an important step to fuller membership in the institutions of the European Union–requires ratification of the *European Convention on Human Rights*. A resolution of the European Parliament in 1998 stated that consent to any country joining the European Union would be refused if they violated the human rights of lesbians or gay men through laws or policies, and particularly criticised Austria, Bulgaria, Cyprus, Estonia, Hungary, Lithuania and Romania in this regard.[77] The political carrot of EU membership could be seen as encouraging and even requiring the introduction of domestic GLBT rights. However, the problem of finding a sufficient beachhead in the relevant instruments to launch a GLBT offensive against discriminatory domestic laws and practices still remains elusive precisely because the problems of process and structure referred to above persist. Despite the remarks in the *Toonen* and *Joslin* decisions that the term "sex" in Article 2(1) of the *ICCPR* includes "sexual orientation," the European Court of Justice has refused to follow this view,[78] and has also held that the term "spouse" in the context of entitlement to employment benefits does not include a same-sex partner despite the fact that the two men concerned had gone through a registered partnership under Swedish law.[79] States have frequently resorted to the health and morals exceptions to justify repressive action or legislation, as do other countries even when those arguments have already been judicially discredited.[80] What is happening now, however, is that international tribunals can take, and are increasingly taking, the issue to a wider cultural context than has occurred in the past,[81] but most still baulk at perceived no-go areas considered too sensitive, such as same-sex marriage.[82] In the process the very notion of democracy as something inclusive, rather than as merely the rule of the majority, is slowly emerging.[83] That emergence, however, is slow in many areas: not only with respect to marriage,[84] but in other areas such as adoption[85] and transgender rights.[86]

The approach to GLBT rights by these bodies unfortunately remains patchy and inconsistent.

In some regions, antipathy to GLBT rights can be so strong that nice questions of legal definition and process do not have an opportunity to arise, and even the political carrot-and-stick approach is stymied. In 1995 the African Commission on Human Rights was sent a petition to open an inquiry into Zimbabwe's laws and policies on homosexuality. This petition was withdrawn at the specific request of Zimbabwe's largest gay and lesbian organisation. The reason for this was the fear of reprisals against GLBT communities by the government, which has claimed that homosexuality is not part of African culture.

CONCLUSION

The application of GLBT communities to existing categories recognised as entitled to protection is a growing trend. Reports such as that of the Committee on Legal Affairs and Human Rights of the Parliamentary Assembly of the Council of Europe[87] prompted resolutions of the Parliamentary Assembly on the refugee status of people being persecuted because of their sexual orientation, as well as recommendations calling for the prohibition of discrimination based on sexual orientation and the repeal of criminal sanctions for consenting homosexual acts between adults, as well as for equal ages of consent for heterosexual and homosexual acts and the registration of same-sex relationships.[88] This prompted the Committee of Ministers of the Council of Europe to reject openly the formerly common approach that a powerful cultural reaction against homosexuality could justify governments or parliaments remaining passive instead of responding to discrimination and violence against GLBT communities.[89] The UN High Commissioner for Refugees has similarly interpreted the phrase "social group" in the 1950 *Convention Relating to the Status of Refugees* as including lesbians and gay men, as have some domestic courts.[90]

The possibility that violence aimed at GLBT communities might be classified as genocide has been opened up by the jurisprudence of the International Criminal Tribunal for Rwanda which has held that the term "group" in Article 2 of the Genocide Convention 1948 is not necessarily restricted to national, ethnic, racial or religious groups, but can encompass any stable and permanent group.[91]

NGOs, such as Human Rights Watch and Amnesty International, now openly support and work towards GLBT rights internationally and the International Bar Association passed a resolution on non-discrimination in legal practice in 1998 which expressly refers to discrimination based on sexual orientation.[92] GLBT rights are gaining a higher international profile and a flow-on effect between advances in the domestic and international spheres is evident. Much of the reason for this change of heart has been the detailed research and activism of GLBT organisations.[93]

Problems, however, remain, and they are not purely legal in nature. Not only is funding a significant issue for GLBT organisations as well as for international institutions carrying out such programs,[94] but the very visibility and recognition of international GLBT organisations is controversial. While three lesbian and gay organisations were accredited to the UN World Conference on Human Rights in Vienna in 1993–the first time any such organisations were knowingly accredited to any UN event–and the International Lesbian and Gay Association (ILGA) was granted NGO consultative status by the UN Economic and Social Council in 1993, this status was suspended a year later amid controversy that one of ILGA's member organisations supported paedophilia. Expulsion from ILGA of three paedophile organisations and a redrafted constitution committing ILGA to international human rights standards, including those in the *Convention on the Rights of the Child*, has not prompted a reinstatement of consultative status. ILGA accreditation to the UN World Conference on Racism, Racial Discrimination, Xenophobia and Related Intolerance held in South Africa in 2001 was defeated by a tied vote. In the same year, the UN General Assembly Special Session on HIV/AIDS was delayed over a debate as to whether a representative of the International Lesbian and Gay Human Rights Commission would be allowed to address the session. Eventually this was allowed, but the final document approved by the Special Session omitted any mention of homosexuality, or even of the phrase "men who have sex with men."

It has been suggested that to expand international human rights law to expressly include GLBT issues would involve a broad interpretation of human rights norms by national and international bodies, or the adoption of separate protocols or of a new specific convention.[95] There is considerable antipathy to this course, however. A proposed resolution of the UN Commission on Human Rights on "Human Rights and Sexual Orientation," which was to be voted upon in April 2003, and which did little more than affirm that everyone (including GLBT people) has human rights, has now been postponed until 2004 as a result of pressure from member nations opposing it. As the adoption of a clear instrument is unlikely in the short or medium term, the interaction between the existing international norms and domestic legal systems becomes crucial. The symbiotic relationship between the international norms and domestic legal systems mentioned above is thus even more significant. However, lest this become apologia for cultural relativism (and the discrimination and violence against GLBT communities tolerated or promoted by the domestic legal systems in many countries) or a surrender to the systemic problems of hierarchy and silence faced by those communities when heterosexuality is the presumed "norm," the domestic systems must be fused with broadly based principles arising from the international norms. As the norms themselves may clash–in this context, the clash between the right to freedom of religion and the rights to freedom of expression and privacy is illustrative–the fusion needs to be with something more fundamental. Arguments based on equality are common in the traditional western liberal conception of law and law reform. However, the use of liberal discourse has been criticised by some voices in the GLBT movement, who draw on critiques from post-modernism, critical legal theory and feminism, giving rise to a school of thought known as queer law[96] and lesbian feminist legal theory.[97] These theorists argue that a liberal approach cannot truly challenge discrimination against sexual minorities. They argue that GLBT activists may be co-opted by the system into piecemeal law reforms which do not fundamentally change the system itself and even suppress the diversity within GLBT communities. Adherents to the liberal approach counter that the queer theorists are unrealistic and that concrete change of some kind is necessary if the very concept of human rights is not to become merely quixotic.[98] The international decisions with respect to the rights of transgender people, discussed above, may indicate that there is a kernel of truth in both points of view. Some commentators talk of a "site of struggle," a "site of dialogue" or of a "process of conversation" when explaining rights discourse, the clash of norms and the competing aims of rectifying disadvantage or protecting privileged positions.[99] It is not only the ambiguity of international human rights norms but also their negotiability which is "inherent" in their nature when they are used to promote reform.

Because of the problems with which the notion of equality is fraught, a more useful notion, also to be found underlying international human rights norms, is that of diversity. Instead of an approach which simply tolerates diversity, we need to develop one which actually values diversity. However, resort to a fundamental principle of valuing diversity alone will not solve this problem. But it may be one way of forging a space in legal (and social) discourse so that silence is no longer the predominant circumstance, enabling heterosexism to remain the privileged viewpoint. This must start with local activism challenging domestic laws. It is for this reason that the papers in this volume are important as they represent what is happening locally, but with a view to a true valuing of diversity. As with the ancient view of Equity in Common Law systems being used to mollify the unfairness in the application of domestic legal norms, the growing references to international human rights norms in domestic adjudication illustrate their use *infra legem* (when the norms are recognised as already having been incorporated into the domestic system) and *praetor legem* (where they are used to interpret domestic laws in cases of ambiguity) but rarely, if ever, are international norms used *contra legem* (to actually overturn a clear provision in domestic law). This is not only because of a transformationist approach to the application of international norms in domestic legal systems, but because the dominant legal values do not facilitate an appreciation that the law applies unfairly, much less enable the recognition that such a law is no longer acceptable. Resort to a touchstone of the fundamental value of diversity may assist such a development. Any legal system which shirks its responsibility in balancing fairly the legitimate claims of its diverse stakeholders cannot claim to have justice as its true objective.

NOTES

1. 3 UNGAOR 962 (1948), Res. 217 III (C)
2. (1966) UNTS Vol.999 p. 171
3. Article 6
4. Article 7
5. Article 9
6. Article 17
7. Article 18
8. Article 19
9. Article 21
10. Article 22
11. Article 23
12. Article 26
13. (1966) UNTS Vol. 993 p. 3

14. Article 6
15. Article 9
16. Article 11
17. Article 12
18. Article 13
19. (1951) UNTS Vol.189 p. 150
20. Article 1A
21. See, for example, J Roland Pennock, "Rights, Natural Rights and Human Rights–A General View," in *Human Rights* (J Roland Pennock & John W Chapman, eds, 1981).
22. Jerome J Shestack, "The Legal Profession and Human Rights: Globalisation of Human Rights Law" (1997) 21 *Fordham International Law Journal* 558
23. See below.
24. See R.J. Vincent: *Human Rights and International Relations* (1986, Cambridge U.P.) who writes at p. 19 that: "human rights did not just happen, they had to be invented."
25. See John Humphrey: *Human Rights and the United Nations: A Great Adventure* (1984, Transnational).
26. The *International Covenant on Civil and Political Rights*, the *Convention on the Elimination of All Forms of Discrimination Against Women* and the *Convention on the Rights of the Child*.
27. See, for example, Articles 1 and 2 of the Optional Protocol to the International Covenant on Civil and Political Rights.
28. Communication No. 488/1992, views given on 31 March, 1994, UN Doc CCPR/C/50/D/488/1992. For a commentary, see Wayne Morgan, "Sexuality and Human Rights" (1993) 14 *Australian Yearbook of International Law* 277.
29 A/37/40, p. 61
30. It passed the *Human Rights (Sexual Conduct) Act 1994* which used the federal government's power to enact legislation based on treaties and the Act applied to all of the Commonwealth.
31. ETS No.5 (1950), as amended by Protocol No.2 (ETS No. 44, 1963), Protocol No.3 (ETS No.45, 1963), Protocol No.5 (ETS No.55, 1966) and Protocol No.8 (ETS No.118, 1985).
32. (1981) 4 E.H.R.R. 149
33. (1991) 13 E.H.R.R. 186
34. (1993) 16 E.H.R.R. 485
35. *Sutherland v United Kingdom*, Commission Report, July 1, 1997.
36. *L & V v Austria* (9 January, 2003, Application Nos. 39392/98 & 39829/98); *SL v Austria* (9 January, 2003, Application No. 45330/99)
37. *Smith v United Kingdom* (2000) E.H.R.R. 493; *Lustig-Prean v United Kingdom* (2000) E.H.R.R. 548
38. See, for example, *X and Y v United Kingdom* (App. No.9369/81, (1983 32 Eur. Comm. H.R. Decisions and Reports, 220.
39. *Salgueiro Da Silva Mouta v Portugal* (Case no. 33290/96, December 21, 1999)
40. *B v France* (1992) E.H.R.R. 1: changing names and sexual information on official documents.
41. *X, Y and Z v United Kingdom*, Case No. 75/1995/581/667 (1997): birth certificate of a child born as a result or artificial insemination of the mother would not show the mother's partner, a female-to-male transsexual, as the father of the child.

42. *Karner v Austria*, No.40016/98: surviving same-sex partner entitled to maintain a tenancy on the basis of Article 14 (prohibition of discrimination) and Article 8 (respect for the home).
43. See Report of the Committee on Legal Affairs and Human Rights, *Situation of Lesbians and Gays in Council of Europe Member Countries*, 6 June 2000, Doc. No.8755 (*http://stars.coe.fr/doc/doc00/edoc8755.htm*).
44. 2000 O.J. (C364)
45. *Annual Report 1999*, Chapter 4, OEA/Ser.L/V/II.106 Doc. 6 rev (13 April, 1999).
46. *Marta Alvarez Giralda v Columbia*, Case 11,656, 4 May 1999, Report No.71/99.
47. Individuals can be given direct rights under a treaty, but only if the contracting parties (i.e., States) clearly allow this: *Advisory Opinion on the Postal Service in Danzig* P.C.I.J. Rep., Series B, No. 11, 1925.
48. For example, as did Liberia and Ethiopia in the *South West Africa Case* ICJ Rep, 1960.
49. See Article 4 of the ICCPR. In any event, the right to privacy, which is so far the principal right successfully argued in GLBT related cases, is not expressed to be non-derogable.
50. See General Comment 10, 29/06/83
51. *Ibid*.
52. ICCPR Art.23(2)
53. General Comment 19, UN Doc. CCPR/C/21/Rev.1/Add 1-4, 27/07/90, paragraph 2.
54. 75/1995/581/667, 22 April 1997
55. 16/1989/176/232 (1990)
56. 31-32/1997/815-816/1018-1019 (1998)
57. See *Marcks v Belgium* Series A No. 31, p. 14 (1979); *Keegan v Ireland* Series A No. 290, p. 17 (1994)
58. CCPR/C/75/D/902/1999, 30 July 2002
59. See W. Eskridge, "A History of Same-Sex Marriage" (1993) 79 *Virginia Law Review* 1419.
60. An appeal from the decision of the New Zealand Court of Appeal to the Privy Council was possible, but as New Zealand made no formal submissions as to admissibility, the Committee decided that the communication was admissible. This in itself further illustrates the privileged position of States in this process as the Committee adopts no proactive approach.
61. Paragraph 8.2
62. For example, the interpretation of the word "and" as a disjunctive and a conjunctive term depending on the context: see generally John Bell and Sir George Engle: *Cross on Statutory Interpretation* (3rd ed, 1995). The *Vienna Convention on the Law of Treaties 1969* provides in Article 31(1): "A treaty shall be interpreted in good faith in accordance with the ordinary meaning to be given to the terms of the treaty *in their context* and in *the light of its object and purpose*" (emphases added).
63. *Karner v Austria*, above.
64. Rajsoomer Lallah and Martin Scheinin
65. *In re Kevin* [2001] Fam.C.A. 1074 (12 October, 2001)
66. *Bellinger v Bellinger* [2002] Fam. 150: a male-to-female transsexual was refused a declaration that she had contracted a valid marriage with a man, but the Court of

Appeal noted the "profoundly unsatisfactory nature of the present position." (at p. 178). Leave to appeal to the House of Lords has been granted.

67. *Goodwin v United Kingdom* (2002) 35 EHRR 18
68. At para. 103
69. Case No. 109/1995/615/703-705 (1997)
70. General Comment 16, 08/04/88, paragraph 4
71. Law of 21 December 2000 (Staatsblad 2001, nr.9)
72. Law of 30 January 2003
73. *Halpern v Canada (Attorney-General); Metropolitan Community Church of Toronto v Canada (Attorney-General)* (2002-07-12) ONSC 68400; 392001
74. For example, *An Act Relating to Civil Unions* (Vermont), (Act 91, H.847) (2000)
75. *National Coalition for Gay and Lesbian Equality v The Minister of Justice* Case CCT 11/98 Citation
76. *Lawrence & Garner v Texas* No. 02-102 (June 26, 2003), unreported.
77. Res. B4-0824 and 0852/98 (17 September, 1998)
78. *Grant v South-West Trains* [1998] ECR I-621
79. C-122/99 P and C 125/99 P, May 31, 2001
80. For example, the argument of the United Kingdom in *Dudgeon v United Kingdom*, above, and the argument of Australia in the *Toonen Case*, above.
81. For example, the view of the Human Rights Committee in *Toonen v Australia*, above, and the European Court of Human Rights in *Karner*, above.
82. *Joslin et al. v New Zealand*, above.
83. For example, the *Smith* and *Lustig-Prean* cases, above, where it was held that discrimination against homosexual people in the military could not be justified in a democratic society.
84. See, for example, the public statements by US President George W. Bush, as well as the Pope, reiterating the heterosexual nature of marriage (New York Times, July 31, 2003).
85. In *Frette v France* 26/2/02 citation the European Court of Human Rights ruled that France could refuse to allow gays and lesbians to adopt children.
86. In *B v France* (1992) EHRR 1 it was held that some accommodation must be made in allowing the change of names and sexual information on official documents. However, in *Sheffield and Horsham v United Kingdom* citation, the United Kingdom's refusal to alter birth certificates was upheld.
87. *Situation of Lesbians and Gays in Council of Europe Member States*, Document 8755, 6 June 2000 (http://stars.coe.fr/doc/doc00/edoc8755.htm)
88. See http://stars.coe.int/asp/DocByDate.asp
89. See http://stars.coe.fr/ta/ta00/EREC1474.htm
90. For example, the Supreme Court of Canada in *Canada v Ward* [1993] 2 SCR 689
91. The jurisprudence of the Tribunal can be accessed at www.ictr.org/default.htm
92. See Tahmindjis, "An International Resolution on Non-Discrimination in Legal Practice" (2000) 4 *International Journal of Discrimination and the Law* 73.
93. For example, ILGA-Europe submitted research on the treatment of GLBT communities in Hungary, Poland, Romania and Slovenia to the hearings of the Parliament intergroup on gay and lesbian rights which held hearings on "EU Enlargement: A Gay Perspective" in June 2001.

94. For example, European Union funding led to the production of important publications such as Waaldijk and Clapham's *Homosexuality: A European Community Issue* (1993, Nijhoff).

95. See Debra L. DeLaet, "Don't Ask Don't Tell: Where is the Protection Against Sexual Orientation Discrimination in International Human Rights Law?" (1997) 7 *Law and Sexuality* 31 at 35. For a suggested international instrument, see Eric Heinze: *Sexual Orientation: A Human Right* (1995, Kluwer), "Model Declaration of Rights Against Discrimination on the Basis of Sexual Orientation," pp. 291-303.

96. For a summary, see Wayne Morgan, "Queer Law: Identity, Culture, Diversity, Law" (1995) 5 *Australasian Gay and Lesbian Law Journal* 1.

97. See L Harne & E Miller (eds): *All the Rage: Reasserting Radical Lesbian Feminism* (1996, Women's Press).

98. See Robert D. Sloane, "Outrelativising Relativism: A Liberal Defense of the Universality of International Human Rights" (2001) 34 *Vanderbilt Journal of Transnational Law* 527.

99. For example, John Hannaford, "Truth, Tradition and Confrontation: A Theory of International Human Rights" (1993) 31 *Canadian Yearbook of International Law* 151.

Sexuality and Australian Law

The Hon. Justice Michael Kirby, AC, CMG

High Court of Australia

SUMMARY. The author describes the changing legal environment concerning same-sex relationships in the common law world with special reference to Australia. He refers to shifts in public opinion recorded in opinion polls; important decisions of human rights courts and tribunals; and changes in national law and court decisions. He then reviews the Australian constitutional setting which divides lawmaking responsibility on such subjects between the federal, State and Territory legislatures. He describes initiatives adopted in the States and Territories and the more modest changes effected in federal law and practice. He concludes on a note of optimism concerning Australia's future reforms affecting discrimination on the grounds of sexuality. *[Article copies available for a fee from The Haworth Document Delivery Service: 1-800-HAWORTH. E-mail address: <docdelivery@haworthpress.com> Website: <http://www.HaworthPress.com> © 2005 by The Haworth Press, Inc. All rights reserved.]*

The Hon. Justice Michael Kirby is Justice of the High Court of Australia and one-time President of the International Commission of Jurists. In 1999, the author included in his entry in *Who's Who in Australia* details of his relationship with his partner of thirty years, Johan van Vloten. Such entries had not been previously included in the publication. This fact was noted in due course by sections of the media in Australia with predictable results. Based on a paper presented to the conference of the International Bar Association, Amsterdam, 2000, and derived from a chapter in Robert Wintemute & Mads Andenas (eds): *The Legal Recognition of Same-Sex Partnerships* (Hart, 2000). Published in its original form (1999) 19 *Australian Bar Review* 4.

[Haworth co-indexing entry note]: "Sexuality and Australian Law." Kirby, Michael. Co-published simultaneously in *Journal of Homosexuality* (Harrington Park Press, an imprint of The Haworth Press, Inc.) Vol. 48, No. 3/4, 2005, pp. 31-48; and: *Sexuality and Human Rights: A Global Overview* (ed: Helmut Graupner, and Phillip Tahmindjis) Harrington Park Press, an imprint of The Haworth Press, Inc., 2005, pp. 31-48. Single or multiple copies of this article are available for a fee from The Haworth Document Delivery Service [1-800-HAWORTH, 9:00 a.m. - 5:00 p.m. (EST). E-mail address: docdelivery@haworthpress.com].

http://www.haworthpress.com/web/JH
© 2005 by The Haworth Press, Inc. All rights reserved.
Digital Object Identifier: 10.1300/J082v48n03_04

KEYWORDS. Human rights, sexual orientation, discrimination on the grounds of homosexual orientation and same-sex relationships, Australia, legal developments in statute and common law, federal constitutional arrangements, amendments to State and Territory laws concerning discrimination, property relationships and benefits and entitlements, changes in federal law concerning superannuation and pensions, immigration and federal public service, likely future changes

A CHANGING LEGAL ENVIRONMENT

My participation in a publication on this topic could not, and would not, have happened even a few years ago. The participation of many senior judges and lawyers from a number of countries, considering this question, would have been unthinkable. Same-sex relationships were the outward manifestation of impermissible emotions. Such emotions, or at least the physical acts that gave them expression, were criminal in many countries. If caught, those involved would be heavily punished, even if their acts were those of adults, performed with consent and in private. Needless to say, such laws, whether enforced or not, led to profound alienation of otherwise good citizens, to serious psychological disturbance when people struggled to alter their natural sexual orientation, to suicide, blackmail, police entrapment, hypocrisy and other horrors.

It is fitting that, as the modern criminalisation of homosexual conduct can largely be traced to the laws of England, which were copied faithfully throughout the old British Empire (even in places where the previous developed law had made no such distinctions), leadership in the direction of reform should eventually have come from the United Kingdom. The Wolfenden Report[1] and the reform of the law which followed[2] became the model whose influence gradually spread throughout the jurisdictions of the Commonwealth of Nations, or at least amongst the old Dominions. Some of the more autocratic societies within the Commonwealth have rediscovered the sodomy offences and utilised them against political critics.

The Wolfenden reforms in England, and their progeny, both responded to and stimulated changes in community opinion about homosexual conduct. These changes, in turn, influenced social attitudes to people who are homosexual, bisexual or transgender in their sexual orientation. Once the lid of criminal punishment and social repression was lifted, people came to know their gay and lesbian fellow citizens. They came to realise that, boringly enough, they have all the same human needs as the heterosexual majority. The needs for human love, affection and companionship; for family relationships and friendships; for protection against irrational and unjustifiable discrimination; and for equal legal rights in matters where distinctions cannot be affirmatively justified.

A measure of the continuing erosion of public opposition to legal change in this area, and of strong generational differences in attitudes to such subjects, can be seen in a survey conducted in the United States of America.[3] Accepting that country as probably the most conservative on this subject amongst the Western democracies, what is notable in the comparison with the results of a similar survey conducted thirty years ago is the strong shift towards acceptance of the legalisation of homosexual relations (then 55%; now 82%), and the support amongst younger people for legalising homosexual relations. The young tend to be those who know someone who identifies openly as gay or lesbian. Similar surveys in other Western countries, including my own, indicate generally similar shifts in public opinion, although the current debate with respect to gay marriage indicates that even "liberal" public opinion generally hesitates at full recognition of same-sex marriages.

Significantly, the principal reason given in the American survey by those personally opposed to homosexuality is "religious objections" (52%). Yet even amongst the major religions in many Western countries, there has been a cautious shift to recognition of the need for change. Many commentators on the Pope's visit to the United States in January 1999 remarked on the "sharp generational polarisation" on issues such as homosexuality, premarital sex and the ordination of women priests.[4] In Australia, some thoughtful commentators within the Catholic Church (now the largest religious denomination in the country) have begun to talk of sexuality beyond the proposition that would insist upon acceptance of sexual orientation but prohibit all of its physical and emotional manifestations. Thus Bishop Patrick Power in Canberra, Australia, has called for "solidarity with the poor, the marginalised, the oppressed."[5] He said: "[There] is a very real difficulty for the Church in terms of its credibility in the wider community. Some members of the Church community and hierarchy appear to act quite cruelly towards people such as single parents, homosexuals, divorced and remarried couples . . ."

The advent of the Human Genome Project and the likelihood that, in many cases at least, sexual orientation is genetically determined, make it unacceptable to impose upon those affected unreasonable legal discrimination or demands that they change. It was always unacceptable; but now no informed person has an excuse for blind prejudice and unreasonable conduct. If we are talking about the unnatural, demands that people deny their sexuality or try to change it, if it is part of their nature, are a good illustration of what is unnatural. An increasing number of citizens in virtually every Western democracy are coming inexorably to this realisation. People are not fools. Once they recognise the overwhelming commonalities of shared human experience, the alienation and demand for adherence to shame crumbles. Once they reflect upon the unreasonableness of insisting that homosexuals change their sexual orientation, or suppress and hide their emotions (something they could not demand of themselves), the irrational insistence and demand for legal sanctions tends to fade away. Once they know that friends and family, children, sisters or uncles are gay, the hatred tends to melt. In the wake of the changing social attitudes inevitably come changing laws: both statutes made by Parliaments and the common law made by judges.

Virtually every jurisdiction of the common law is now facing demands for the reconsideration of legal rules as they are invoked by homosexual litigants and other citizens who object to discrimination. To some extent the standards of change have been set by regional bodies such as the European Court of Human Rights,[6] and international bodies such as the United Nations Human Rights Committee.[7] In the past, litigants could not be found to prosecute these issues. This was because of various inhibitors: the risk of criminal prosecution; the fear of social or professional stigmatisation; the desire to avoid shame to themselves or their families. Now that these controls are in decline, it must be accepted that courts and legislatures will face increasing demands that legal discriminations be removed and quickly. The main game of shame is over. Reality and truth rule. Rationality and science chart the way of the future. The same thing happened earlier to laws and practices which showed discrimination on the grounds of race and gender. The same opposition was mooted in the name of religion, of nature or of reason. No one of value believes the myths of racial or gender inferiority anymore. There is no reason to believe that it will be different in respect of discrimination on the ground of sexuality.

Sometimes litigants will be able to invoke a national charter of rights, as has happened in Canada.[8] Sometimes their cases will involve very large questions as in a case in New Zealand.[9] At other times they will involve something as tedious as the construction of the *Rent Act*, as occurred recently in England.[10] Australia has also been affected by these developments. The purpose of this contribution is to explain some of the developments.

THE AUSTRALIAN CONSTITUTIONAL SETTING

In order to approach Australian legal developments it is necessary to appreciate the nature of the Australian federation. The Constitution divides the lawmaking power in Australia between the Commonwealth (the federal polity) and the States. Generally speaking, as in the United States of America, if a legislative power is not expressly granted by the Constitution to the federal Parliament, it remains with the States. The result of this arrangement, again speaking very generally, is that large areas of private law–and especially of criminal law–are left to State lawmaking. The federal Parliament, outside the Territories where it ultimately enjoys plenary constitutional powers,[11] has tended to be concerned in matters of lawmaking on subjects of national application and in federally specified areas.

This general description must be modified by appreciation of three important developments which have gathered pace in recent decades. First, the federal Parliament, encouraged by expansive decisions on the grants of federal constitutional power, has extended its legislation into areas which almost certainly were not expected to be regulated federally when the Constitution was enacted in 1900.[12] Thus, by the use of tax incentives, a large framework of federal legislation has recently been enacted governing the law of superannuation (contributory retirement benefits) in Australia.[13]

Secondly, although Australia (now almost alone) does not have either a comprehensive constitutional charter of rights, nor a statute-based guarantee of fundamental civil entitlements, much anti-discrimination legislation has been enacted, including at the federal level. Some of this has been supported by the federal power to make laws with respect to external affairs. International treaties to which Australia has subscribed have become a means of supporting the constitutional validity of federal legislation outside traditional federal fields. It was in this way, in reliance upon Australia's obligations under the International Covenant on Civil and Political Rights that the federal or Commonwealth Parliament enacted the Human Rights (Sexual Conduct) Act 1994. That Act was adopted in response to the decision of the United Nations Human Rights Committee in *Toonen* v. *Australia*.[14] That decision found that the sodomy laws of Tasmania, the sole Australian State then to retain such laws, imposed an arbitrary interference with Mr. Toonen's privacy in respect of his adult, consensual, private sexual relationship with his partner. Following a decision of the High Court of Australia in favour of Mr. Toonen and his partner, upholding the constitutional viability of the proceedings,[15] the Tasmanian Parliament repealed the offending provisions of the Criminal Code. It has since enacted a non-discriminatory offence which makes no distinction on the basis of sexuality.

Thirdly, there has been a rapid growth in the number and importance of federal courts and of federal jurisdiction in Australia over the past twenty years. This has been, in part, a response to the general enlargement of federal law, the growth of the federal bureaucracy, the expansion of federal administrative law rights,[16] and the need for effective judicial supervision to bring the rule of law into every corner of federal administration in Australia.

There are six States in Australia. As well, there are two mainland Territories (the Northern Territory of Australia and the Australian Capital Territory) which have been granted substantial self-government under federal legislation. Accordingly, outside the areas regulated directly by federal law in Australia, there are eight significant legal jurisdictions. All have their own separate statutory regimes dealing with the vast array of private law matters, local administrative law and most matters of criminal law. It is beyond the scope of this chapter to review the legislation in each of the eight sub-national Australian jurisdictions. I will therefore concentrate on the State of New South Wales, which is the most populous State in Australia.

CHANGES IN STATE LEGISLATION

As in most jurisdictions which inherit statutes going back to much earlier colonial times, a large number of enactments of the New South Wales Parliament (and some of them not so old) reflect discrimination against homosexual citizens. This has been called to notice by the State Anti-Discrimination Board.[17] The examples are many and found in every corner of the law–even unexpected corners. Thus, the Stamp Duties Act 1920 (NSW) provides that, if a share of a jointly owned property is sold by one party in a heterosexual relationship following the end of that relationship, and if so ordered by a court, the remaining partner may be exempted from paying stamp duty. There is no such entitlement to exemption for a same-sex partner. Similarly, the Superannuation Act 1916 (NSW) contains a definition of "spouse," in relation to a death benefit, which has the consequence that, where a contributor to a superannuation scheme dies without leaving a legally recognised "spouse" (or, in some cases, children), the deceased contributor will receive only a refund of contributions without interest. This involves less favourable treatment for partners of the same sex and some others who are less likely to have a lawful "spouse" or child.

The Adoption of Children Act 1965 (NSW) provides that a court may make an adoption order in favour of a married couple or, in certain circumstances, to a man and a women in a de facto relationship. Such an order cannot be made in favour of persons in a same-sex relationship, whatever its duration and whatever the exceptional circumstances of the case. The Evidence Act 1995 (NSW) contains certain legal privileges in respect of opposite-sex couples which are not extended to same-sex partners. The New South Wales Anti-Discrimination Board has repeatedly submitted to the State Parliament and Government that the legislation of the State needs to be changed to afford wider recognition to relationships involving same-sex partners and persons in non-traditional and/or extended family relationships. Because of the growing numbers of persons in a variety of human relationships who fall outside the protection of the present law, reform of the law is needed. The first, partial and limited reforms took place in 1998 and 1999.

The Equal Opportunity Tribunal established by the Anti-Discrimination Act 1977 (NSW) is empowered to hear complaints in certain circumstances where a person claims to have suffered discrimination on the ground of his homosexuality. Such complaints are now regularly taken to the Tribunal. In 1995, it found that a health fund which had refused to allow the complainants a "family" or "concessional" rate was guilty of unlawful discrimination. The complainants were two males bringing up the son of one of them. They had joint bank accounts, joint ownership of a motor vehicle and a joint mortgage. Although the couple did not fit within the "spouse" relationship under the rules of the fund, they did come within the "family" relationships as defined. They were entitled to the concessional rate. An appeal by the fund to the Supreme Court of New South Wales failed.[18]

As a background to what now follows, it is appropriate to say that such studies as have been conducted in Australia to sample the opinion of same-sex partners seem to indicate that the majority surveyed (80%) do not consider that marriage or marriage equivalence is desirable in their cases.[19] However, they want the discrimination removed and the provision of legal protections against discrimination. At least in New South Wales, the legislators are responding.

In 1998 the Same-Sex Relationships (Compassionate Circumstances) Bill 1998 (NSW) was introduced into the New South Wales Parliament, to meet what were described as "urgent areas of need which relate to wills, family provision and hospital access" for same-sex partners.[20] The purpose of that Bill, a Private Member's measure, was to pick up on a commitment given by the State Premier to the President of the AIDS Council of New South Wales prior to the election in which his party achieved Government in 1995. That commitment was:[21]

> Labor is committed to reform of legislation around same-sex relationships so that same-sex partners have the same rights and responsibilities as heterosexual *de factos* when their partner is hospitalised or incapacitated. We will also ensure that same-sex partners are not discriminated against in the operation of the will and probate and family provisions.

This measure was not enacted when the Government cancelled the allocation of time to Private Members for the remainder of the parliamentary session. Several other Private Member's Bills or related topics also lapsed when the New South Wales Parliament was dissolved for a State election held in March 1999.

The new State Parliament, which convened after the re-election of the Australian Labor Party Government led by Mr. Carr, moved quickly to enact the Property (Relationships) Legislation Amendment Act 1999 (NSW). The Bill for that Act was introduced into the Legislative Council by the State Attorney-General (Mr J W Shaw QC). It was passed by that Chamber by 37 votes to 3. In the Legislative Assembly, it was passed without division. The debates were notable for enlightened views expressed by members of both Houses and both sides of politics, although there were also expressions of prejudice and ignorance.[22] Mr Shaw described the legislation as "historic," which for Australia it certainly is. He went on:[23]

> In an open and liberal society, there is no excuse for discrimination against individuals in our community based on their sexual preference. To deny couples in intimate and ongoing relationships within the gay and lesbian community the same rights as heterosexual *de facto* couples is clearly anomalous.

A speech by a National Party member of the Lower House, representing a rural electorate and a party sometimes described as conservative (Mr. Russell Turner MP), was specially striking:[24]

> Generally, they [people in same-sex relationships] have faced life, they have been through agonies and they, in a lot of instances, are probably far better adjusted than many married couples who are living in a state of acceptance by the community, the church, and the laws of this country.

The legislation broadly assimilated same-sex partners within the De Facto Relationships Act 1984 (NSW), which has been renamed the Property (Relationships) Act–itself a sign of how common *de facto* relations of all kinds are in Australia today.[25]

The thrust of the New South Wales Act is to allow for court orders adjusting property relations on the termination of a domestic relationship. The rights affected include real and personal property rights, such as rights of inheritance upon intestacy, taxes in relation to property transfers between partners, insurance contracts, protected estates, family provision (following inadequate testamentary provision), and State judges' pensions. Non-property rights are conferred in relation to human tissue and medical treatment decisions, coroner's inquest participation, decisions about bail for arrested persons, guardianship and mental health decisions, rights in retirement villages and accident compensation.

A number of New South Wales Acts are amended by the 1999 Act to impose on same-sex couples the same obligations to disclose interests as would exist in the case of spouses. Areas acknowledged as still requiring attention include adoption, foster parenting and superannuation for State government employees. The New South Wales Legislative Council's Standing Committee on Social Issues (chaired by Ms. Jan Burnswoods MLC) has a reference from the New South Wales Parliament on relationships law reform. The Committee has called for submissions on the ways in which the Property (Relationships) Amendment Act 1999 does not adequately address legal concerns necessary to remove residual legal discrimination. In 2003, New South Wales amended the age of consent laws. Previously, as in England until 2000, the law discriminated between sexual activity that is male-male (18 years), male-female (16 years) and female-female (16 years). By legislation enacted in 2003, a uniform general age of consent of 16 years was substituted.

Following the New South Wales legislation, the Parliament of the State of Queensland, amongst others, enacted broadly similar legislation.[26] However, the New South Wales model has been rejected by one New Zealand commentator as not going far enough.[27] On a national level, the importance of the New South Wales and Queensland Acts should not be exaggerated. But they are significant and symbolic. In a Federation such as Australia, reforms enacted in one jurisdiction tend, in time, to influence developments in others. Once it was South Australia that led the way in such matters (including decriminalisation of homosexual acts and the enactment of anti-discrimination legislation). This time it has been New South Wales.

Even before the 1999 reforms were adopted, legislation was enacted by the New South Wales Parliament which provided an interesting model to afford protection to people in same-sex relationships under State law. Thus, the Workers' Compensation Legislation Amendment (Dust Diseases and Other Matters) Act 1998 (NSW) contained, in Schedule 6, a number of amendments to the Workers' Compensation (Dust Diseases) Act 1942 (NSW). Amongst those changes is a new definition of "de facto relationship" in s. 3(1) of the 1942 Act. The redefinition is broad enough to encompass same-sex relationships:

> *De facto relationship* means the relationship between two unrelated adult persons:
>
> a. Who have a mutual commitment to a shared life, and
> b. Whose relationship is genuine and continuing, and
> c. Who live together, and who are not married to one another.

This provision allows for definitional flexibility as social considerations develop and change. Much work remains to be done. But significant reforms have been accepted in Australia's most populous State. A model has been provided for the rest.

CHANGES IN FEDERAL LEGISLATION

The Australian Constitution, which celebrated its centenary in 2001, is one of the four oldest documents of its kind still in operation in the world. When adopted, it did not contain a general Bill of Rights, such as became common in the post-independence constitutions of other countries of the Commonwealth of Nations. There is therefore no precise equivalent to the Bill of Rights in the United States Constitution, or the Charter of Rights and Freedoms in the Canadian Constitution, to stimulate and facilitate challenges to discriminatory provisions in federal law. Generally speaking, in such matters Australians must rely on the Federal, State and Territory Parliaments and Governments to secure changes. Only rarely can the aid of the courts be involved.

Under the Australian Constitution, one matter upon which the federal Parliament enjoys legislative power is "immigration and emigration."[28] Since 1984, in part because of lobbying by the Gay and Lesbian Immigration Task Force (GLITF), changes have been introduced into Australian migration law and practice which have expanded the rights of entry into Australia of persons in same-sex relationships.

The main breakthrough occurred in 1985 when Mr. Chris Hurford was Minister for Immigration. Upon his instructions, regulations and practices were adopted which, to a very large extent, removed discrimination and provided for the consideration of applications for migration to Australia largely (but not entirely) on an equal footing.

Entry into Australia of non-residents is governed by the Migration Act 1958 (Commonwealth) and the regulations made under that Act. The regulations now provide for visa subclasses to permit the entry into Australia of people in "interdependent" relationships. This is the adjectival clause which has been adopted to describe same-sex partners. The relevant Australian visa classes are 310 and 301. They permit migration to Australia of a person sponsored by his or her partner. Comparable visas to allow change of status within Australia are visa classes 826 and 814.[29] The two categories mirror, in turn, those applying to persons seeking entry to Australia on the basis of a *de facto* heterosexual relationship.

The annual migration programme (RAM) for Australia contains an allocated number of places available to persons in the "interdependent" categories. By comparison to the total size of Australia's migration programme, the numbers are very small. For the financial year 1996-97, 400 places were reserved for "interdependency visas."

Some discrimination remains in migration law and practice. Thus, for heterosexual *de facto* relationships and "interdependency relationships," the partners must be able to prove a twelve-month committed relationship before being eligible to proceed with the application. In the case of heterosexual relationships, this precondition can be overcome, quite simply, by marriage, an event substantially within the control of the persons themselves. A similar shortcut is not available to same-sex couples. In some countries which still criminalise, prosecute or stigmatise persons who establish a same-sex household, proof of twelve months' cohabitation, especially with a foreigner, may be difficult or even impossible. Provision is made for waiver of this requirement in compelling circumstances.

A second important omission from current immigration law is that persons from overseas, who are not Australian or New Zealand citizens and seek either to migrate or enter Australia temporarily, are unable to include in their application as members of their family unit (and thus bring with them) persons with whom they presently reside in their country of origin in a same-sex relationship. GLITF has made representations for the amendment of the law in this regard. However, the Minister has indicated that a same-sex partner of an applicant for immigration must apply for a visa in their own right if they wish to enter Australia with their partner. Only a person in a same-sex relationship with an Australian citizen (or a permanent resident or an eligible New Zealand citizen) is able to apply for an interdependency visa for migration to Australia, sponsored by the Australian partner.[30]

Notwithstanding these defects, it is clear that Australian immigration law is comparatively enlightened on this subject. As yet, only a dozen countries (the United Kingdom, the Netherlands, Belgium, Iceland, Norway, Denmark, Sweden, Finland, Australia, New Zealand, South Africa and Canada) have a policy of recognising same-sex relationships for immigration purposes. In the case of the United Kingdom, only in October 1997 did the Immigration Minister announce a "concession" whereby most couples legally unable to marry, including same-sex partners (a category formally rejected) would be recognised for purposes of immigration to the United Kingdom.[31]

In the field of refugee law, Australia is a party to the 1951 Refugees Convention, which is incorporated into domestic law.[32] One of the categories of persons entitled to enjoy refugee status is one who "owing to a well-founded fear of being persecuted for reasons of . . . membership of a particular social group . . . is outside the country of his nationality and is unable or, owing to such fear, is unwilling to avail himself of the protection of that country." The possibility that in some countries homosexuals and others in same-sex relationships would be so categorised has been recognised in a number of decisions in Australia and the United Kingdom.[33] In Australia, for at least five years, both the Department of Immigration at the primary level and the Refugee Review Tribunal have granted refugee status to both male and female homosexuals who could establish a well-founded fear of persecution if returned to their country of nationality.[34] Various difficulties arise in such a case, because of views sometimes taken in the Tribunal concerning the need for applicants to prove their sexual orientation, and because of a paucity of information about the persecution of homosexuals in some countries. Australia has developed policies for the group "women at risk." There may be a need for similar supportive programmes for homosexual refugees and also for their same-sex partners.[35] Many of them are at serious risk in their countries of origin or temporary residence.

Superannuation is now largely regulated in Australia by federal laws. The Senate Select Committee on Superannuation of the Australian Parliament reported in September 1997.[36] The Committee put forward "as a general proposition" a proposal earlier made to it, in the context of a review of superannuation: that persons without defined dependents (such as their widow, widower or eligible children) should have an entitlement under federal law to nominate a beneficiary, so that they do not lose entirely the benefit of entitlements which would otherwise accrue to them were they in a currently eligible relationship. The Senate Committee recognised that the present provisions were a "discrimination against those . . . not in a recognised relationship."[37] The Committee held back from making a recommendation that provision should be made for the "nomination of a dependent" because of reconsideration of the current structure of the scheme established by the Act.[38] However, as in the case of the Parliamentary Scheme, applicable to federal politicians, the Committee recommended[39] that the rules under which the benefits were paid "should be reviewed to ensure that they are in accordance with community standards."

A Private Member's Bill,[40] introduced into the House of Representatives of the federal Parliament by an Opposition member, sought to remove discrimination against same-sex couples in the sphere of superannuation. Earlier, a larger measure was introduced into the Australian Senate,[41] also by an Opposition Senator. It was referred to the Senate Legal and Constitutional References Committee. In December 1997, that Committee tabled a report recommending that couples or partners should be protected by superannuation entitlements regardless of their sexuality or gender. Neither of the foregoing Bills has yet attracted the support of the Australian Government. In March 2000, a further Private Member's Bill identical to the one that had stalled in the House of Representatives was introduced into the Australian Senate in the hope of advancing consideration of its proposals in the Parliament. It remains under consideration.

The discrimination in the field of superannuation and like benefits has become more noticeable as other federal legislation, and legislatively encouraged moves in Australia, have come to recognise and protect the "employment packages" of persons governed by federal law. Nowadays, it is much more common to look to a person's total employment "package" rather than just their base salary. Where there is a significant differentiation in superannuation and like benefits, unconnected with the quality of their professional performance and concerned only with their private domestic arrangements, unjust discrimination can be seen in sharp relief.[42] According to news reports, politicians of most political alignments in Australia have begun to perceive the serious injustice which is worked by current superannuation and like laws in the case of persons living in stable same-sex relationships.[43]

However, in 2003 the Australian Government introduced legislation to change superannuation laws in Australia in significant ways. This legislation withheld important benefits from same-sex partners. Opposition attempts to amend the legislative package, to insist on equality of treatment of all people in domestic relationships, narrowly failed in the Australian Senate in October 2003. The withholding of benefits to same-sex couples was apparently deliberate.

In 1999, an Australian Ambassador, presenting his credentials to the Monarch of the country to which he was accredited by Australia, took along his same-sex partner. Such relationships are legally recognised in that country, where the action of the Ambassador would have been unremarkable. Yet the diplomat and his partner had to suffer the indignity in Australia of a tabloid headline reducing his serious professional career to the insult: "Three Queens in One Palace."[44] It took more courage and honesty for the Ambassador to do as he did than to continue with pretence. It took more courage and integrity than the anonymous byline writer exhibited in the newspaper concerned. And it must be acknowledged that the Australian Department of Foreign Affairs and Trade has, in this respect, observed a non-discriminatory policy. The certified agreement adopted by the Australian Department of Foreign Affairs under the Workplace Relations Act 1996 (Cth)[45] states:

> The conditions regarding the official recognition of *de facto* relationships for the purpose of the conditions of service apply regardless of sexual preferences.

Similar statutory "certified agreements" have been adopted by other federal departments and agencies in Australia. In practice, this means that for most benefits of office (but not yet superannuation), same-sex partnerships enjoy equal employment benefits in the federal public service in Australia. Thus, in the Australian foreign service, they include: airfares to and from posting; the payment of supplementary living allowances as a couple whilst overseas; the payment of other incidental allowances on the same basis where an entitlement arises (e.g., clothing allowances); and the payment of health cover by the Federal Government for both partners during the posting. It is necessary to have the relationship officially recognised by the relevant Department before the partners proceed to the posting, by the provision of a statutory declaration with accompanying evidence. But these and other benefits are closely assimilated to those of any other non-married *de facto* partner. The achievement of such entitlements and practices evidences a commitment by those in charge to the principle of non-discrimination in the matter of sexuality and federal public employment.

The Parliament of Australia in respect of its members, and in some areas of its legislative responsibility, has begun to act. The agencies of the federal Government in Australia have moved, in respect of federal officers, to abolish discrimination in employment benefits, and to exercise their powers under delegated legislation in a non-discriminatory way.[46] Even the federal Judicature has begun to provide benefits of domestic and international travel for non-married partners of federal judges of whatever sex. But the federal Judges' Pensions Act 1968 remains resolutely unchanged.[47]

THE JOURNEY OF ENLIGHTENMENT

There are other changes which are occurring in the statutory regimes governing the benefits of same-sex partners in Australia. The changes are occurring bit by bit and piece by piece. This is what happened earlier with racial and gender discrimination. It is still happening in those fields. The end of unfair discrimination has not yet been achieved. Australia, like other countries, is on a journey of enlightenment. It has taken important steps, but many more remain to be taken. It seems likely that progress towards the removal of discrimination which cannot be rationally justified will continue. As it serves a people generally committed to equal justice for all under the law, I have confidence that the Australian legal system, and those who make the laws in Australia, will, in due course, eliminate unfair discrimination on the basis of sexual orientation. The scales are dropping from our eyes. Injustice and irrational prejudice cannot long survive the scrutiny of just men and women.

It would appear to be in the interests of society to protect stable and mutually supportive relationships and mutual economic commitment. It would seem against society's interests to penalise, disadvantage and discourage them. Australia is gradually accepting this truth. There remain stubborn opponents. Various reforms remain to be achieved. And beyond Australia, there is a world of discrimination and oppression to be shamed and cajoled into action. Clearly, this will be one of the big issues of human rights in the coming decades. It is therefore a topic important to the lawyers and citizens of the world.

NOTES

1. *Report of the Committee on Homosexual Offences and Prostitution*, Cmnd. 247 (London, HMSO, 1957) (chaired by Sir John Wolfenden).
2. *Sexual Offences Act* 1967 (England and Wales). The *Sexual Offences (Amendment) Act 2000* removed discrimination from the age of consent in sexual offences in the whole of the United Kingdom in Nov. 2000. In Australia, the discriminatory statutory provisions on the age of consent for sexual activity have gradually begun to disappear. In 2002, the Parliament of Western Australia abolished the differential age of consent of 21 years for males, substituting a common age of consent at 16 years. See *Acts Amendment (Lesbian and Gay Law Reform) Act 2002* (WA). In New South Wales, by the *Crimes Amendment (Sexual Offences) Act 2003* (NSW), the age of consent for males was reduced from 18 years to 16 years, the same as for females.
3. See *Washington Post* (26 December 1998) A12 (survey conducted by the *Washington Post*, Kayser Family Foundation, and Harvard University).
4. G Niebuhr, "In US Pontiff to look to the new generation" *International Herald Tribune* (26 January 1999) 2. For parallels between discrimination against women and against homosexuals, see Martha Nussbaum, *Sex and Social Justice* (New York, Oxford University Press, 1998).
5. Citing *Instrumentum Laboris* No. 3. Bishop Patrick Power, "Marginalised People: In Society and in the Church," address to the Oceania Synod of Bishops, 1998.
6. *Dudgeon v. United Kingdom* (1981) 4 European Human Rights Reports (EHRR) 149; *Norris v. Republic of Ireland* (1988) 13 EHRR 186; *Modinos v Cyprus* (1993) 16 EHRR 485.
7. *Toonen v. Australia* (1994) 1 International Human Rights Reports 97.
8. *Egan v Canada* [1995] 2 SCR 513; *M v H* [1999] 2 SCR 3. See generally Robert Wintemute, "Discrimination Against Same-Sex Couples: Sections 15(1) and 1 of the Charter: *Egan v. Canada*" (1995) 74 *Canadian Bar Review* 682, "Sexual Orientation Discrimination as Sex Discrimination: Same-Sex Couples and the *Charter* in *Mossop, Egan* and *Layland*" (1994) 39 *McGill Law Journal* 429. See now *Halpern & MCCT v Canada (AG)* [2003] O.J. No.2268 (C.A.).
9. *Quilter v Attorney-General* [1998] 1 NZLR 523.
10. *Fitzpatrick* v. *Sterling Housing Association Ltd* [2001] 1 AC 27 (House of Lords).

11. Australian Constitution, section 122.

12. For example, in *Re Wakim, ex parte McNally* (1999) 93 ALJR 839 at 850, McHugh J remarked that the "marriage" power in the Australian Constitution (section 51(xxi)) might today "or in the near future" mean "a voluntary union for life between two *people* to the exclusion of others," so as to permit the Parliament of the Commonwealth to "legislate for same-sex marriages."

13. *Attorney-General of the Commonwealth* v. *Breckler* (1999) 197 CLR 83 at 115-119 (High Court of Australia).

14. *Supra* n. 8.

15. *Croome* v. *Tasmania* (1997) 191 Commonwealth Law Reports 119.

16. Administrative Appeals Tribunal Act 1975 (Commonwealth); Administrative Decisions (Judicial Review) Act 1977 (C'wealth).

17. New South Wales Anti-Discrimination Board, Newsletter, *Equal Time*, Feb. 1999.

18. *NIB Funds Limited* v. *Hope* (15 Nov. 1996), Supreme Court of New South Wales, unreported.

19. Sotirios Sarantakos, "Legal recognition of same-sex relationships" (1998) 23 *Alternative Law Journal* 222, "Same-Sex Marriage: Which Way to Go?" (1994) 24 *Alternative Law Journal* 79.

20. C Moore MP (NSW), *Media Release*, 20 October 1998.

21. Letter by the Hon. R Carr MP to the President, AIDS Council of NSW, 22 February 1995. See Statement by Ms. Clover Moore MP to the Legislative Assembly of New South Wales in New South Wales Parliamentary Debates (Legislative Assembly), 22 October 1998, at 59.

22. See Millbank & Morgan, in their chapter in Wintemute & Andenas, *supra* note 1.

23. See New South Wales Parliamentary Debates (Legislative Council) 13 May 1999, 228; 26 May 1999, 36.

24. See New South Wales Parliamentary Debates (Legislative Council), 1 June 1999, 740 at 741. Subsequently the Leader of the National Party was reported as predicting that there would be "no more watering down our opposition to indulgent and selfish gay rights laws": *Sydney Morning Herald* (19 June 1999) 11.

25. Jenni Millbank & Kathy Sant, "A Bride in Her Every-day Clothes: Same Sex Relationship Recognition in N.S.W.," (2000) 22 *Sydney Law Review* 181.

26. Property Law Amendment Act 1999; Industrial Relations Act 1999, Schedule 5, definitions of "spouse" and "discrimination." Substantial legislation has also been enacted by the Parliaments of Victoria and Western Australia and a package of laws has also been enacted by the Parliament of Tasmania.

27. D.F. Dugdale, "Same-Sex Relationships" (Feb. 2000) *New Zealand Law Journal* 3.

28. Australian Constitution, section 51(xxvii). The Commonwealth also enjoys power with respect to naturalisation and aliens (section 51(xix)) and external affairs (section 51(xxix)).

29. D Bitel, "Recognition of Same-Sex Relationships in Australian Immigration Law," unpublished paper, International Bar Association Conference, Vancouver, September 1998, at 3. See especially the federal Migration Regulations, reg. 1.09A ("Interdependent relationships").

30. GLITF (NSW), *Same-Sex Couple Discrimination for Independent and Business Visa Applications*, submission to the Australian Human Rights and Equal Opportunity Commission (June 1997).

31. Wesley Gryk, "The Recognition of Unmarried Relationships Under British Immigration Law–An Evolving Process?", unpublished paper, International Bar Association Conference, Vancouver, 16 September 1998, at 2.

32. Migration Act 1958 (Commonwealth), section 4(1).

33. Cf *Applicant A v. Minister for Immigration and Multicultural Affairs* (1997) 190 Commonwealth Law Reports 225 at 304 (n.296). See also *R v. Immigration Appeal Tribunal, ex parte Shah* [1999] 2 AC 629 at 663 per Lord Millett (". . . [g]iven the hostility encountered by all homosexuals in such a society and the obvious problems the applicant would have in satisfying his tormentors of his own sexual abstinence, I doubt that the difficulty [of establishing that a fear of persecution was well founded] would be a real one").

34. Bitel, *supra* n 30 at 4-5.

35. Cf Bitel, *ibid.* at 5.

36. Australian Parliament, Senate Select Committee on Superannuation, *The Parliamentary Contributory Superannuation Scheme and the Judges' Pensions Scheme*, 25th Report, Canberra, September 1997.

37. *Ibid.* at para. 4.6.

38. *Ibid.* at para. 4.7.

39. *Ibid.*, Recommendation 4.1.

40. Superannuation (Entitlements of Same-Sex Couples) Bill 1998. The member introducing the Bill (Mr. A Albanese MP) gave the Second Reading Speech for the Bill on 7 June 1999, which has not yet been enacted. The speech followed shortly after a report of the Australian Human Rights and Equal Opportunity Commission, *Superannuation Entitlements of Same-Sex Couples* (June 1999), was tabled in the Federal Parliament by the Attorney-General. The Commission found that present Australian superannuation law was in breach of two international conventions to which Australia is a party, the International Covenant on Civil and Political Rights and the ILO Discrimination (Employment and Occupation) Convention. In August 2000, the conference of the Australian Labor Party (ALP) adopted the removal of discrimination against same-sex couples in the context of superannuation as party policy. The ALP is the main Opposition Party in the Australian Federal Parliament.

41. Sexuality Discrimination Bill 1995.

42. See D McCarthy, "Superannuated" *Brother-Sister* (Melbourne) (No 182, 15 April 1999) 7.

43. C Pearson, "Saving not such a super idea for same-sex couples," *Australian Financial Review* (3 May 1999) 19. Cf. the motion of Ms. Leane Burke MP (Prahran) in the Victorian Parliament, adopted by the Victorian conference of the Liberal Party of Australia, which urged the Federal Government to "ensure same-sex partners are given equality of treatment with respect to superannuation payments as those given to opposite-sex *de facto* partners." See also J McKenzie, "Super Boost for Equality Campaign", *Brother-Sister* (No. 182, 15 April 1999) 3.

44. *Daily Telegraph* (Sydney) (26 February 1999) 7.

45. Australia, Department of Foreign Affairs and Trade, Certified Agreement, 1998-2000.

46. See Australia, Remuneration Tribunal, Determination No 2 of 1998, Members of the Parliament–Travelling Allowance, para. 2.8: "A senator or member may nominate to the Special Minister of State one nominee as eligible to receive travel privileges under this entitlement, and, subject to any procedural rules made by the Special Minister of State, may vary that nomination from time to time."

47. Cf. Carl Stychin, "*Grant*-ing Rights: The Politics of Rights, Sexuality and the European Union" (2000) 51 *Northern Ireland Legal Quarterly* 281 at 282, 300.

Transsexuals and European Human Rights Law

The Hon. Lord Robert Reed

Court of Session and High Court of Justiciary, Scotland

SUMMARY. Sexual identity is a legal status, and as such it is as much dependent on public policy as on self-identification. However, because this status can be crucial to one's role in society, a conflict between the legal status and an individual's perceptions or aspirations creates a dilemma if society is committed to individual freedom. This difficulty can become particularly acute where it is technically possible for an individual to alter some of the factors used socially or legally to determine sexual identity. This paper analyses these difficulties, both from the situation of endocrine disorder and with respect to gender identity. It argues that this distinction in approach may not be a valid basis for different legal treatment. It considers four major issues: the stage at which a change of gender should be recognised; any preconditions to which a legal change of gender should be made subject; whether legal recognition should be made for all purposes or only for specific areas of the law; and the confidentiality of a person's previous sexual identity. The paper particularly analyses the law in the United Kingdom and then considers other jurisdictions before focusing on the treatment of transsexuals under the European Convention on Human Rights. *[Article copies available for a fee from The Haworth Document Delivery Service:*

The Hon. Lord Robert Reed is Judge of the Court of Session and High Court of Justiciary in Scotland.

[Haworth co-indexing entry note]: "Transsexuals and European Human Rights Law." Reed, Robert. Co-published simultaneously in *Journal of Homosexuality* (Harrington Park Press, an imprint of The Haworth Press, Inc.) Vol. 48, No. 3/4, 2005, pp. 49-90; and: *Sexuality and Human Rights: A Global Overview* (ed: Helmut Graupner, and Phillip Tahmindjis) Harrington Park Press, an imprint of The Haworth Press, Inc., 2005, pp. 49-90. Single or multiple copies of this article are available for a fee from The Haworth Document Delivery Service [1-800-HAWORTH, 9:00 a.m. - 5:00 p.m. (EST). E-mail address: docdelivery@haworthpress.com].

http://www.haworthpress.com/web/JH
© 2005 by The Haworth Press, Inc. All rights reserved.
Digital Object Identifier: 10.1300/J082v48n03_05

1-800-HAWORTH. E-mail address: <docdelivery@haworthpress.com> Website: <http://www.HaworthPress.com> © 2005 by The Haworth Press, Inc. All rights reserved.]

KEYWORDS. Transgender, human rights, gender identity, European Convention on Human Rights, legal indicia for sexual identity

INTRODUCTION

Rejection of sex discrimination may incline us to assume that a person's sex is, or should be, irrelevant to his or her legal rights. Indeed, in a case before the European Court of Justice, the Advocate-General appealed to what he described as "a universal fundamental value, indelibly etched in modern legal traditions and in the constitutions of the more advanced countries: *the irrelevance of a person's sex with regard to the rules regulating relations in society.*"[1] Over a very large area, the law of a modern western society, such as the United Kingdom, is indeed indifferent to sex. Sex is irrelevant to most of the legal relationships which give rise to rights and obligations under the law of contract or the law of delict, and to most of the criminal law. It is however relevant to some legal relationships and concepts, because it is considered to be material in fact. For example, it is considered relevant to contracts of life assurance, because women generally live somewhat longer than men. It is relevant to the age of legal capacity in some legal systems, because puberty tends to occur earlier in girls than in boys. In some situations, sex is an essential ingredient of a legal relationship or concept. For example, in Scotland only a woman can be the victim of rape (the corresponding offence, where the victim is male, being distinct), and only a man can commit rape (other than as an accessory). A traditional example is the contention that marriage can be entered into only by a man and a woman.

The particular legal relationships or concepts to which sex is relevant, or of which it is an essential ingredient, vary from one legal system to another, depending to some extent on the degree to which the society expects different social roles and behaviour of the sexes; but it is difficult to envisage a legal system which was entirely indifferent to sex, just as it is difficult to imagine a society in which a person's sex would not be important to his or her personality and relationships with others. The legal significance attached to a person's sex can of course give rise to a variety of issues; but the most fundamental difficulty arises insofar as the assignation of a person to a particular sex is itself problematical.

Since sexual identity is a legal status, it is not determined by the individual, but is dependent on public policy. At the same time, because it is an aspect of status which is critical to an individual's role in society, to an even greater extent than some other aspects of status (such as legitimacy or marriage), it is difficult to separate from an individual's personality and has a particular impact upon an individual's self-determination. To the extent that there is a conflict between individuals' perceptions or aspirations in respect of their own sexual identity, and their legal status as a member of one sex or the other, that conflict will give rise to difficulties in a society committed to individual freedom. Such difficulties become acute under circumstances in which it is technically possible for an individual to choose to alter certain (but not all) of the factors used socially or legally as criteria of sexual identity. In the great majority of cases there is of course no difficulty in determining the sex to which a person belongs. But there are cases in which the issue is problematical. Such cases are of interest to medicine as well as to the law; and the legal approach to such cases has, inevitably and properly, been influenced by the state of medical understanding and the nature of medical treatment.

Modern medicine would, I understand, divide such cases into two broad categories: cases involving an endocrine disorder causing non-conventional physiological sexual differentiation; and cases involving a condition known as gender dysphoria syndrome or gender identity disorder. It may be helpful to say something about these medical matters before going further.[2]

Irregularities of physiological sexual differentiation are characterised by an abnormality in the formation of the internal or external genital structures. Most are genetically determined and are associated with an ambiguous appearance of the external genitalia. Some persons in this category are genetically female and have ovaries; others are genetically male and have testes; and the remainder have both ovarian and testicular tissue. The medical treatment of such persons generally begins in childhood. Advice as to the appropriate sex-of-rearing is based mainly on the appearance of the external genitalia and on the likely pattern of secondary sexual development at puberty (based on the likely diagnosis of the condition). Gender conversion after puberty remains a possibility. The treatment of a person subject to such a condition may involve the use of hormones to promote the characteristics of the sex regarded as more appropriate, and surgical treatment to render the body more "normal" in its appearance. The sex which treatment aims to consolidate will usually be that which the person has adopted psychologically and socially, which may be different from the person's chromosomal sex.

Gender dysphoria syndrome, on the other hand, is a condition of persons who are anatomically "normal" and who experience a strong and persistent cross-gender identification. This may manifest itself in persistent discomfort about the person's birth sex or a sense of inappropriateness in the gender role of that sex, and as a result suffer clinically significant distress or impairment in social, occupational or other important areas of functioning. It is to persons in this category that the term "transsexual" is usually applied: persons who belong physically to one sex (prior to treatment, at least) but believe that they belong to the other sex, and who often seek medical and surgical treatment so as to adapt their physical characteristics to their psychological nature, and thereby achieve a better integrated identity. The treatment of such persons may involve gender re-assignment treatment, by means of hormones and surgery, to give them a physical appearance resembling that of the sex with which they identify. Other procedures may also be undertaken, such as breast implants, electrolysis for the removal of hair, reshaping of the nose, and speech therapy. Such treatment can enable a transsexual person to have sexual relations with a member of his or her original sex, but not to procreate (other than through the use of preserved gametes) and the chromosomes of a post-operative transsexual remain those of the original sex. Scottish and Dutch data suggest that approximately 1 in 12,400 males over 15 years of age and 1 in 50,000 females are transsexual. There is no necessary connection between transsexualism and sexual orientation: the great majority of transsexuals are said to be heterosexual.

It should be noted that the account given in the preceding paragraph is a generalisation: transsexuality is infinitely varied, and all individuals in this category do not all raise identical issues. For example, although most transsexuals identify with the opposite gender from early childhood, several of the leading cases have concerned male to female transsexuals who had led "conventional" lives, having married women[3] and in some cases fathered children.[4] Similarly, although most transsexuals seek gender re-assignment treatment, one of the cases has concerned a transsexual who refused to undergo such treatment.[5] There is also a variation in the extent to which treatment is taken: most of the cases have concerned situations where there had been full reconstructive surgery, but one of the cases concerned a situation where only partial surgery had been carried out, affecting the secondary sexual characteristics only.[6] For medical reasons it is common for female-to-male transsexuals, in particular, not to undergo full re-assignment surgery. It would also be a mistake to assume that the end result of treatment is always satisfactory, in the sense that a reasonable approximation to the desired gender is achieved. This is reflected in Portuguese law, where (as I understand the position) gender re-assignment surgery cannot lawfully be performed, but persons operated upon elsewhere can request a court's authorisation to have civil status amendments made. The court's decision in such a case is influenced by the success of the treatment as reflected in the transsexual's appearance and the consequent likelihood of social acceptance in the new gender.[7]

Physiological disorders have long presented a problem to legal systems requiring an exhaustive classification of persons as either male or female. The problem was discussed, for example, in Roman law.[8] Gender dysphoria, on the other hand, although not a new condition, has only in relatively recent times been the subject of medical study and it has given rise to acute legal difficulties only since the advent of gender re-assignment treatment. Those who have undergone such treatment will generally wish to be legally recognised as belonging to the sex with which they identify: indeed, their condition may well cause them to suffer continuing psychological distress unless such recognition is granted. It is with such persons that the present paper is principally concerned.

With physiological conditions which can lead to difficulty in deciding the biological sex to which a person belongs, once the most appropriate sex has been decided, medical and surgical treatment can be used to remove any apparent features of the other biological sex. Any "change" of sex–if, for example, the individual was registered at birth as belonging to one sex, and it is subsequently decided that the other sex is more appropriate–can be regarded as the correction of a mistake. The public response to such individuals can be expected to be, in general, one of sympathy and acceptance that treatment is appropriate.

Transsexuals, on the other hand, are (so far as present understanding goes) persons whose treatment involves the alteration of a body of one sex so as to create the appearance of a body of the opposite sex. The surgery does not alter their biological sex, which is fixed at birth, but brings their physical appearance into conformity with their psychological convictions. One might hope, in a humane society, that such individuals would also be regarded as entitled to a sympathetic acceptance of the appropriateness of medical or surgical treatment. In the past, however, in the United Kingdom at least, they have at times been treated with hostility and derision. The disjunction between biological sex and the desire to live and be accepted as a member of the opposite sex appears to have offended against a taboo, and to have been perceived to some extent as unnatural and distasteful. I have the impression that, in more recent times, antipathy has waned and there has to some extent been a more compassionate attitude,[9] although transsexuals are still sometimes treated in the press and in advertising in a humorous fashion.[10] Nevertheless, there remains a degree of prejudice and stigmatisation. In consequence, the desire of post-operative transsexuals to be accepted socially in their new sexual identity has been capable of realisation only if the fact of their being post-operative transsexuals has remained concealed: something which depends, in part, upon the legal regime under which sexual identity is given official recognition. At the same time, the endeavours of transsexuals to obtain legal recognition of their new identity have not received the support of the legislature in the United Kingdom,[11] possibly reflecting a more general lack of support. It would be inaccurate, however, to criticise such a lack of support as simply unthinking hostility and prejudice, as significant legal, social, ethical and symbolic issues are raised. Nor is an unwillingness to accept a change of sex peculiar to the popular press or the less well educated. An all-women college at Cambridge, for example, was divided on the question whether to accept a fellow who was discovered to be a post-operative transsexual.[12] Nor is this attitude unique to the United Kingdom: a series of cases from other Member States of the Council of Europe, the European Commission and Court of Human Rights have recognised the negative reactions to transsexuality.[13]

The distinction drawn between gender dysphoria and physiological disorders, however, is less clear-cut than might be thought, and may prove to be a less defensible justification for a difference in treatment than might be supposed. In some respects, it is difficult to draw a clear distinction between physiological disorders and transsexualism. Testicular feminisation syndrome, for example, involves an apparently normal woman with a vulva but no vagina, no uterus, undescended testes and a male chromosome pattern. Such a person is likely to be raised, and to regard herself, as a woman, and may well undergo surgery and other treatment to create a vagina and other female characteristics, so as to give her a body which corresponds to the gender in which she is socially and psychologically at home. If the position of a male-to-female transsexual is to be distinguished, that must be on the basis that (1) her condition is the result of psychological rather than physical factors, or (2) that she has had all the outward characteristics of one sex–and may have lived socially as a member of that sex, even marrying and fathering children–prior to adopting those of the other sex. So far as the first of these points is concerned, caution has to be exercised about assuming that gender dysphoria is a purely psychological condition. Some relatively recent scientific studies suggest that gender dysphoria may have a physiological basis in the structure of the brain,[14] although whether this is inherent, or due to hormone treatment, environmental or other factors, is a matter of controversy.[15] The second ground of distinction might be considered to be more convincing, if a distinction is to be drawn, but it might really be more relevant to the retrospective effects of any change of sexual identity and the attitudes of third parties.

One aspect of the problem is that sexual identity is part of what one might call the core sense of self. Sexual differentiation is not simply physical. From the subjective viewpoint of the individual concerned, gender must be determined psychologically: usually that determination will be congruent with biological indicia, such as the genitalia and secondary sexual characteristics, but in the case of transsexuals it is not. From the point of view of others, on the other hand, the biological indicia are, even in the case of transsexuals, liable to be of overriding importance. A life insurance company, for example, will want to know whether to assess the risk presented by an individual on the basis of the actuarial data relating to men or those relating to women and the biological criteria may be a more reliable guide to the choice of data than the psychology of the individual involved. The distinction sometimes drawn between sex and gender–i.e., the biological sex on the one hand, and the psycho-social sexual identity[16] on the other hand–is a useful way of differentiating between these concepts.

The way in which a legal system treats transsexuals will inevitably reflect a variety of aspects of that system. This paper will begin by looking at the way in which the relevant law in the United Kingdom has evolved, and will then consider very briefly the law of other jurisdictions, before focusing on the treatment of transsexuals under the European Convention on Human Rights. The European experience is of interest in showing how, even in the absence of any right concerned expressly with sexuality, other rights can have a bearing on the issues raised. The evolution of the European law is also of particular interest in the United Kingdom in view of the implementation of the Human Rights Act 1998 (which came fully into force in October 2000, and gives domestic effect within the United Kingdom to the European Convention on Human Rights), and which may result in a tendency towards the "constitutionalisation" of United Kingdom law (including private law).

UNITED KINGDOM LAW

Traditionally, legal thinking in the United Kingdom is not rights-based, although it might be described as libertarian, or at least *laissez faire*: broadly speaking, everything is permitted that is not expressly prohibited. That approach might be regarded as having facilitated the treatment of transsexuals, insofar as gender re-assignment surgery has been regarded as a matter between patient and doctor, and has not been subject to specific legal regulation.[17] This is different from the position in several other European countries, where gender re-assignment surgery is either prohibited (as in Portugal) or, more commonly, can be carried out only with the authority of a court after strict conditions have been met (as in France and Denmark). Equally, the ease with which names can be changed, and the absence of identity papers from British life, mean that transsexuals are spared the frequent embarrassment to which they have been exposed under, for example, the French system. The relatively informal nature of administrative arrangements in the United Kingdom enables many other potential problems to be avoided through the application of common sense: for example, whether a transsexual sentenced to a term of imprisonment should be held with men or with women;[18] or whether she should be treated in hospital in a male or female ward. Issues of this kind are not dependent on legal status, but are resolved on the basis of individual circumstances, the social status being, in practice, the principal factor. On the other hand, the absence of any fundamental constitutional rights analogous to those contained in the European Convention has had the consequence that problems concerning the legal classification of post-operative transsexuals have been addressed in the specific contexts in which they have arisen, as a matter of interpretation of the legislation or common law principles relevant to that context (which are likely to have been formulated without such problems in mind, or indeed before such problems became a technological possibility). The absence of official identification papers (unlike in many other European societies, where identification papers from British society require to be carried and produced) also has the consequences that, when identity does require to be established, reliance is placed upon documents prepared for some other purpose, such as passports, driving licences and birth certificates. Transsexuals are able to have their passports, driving licences and tax records altered to reflect their new identity without difficulty but, as will appear, birth certificates are regarded as historical records of birth details, and accordingly cannot be altered to reflect a change of sexual identity. Their use as evidence of identity is officially discouraged, but is nonetheless a matter of practice in some contexts.

One of the earliest relevant legal cases in the United Kingdom concerned an application to alter the record of a person's birth details as contained in the official register of births, so as to alter the sex recorded there. It was held that the register was a historical record, and therefore could not be altered in consequence of events occurring subsequent to birth, unless (as in a case where the sex of a child is indeterminate at birth) it was discovered that an error had been made.[19] That decision was based on the interpretation of the legislation establishing the register. The legislation has subsequently been amended to enable certain events occurring subsequent to birth (namely, legitimation and adoption) to be reflected in the register, but not the change of gender of a post-operative transsexual.[20] As will be seen, this has given rise to a number of cases before the European Court of Human Rights.

Other relevant cases have concerned the law of marriage. These cases have been contested between private parties, one of whom has sought to assert, and the other to deny, the validity of a purported marriage entered into between them. Early cases concerned persons born with a physiological disorder, and focused on the requirement of the English common law that the parties to a marriage must be capable of consummating it. The sex of the individuals concerned was not in issue, and it was assumed in each case that one party was male and the other was female. In a case where the woman had undergone surgical treatment to create female genitalia (and to remove male genitalia), it was held that a female with surgically created genitalia was incapable of normal sexual relations and therefore could not marry.[21] Doubts as to the correctness of that decision were however expressed in a subsequent case in the Court of Appeal.[22]

This formed the background to the important case of *Corbett* v *Corbett*,[23] which concerned a purported marriage between a man and a post-operative male-to-female transsexual. In this case the plaintiff founded primarily on the requirement of the English common law that marriage be entered into between a man and a woman: the true sex of the transsexual was thus placed in issue. The capacity of the transsexual to consummate the marriage was also raised as a secondary issue. The medical evidence before the Court was that there were at least four criteria for assessing the sexual identity of an individual. These were:

    i. chromosomal factors;
   ii. gonadal factors (i.e. presence or absence of testes or ovaries);

iii. genital factors (including internal sex organs); and
iv. psychological factors.

Some of the medical witnesses added:

v. hormonal factors, or secondary sexual characteristics.

The court noted that these criteria had been evolved for medical purposes–to determine the sex in which it would be best for the individual to live, rather than to determine the sex to which the individual belonged–and were not necessarily decisive of the legal basis of sex determination. It was common ground among all the medical witnesses that the biological sexual constitution of an individual was fixed at birth, at the latest. At birth, the defendant's chromosomes, gonads and genitals were all of a male character.

In determining whether the defendant was a woman for the purposes of the law of marriage, the court decided that the criteria must be biological (i.e., the chromosomal, gonadal and genital tests). Marriage had always been recognised as the union of man and woman, and the institution on which the family was based. It was biological sex which was critical for the purposes of marriage, because one of the essential elements in marriage was the capacity for natural heterosexual intercourse. Only someone who was biologically female was capable of having natural sexual intercourse with a man. Since both the plaintiff and the defendant were biologically male, it followed that the purported marriage was void.

The Court recognised that the defendant was treated by society (including the Government) as female for many purposes, such as national insurance and the issuing of a passport, but rejected the argument that it was illogical to refuse to treat her as a woman for the purposes of the law of marriage:

> The illogicality would only arise if marriage were substantially similar in character to National Insurance and other social situations, but the differences are obviously fundamental. These submissions, in effect, confuse sex with gender. Marriage is a relationship which depends on sex and not on gender.[24]

Whether one agrees with the decision in *Corbett* or not, the observation that sex is distinguishable from gender, that one or the other of them may be more or less important in different legal contexts, and that there is therefore no logical requirement to treat transsexuals in the same way in every conceivable legal context, appears to me to be perceptive and important.

Corbett was concerned with the law of marriage, and nothing else. Nevertheless, this decision was applied in the context of sexual offences in *R v Tan*,[25] where a post-operative male-to-female transsexual was treated as a male for the purposes of legislation concerning prostitution. A similar approach was followed in two cases concerning social security legislation, where male-to-female transsexuals were treated by the National Insurance Commissioner as male for the purposes of retirement age.[26] In another case, a female-to-male transsexual, who had not undergone any sex change treatment, was treated by an Industrial Tribunal as female for the purposes of sex discrimination legislation.[27] More recently, it has been observed in the Court of Appeal that *Corbett* might bear re-examination in the light of new insight into the aetiology of transsexualism and legal developments in Europe and elsewhere.[28] Commenting on legislation which had made the criterion of a valid marriage that the parties were "male and female," as compared with the common law requirement that they be a man and a woman, Ward LJ. observed:

> It may be–but I express no view about it–that the choice of the words 'male and female' has left the way open for a future court, relying on the developments of medical knowledge, to place greater emphasis on gender than on sex in deciding whether a person is to be regarded as male or female.[29]

Under European Community law, it has been held that discrimination against a transsexual undergoing gender re-assignment treatment constitutes discrimination on grounds of sex and is therefore prohibited.[30] The case concerned the manager of an educational establishment, whose employers were unwilling to allow him to carry out his duties wearing female clothing as part of his pre-operative "real life" period. The case has been applied in the United Kingdom,[31] but its full implications have yet to be established, particularly in areas of employment calling for a particularly intimate relationship between the transsexual employee and a member of the public. In a subsequent British case, for example, it was held that the police were entitled to reject a post-operative male-to-female transsexual who wished to be a policewoman, since she would be unable–as a person of male sex–to carry out duties which could only be lawfully be carried out by a female, such as intimate searches of female suspects: although she was discriminated against, the discrimination was held to be justified.[32] Although that case turned on the *Corbett* approach to sexual identity, and its implications for statutory requirements imposed upon the police, it raises the issue of whether, regardless of the *Corbett* test, there are any situations in which the unwillingness of a member of the public to accept a transsexual as equivalent to an individual naturally belonging to the same gender should be respected.

OTHER JURISDICTIONS[33]

In some other European countries, such as France[34] and West Germany,[35] transsexuals had at one time equally little success in the courts. In Sweden, however, the legislature enacted in 1972 legislation enabling transsexuals to change their legal sex and, subject to certain conditions, to marry a person of their former sex. Similar legislation was passed in Denmark in 1973-5. Following an important decision of the Bundesverfassungsgericht in 1978,[36] legislation was also passed in West Germany in 1980. Broadly similar legislation was passed in Italy in 1982, and in the Netherlands in 1985. A similar result was also achieved in a number of other European countries through administrative or court practice. As I understand the position, transsexuals now have a right to marry, under certain conditions, in at least twelve Member States of the Council of Europe: Sweden, Germany, Italy, the Netherlands, Denmark, Finland, Luxembourg, Austria, Belgium, France, Portugal and Turkey. The converted transsexual's new identity also appears to be legally recognised, for some purposes at least, and subject to certain conditions being satisfied, in at least 23 of the Member States of the Council of the Europe.[37] The only Member States whose legal systems definitely do not recognise a change of gender are said to be the United Kingdom, Ireland, Andorra and Albania.[38]

The German law is of particular interest in the present context, as the decision of the Bundesverfassungsgericht was based on human rights considerations, and the subsequent legislation gives some idea of the type of conditions to which recognition of a new sexual identity may be made subject. The decision of the court was based in part upon Article 1 of the Basic Law. This provides for the protection of human dignity, which is considered to be the highest of all the principles of German constitutional law:

> (1) The dignity of a human person is inviolable. To respect it shall be the duty of all public authority.

The decision was also based on the right to self-determination, granted by Article 2 of the Basic Law:

> (1) Everybody has the right to the free development of his personality, as long as he does not violate the rights of others and does not contravene the constitutional order or moral laws.

In relation to Article 1, the court said:

> Art. 1(1)BL protects the dignity of a human person as he sees himself in his individuality and self-awareness. Part of this is that the human person can make decisions for himself and can autonomously determine his own fate.

The court also held that Article 6, which guarantees the institution of marriage, protected the right of post-operative transsexuals to marry a person of their former sex, notwithstanding their inability to procreate:

> The ability of a man to produce a child or of a woman to give birth to a child is not a pre-requisite for marriage . . . the partners form this community on the basis of their own ideas and expectations. It is possible that many people reject a marriage between a male transsexual and a man based on the subliminal view that this is morally repulsive. However, irrational opinions cannot stand in the way of marriage.

The subsequent legislation, the Transsexuals Act 1980, offers two options to meet the demands of transsexuals: (a) a change of forename, and (b) the rectification of the sex recorded at birth. A change of forename is permitted when a person has been living as a transsexual for three years and there is a high probability that the feelings of belonging to the other sex will not change. To obtain rectification of public registers a person has to comply with three further conditions: (1) that he or she is unmarried; (2) that he or she is permanently unable to procreate; and (3) that he or she has undergone gender re-assignment surgery. All three of these requirements have given rise to arguments based on human rights concerns.[39] Some other legal systems impose similar requirements; others do not.[40]

Mention can also be made briefly of the law of other common law jurisdictions. *Corbett* has, I understand, been followed in South Africa,[41] but not in criminal cases in Australia. One such case[42] concerned two male-to-female transsexuals, one post-operative and the other not, who were charged with procuring an act of indecency with a male. The post-operative transsexual was held to be female in this context, while the other was held to be male. A similar approach was suggested in a subsequent case,[43] in respect of the rape of a male-to-female transsexual. These decisions focused on the actual behaviour of the individuals in question and the nature of the offences, rather than upon supposed logical consistency with the law of marriage: an approach which appears to me to be more convincing than that followed in *R. v Tan*. Legislation introduced by three Australian States or Territories allows transsexuals to obtain civil status recognition.[44] It appears to be unclear whether that enables them to marry. A change of gender is also recognised in Canada, but transsexuals are not permitted to marry in their acquired gender. The right of transsexuals to marry has been recognised in certain of the United States of America[45] and in New Zealand.[46]

THE EUROPEAN CONVENTION ON HUMAN RIGHTS

The European Convention contains no provision which expressly deals with sexual identity or sexual activity. There are however certain provisions which are relevant to these issues. The cases have concerned principally Articles 8 and 12. Article 8 is in the following terms:

> (1) Everyone has the right to respect for his private and family life, his home and his correspondence.
>
> (2) There shall be no interference by a public authority with the exercise of this right except such as is in accordance with the law and is necessary in a democratic society in the interests of national security, public safety or the economic well-being of the country, for the prevention of disorder or crime, for the protection of health or morals, or for the protection of the rights and freedoms of others.

Article 12 is in the following terms:

> Men and women of marriageable age have the right to marry and to found a family, according to the national laws governing the exercise of this right.

Some of the cases have also touched on Article 3, which provides:

> No-one shall be subjected to torture or to inhuman or degrading treatment or punishment.

In no case, however, has a complaint by a transsexual under Article 3 been successful.

Some reference has also been made to Article 14, which is in the following terms:

> The enjoyment of the rights and freedoms set forth in this Convention shall be secured without discrimination on any ground such as sex, race, colour, language, religion, political or other opinion, national or social origin, association with a national minority, property, birth, or other status.

No complaint by transsexuals under Article 14 has however succeeded.

The first case concerning transsexuals to be considered by the European Court of Human Rights was decided in 1980. The case, *Van Oosterwijck v Belgium*[47] concerned a Belgian female-to-male post-operative transsexual who had unsuccessfully sought to have his birth certificate altered so as to record that he had been born male. His application had been refused on the basis that there was no error in the birth certificate, and no legal provision to enable account to be taken of artificial changes to an individual's anatomy, even if they corresponded to psychical tendencies. The European Commission on Human Rights concluded[48] that there had been a violation of Articles 8 and 12. The Court, on the other hand, upheld a preliminary objection that there had been a failure to exhaust domestic remedies, and therefore did not require to consider the application on its merits.

The report of the Commission in the *Van Oosterwijck* case is of interest, as the issues are analysed in greater detail than in some of the subsequent cases. In relation to Article 8, the Commission noted that the Article was predominantly negative, in that its objective was essentially to protect the individual against arbitrary interference by public authorities in his private or family life. The resulting obligation of the State was therefore, fundamentally, an obligation to abstain from acting:

> There are, however, cases in which the State properly takes action to regulate a situation, confer legal effects on certain facts or cer-

tain documents; but by failing to take account of subsequent changes in such facts or documents, it might in certain circumstances interfere with the respect due to private life without any positive new act of interference.[49]

Article 8 could therefore apply where interferences with private life–in the instant case, the necessity for the applicant to produce a birth certificate incompatible with his male appearance and in consequence to give "humiliating" explanations to third parties about his illness and treatment–were only made possible by the existence in the national legal system of documents concerning civil status or identity. More generally, the Commission noted that although Belgian law permitted the applicant to assume the appearance of a man, it did not recognise him as a member of the male sex:

> In these conditions, consideration must be given to the question whether, apart from possible interferences with privacy which this position may entail, the refusal legally to recognise the applicant as a man does not in itself amount to an interference with the right to respect for private life within the meaning of Article 8.[50]

The Commission considered that it did, adopting a concept of "private life" which went well beyond any question of privacy or confidentiality, and was much closer to the concept of self-determination found in the German Basic Law:

> The concept of private life contained in Article 8 is however wider than the definition given by numerous Anglo-Saxon and French writers, according to which it is the right to live, as far as one wishes, protected from publicity; for the Commission, "it comprises also to a certain degree the right to establish and to develop relationships with other human beings, especially in the emotional field for the development and fulfillment of one's own personality." ... In the instant case and subject to what we have to say later on the question of marriage, the ... State has ... not interfered with the applicant's behaviour and the relationships into which he has freely entered and which express and compose his personality. But it has refused to recognise an essential element of his personality: his sexual identity resulting from his changed physical form, his psychical make-up and his social role. In doing so, it treats him as an ambiguous being, an "appearance," disregarding in particular

the effects of a lawful medical treatment aimed at bringing the physical sex and the psychical sex into accord with each other. As regards institutionalised society . . . it restricts the applicant to a sex which can now scarcely be considered his own. In the Commission's opinion, the failure of Belgium to contemplate measures which would make it possible to take account in the applicant's civil status of the changes which have lawfully occurred, amounts not to an interference in the applicant's exercise of his right to respect for private life, but a veritable failure to recognise the respect due to his private life within the meaning of Article 8 para 1 of the Convention.[51]

The Commission's approach is noteworthy in emphasising that Article 8 guarantees a *right to respect* for private life, and thus imposes a positive obligation on States to show respect for private life, and not merely a negative obligation to abstain from interferences in private life. The Commission also made clear their view that States which recognised the legitimacy of the medical diagnosis and treatment of transsexuals could not ignore the consequences of such a diagnosis and treatment: they could not have it both ways, allowing transsexuals to undergo surgery and to live socially as members of the other sex, but at the same time insisting on treating them for legal purposes as members of their original sex.

The Commission's approach to Article 12 in the *Van Oosterwijck* case is also of interest. Two members of the Commission, in a dissenting opinion, considered that no separate issue arose under Article 12: if Article 8 required that the change of sex be legally recognised, it followed in their view that the applicant must also be treated as a man for the purposes of the law of marriage and therefore must have a right to marry a woman in accordance with Article 12. As I have indicated earlier, this view–that logic demands a consistent treatment of transsexuals in all areas of the law–is one which appears to me to be fallacious (although that is not to say that consistency may not be justified on practical grounds). Two other members were unconvinced that the sexual conversion had conferred on the applicant "the masculine sex in the full sense of the term": in other words, apparently, they considered that a distinction might be drawn between sexual identify in general and sexual identity under the law of marriage. The majority of the Commission merely expressed the opinion that the State could not refuse the applicant the right to marry solely on the basis of the contents of a birth certificate, and a general theory of the rectification of civil status certificates, without examining the issue more thoroughly.[52] The diversity of views in relation to Article 12, and the greater reluctance to find a definite right to marry on the part of transsexuals, has remained a feature of the case law under the Convention.

The Commission's report was notably innovative, Sweden and Denmark being the only Member States which appear to have legislated by then to give legal effect to sex changes. The Commission's approach under Article 8 was however similar to that taken by the Bundesverfassungsgericht, in the decision already discussed. At about the same time as the *Van Oosterwijck* case, the Commission also dealt with a case from West Germany.[53] Following the decision of the Bundesverfassungsgericht, the parties reached a friendly settlement on the basis that the applicant's birth registration and identity documents had been corrected to show her as being of the female sex (although not with retrospective effect), and that the Government had introduced legislative proposals concerning the status of transsexuals (which became the 1980 legislation already discussed).

The next case concerning transsexuals to be considered by the European Court of Human Rights was decided in 1986. The case, *Rees v The United Kingdom*,[54] concerned a British post-operative female-to-male transsexual. His complaint concerned his inability to obtain a birth certificate describing him as male, due to the historical nature of the information recorded in the register of births, as explained above; and also his inability to marry a woman, due to the law of marriage as explained in *Corbett v Corbett*.

In its opinion on the case, the Commission unanimously supported the first complaint, on the basis that the right to respect for private life under Article 8 imposed on the State a positive obligation to recognise the new status of a post-operative transsexual (following its opinion in the *Van Oosterwijck* case and the German case, and also in a case from Italy),[55] and in particular a duty to enable the transsexual to confirm his new status by the necessary documents:

> [S]ex is one of the essential elements of human personality. If modern medical research . . . has made possible a change of sex as far as the normal appearance of a person is concerned, Article 8 must be understood as protecting such an individual against the non-recognition of his/her changed sex as part of his/her personality.[56]

The Commission noted that legislation having this effect had by then been introduced in several Member States of the Council of Europe, and that no reasons of public interest had been put forward to justify the refusal to amend the birth register. On the other hand, the Commission unanimously rejected the complaint relating to marriage, half of the members taking the view that no separate issue arose, but the other half taking the view that Article 12 raised separate issues, and in particular did not prevent a State from excluding from marriage persons whose sexual category implied a physical incapacity to procreate.

Before the Court, the complaint under Article 8 was more fully explained: the applicant's complaint was that there were constraints upon his full integration into social life which were a result of the State's failure to provide measures which would legally constitute him as a male. In particular, his birth certificate, revealing as it did the discrepancy between his apparent and his legal sex, caused him embarrassment and humiliation whenever social practices required its production. The Commission's submission to the Court was that, since the applicant had been socially accepted as a man, it followed from Article 8 that the change in his sexual identity must be given legal recognition. The Government, on the other hand, maintained that the whole matter depended on the balance that had to be struck between the competing interests of the individual and of society as a whole. The introduction of some kind of official documentation of current social gender, which would be sufficiently widely used not to be associated exclusively with transsexuals, would run counter to the United Kingdom's popular and long-standing concept of civil liberties and its non-reliance on any identity card system.

The Court's approach to the issue distinguished between, on the one hand, *interferences* by public authorities with the right to respect for private life, which are prohibited by Article 8 unless they can be justified on one of the grounds set out in Article 8(2); and, on the other hand, the *positive* obligations which are inherent in an effective respect for private life. In the Court's view, the *Rees* case was concerned with positive obligations. The Court considered that the content of such positive obligations would vary considerably from case to case, having regard to the diversity of practices followed and the situations pertaining in Member States. In that connection, the Court noted that several States had given transsexuals the option of changing their status to fit their new identity, but had done so subject to conditions of varying strictness and subject to a variety of reservations. In other States such an option did not exist. There was little common ground between the States in this area, which was therefore an area in which States enjoyed a wide margin of appreciation. In deciding whether a positive obligation existed, regard had to be had to the fair balance which had to be struck between the general interest of the community and the interests of the individual.

On the merits of the case under Article 8, the Court held (by 12 votes to 3) that there had been no violation. The Court noted that the applicant's difficulties arose from the absence in the United Kingdom of any type of documentation establishing current civil status, and reliance instead upon a public register of an historical nature. The purpose of the register was not to define the present identity of an individual but to record a historical fact; and, even if it were made possible to make subsequent corrections or additions to the register, the public character of the register would make the protection of private life illusory. Since English law provided for the possibility of changing forenames, and of deleting indications of sex from most documents used as identity papers, the difficulties encountered by transsexuals were not especially serious. Article 8 could not require the United Kingdom to establish an entirely new system of documentation to prove civil status, which would have major administrative consequences and would impose new duties on the entire population. The alternative possibility, of recording changes in sex in the register of births, and keeping secret the fact that there had been such a change, would require detailed legislation as to the effects of the change in various contexts (e.g., in the fields of family and succession law) and as for the circumstances in which secrecy should yield to some more compelling interest. The positive obligations arising from Article 8 could not be held to extend that far.

In relation to Article 12, the Court in *Rees* held unanimously that there had been no violation:

> In the Court's opinion, the right to marry guaranteed by Article 12 refers to the traditional marriage between persons of opposite biological sex. This appears also from the wording of the Article which makes it clear that Article 12 is mainly concerned to protect marriage as the basis of the family.[57]

Moreover, Article 12 guaranteed the right to marry and found a family "according to the national laws governing the exercise of this right." The limitations introduced by national law could not restrict or reduce the right in such a way or to such an extent that the essence of the right was impaired; but, in the Court's view, the law in the United Kingdom preventing the marriage of persons who were not of the opposite biological sex could not be said to have an effect of that kind.[58]

The Court's reasoning in relation to Article 12 has been criticised on the basis that United Kingdom law would in practice make it impossible for a post-operative transsexual to exercise any right to marry. There may be greater force in the criticism that the Court's reasoning, in invoking the intention of the 1950 signatories to the Convention, does not address the point that the rights of post-operative transsexuals did not present a legal issue at that time. The principle that the Convention must be interpreted as a living instrument, capable of evolving as society evolves (just as the concept of "family life" has evolved since 1950 away from one based necessarily on marriage),[59] might at some point allow for greater flexibility in the interpretation of Article 12 than the *Rees* judgment might at first sight suggest.

The Strasbourg institutions re-considered these issues in 1990 in the case of *Cossey* v *The United Kingdom*.[60] The applicant was a post-operative male-to-female transsexual whose complaints were the same as in the case of *Rees*. In relation to the complaint concerning birth certificates, the Commission concluded by a majority that the case was indistinguishable from *Rees*, and that there was therefore no violation of Article 8.[61] In relation to the complaint under Article 12, a majority of the Commission purported to accept the Court's decision in *Rees* that Article 12 referred to the traditional marriage between persons of opposite sex (whereas Article 8 protected *de facto* family life irrespective of its legal status), but considered that the applicant could not be regarded as biologically male, since she did not have a male anatomy and was socially accepted as a woman.

The Court, on the other hand, concluded that there was no material difference between the *Cossey* case and the *Rees* case, but nevertheless considered whether it should depart from its *Rees* judgment.

In relation to Article 8, the Court decided by a bare majority (10 votes to 8) that there was no violation, for the reasons given in the *Rees* judgment. The decision of the majority in relation to Article 8 relied on the notion of the margin of appreciation, and on the diversity of practice between the Member States and the absence of common ground. The decision was therefore one which was liable to be revisited in the light of developments in the law of the Member States. The Court made this clear, repeating a statement which it had made in the *Rees* judgment:

> Since the Convention always has to be interpreted and applied in the light of current circumstances, it is important that the need for

appropriate legal measures in this area should be kept under review.[62]

In relation to Article 12, the Court decided by a larger majority (14 votes to 4) that there was no violation, for the reasons stated in the *Rees* judgment. The Court stated that it was not open to it to take a new approach to the interpretation of Article 12 in the absence of a "general abandonment of the traditional concept of marriage."[63]

In a dissenting opinion, Judge Martens expressed himself in terms reminiscent of those used by the Bundesverfassungsgericht in the *Transsexuals* case:

> The principle which is basic in human rights and which underlies the various specific rights spelled out in the Convention is respect for human dignity and human freedom. Human dignity and human freedom imply that a man should be free to shape himself and his fate in the way that he deems best for his personality. A transsexual does use those very fundamental rights. He is prepared to shape himself and his fate.[64]

It might be argued, against this approach, that individuals cannot be treated simply as free agents, since they are also members of a community: society, in other words, is more than a collection of self-determining individuals, but is united by prevailing ideas, which may encompass such matters as sexual identity and marriage. On the other hand, since adherence to the Convention commits Member States to such values as tolerance and pluralism, Member States cannot expect the Court to legitimate practices which do not reflect those values as assessed by the Court, whether or not they accord with prevailing ideas at the domestic level. In interpreting an international convention couched in terms which are both general and value-laden, an international court has to judge what its provisions entail according to the prevailing values of the States adhering to the convention. The Court's circumspection, awaiting an alignment of prevailing ideas, rather than seeking to impose ideas which do not command general acceptance, seems to me to be in principle appropriate. There is however a difficult judgement to be made, in this as in other areas affected by the Convention, as to whether a social evolution has progressed sufficiently far throughout the Member States to be reflected in the interpretation and application of the Convention. There might be thought to have been force in the dissenting opinion of Judges Palm, Foighel and Pakkanen, to the effect that developments in

European society indicated growing acceptance of transsexuals, and a prevailing view that transsexuals should have their new sexual identity recognised by the law. Reference was made in that regard to a resolution of the European Parliament and to a recommendation by the Parliamentary Assembly of the Council of Europe, as well as to legal developments in several Member States.

The European Court of Human Rights re-examined transsexualism in 1992, in a case from France.[65] The case concerned a male-to-female post-operative transsexual who wished to marry a man, and with that in mind applied to the French courts for a declaration that she was of female sex, that her birth certificate should be rectified and that she was entitled to bear female forenames. Her application was refused on the basis that she had not undergone a true change of sex. French law provided for the updating of entries in the civil status register by marginal annotations, and access to such information was strictly regulated. The situation therefore differed from that in United Kingdom cases, where there was no civil status register, and the registers which existed were (in general) historical records accessible to the general public. A further difference was that French law prevented a change of forename unless authorised by a court order in the event of a legitimate interest, whereas in the United Kingdom anyone is entitled to change their name at will. These aspects of French law, together with references to gender in official documents, created more frequent problems, arising from the discrepancy between appearance and official gender, than a British transsexual would be likely to experience.

The Commission noted the Cour de Cassation's view that "even where transsexualism is medically recognised, it cannot be interpreted as a real sex change since, although the transsexual has lost certain characteristics of his original gender he has still not acquired those of the opposite sex" and that Article 8 of the Convention "does not stipulate that a transsexual must be assigned a gender which is not in fact his own."[66] The Commission commented:[67]

> The State thus refused to acknowledge a decisive component of the applicant's personality: her gender identity as formed by her changed morphology, psychological state and role in society. The combination of all those factors gives rise to disruption in the applicant's daily life of such a serious nature that it cannot possibly be justified by concern to protect the rights of others.

The Commission therefore concluded that the French legal system failed to provide the applicant with effective protection of her private life, and was therefore in breach of the positive obligation imposed by Article 8(1). The Commission made it clear however that it was for France, and not the Commission, to decide what measures should be adopted in order to secure respect for the private life of transsexuals. The applicant's complaint of inhuman and degrading treatment, contrary to Article 3 of the Convention, was rejected by a majority.

Before the Court, the applicant sought to persuade the court to reconsider the *Rees* and *Cossey* judgments, particularly in the light of research suggesting that transsexualism might have a physiological explanation, but without success:

> The Court considers that it is undeniable that attitudes have changed, science has progressed and increasing importance is attached to the problem of transsexualism.
>
> It notes, however, in the light of the relevant studies carried out and work done by experts in this field, that there still remains some uncertainty as to the essential nature of transsexualism and that the legitimacy of surgical intervention in such cases is sometimes questioned. The legal situations which result are moreover extremely complex: anatomical, biological, psychological and moral problems in connection with transsexualism and its definition; consent and other requirements to be complied with before any operation; the conditions under which a change of sexual identity can be authorised (validity, scientific pre-suppositions and legal effects of recourse to surgery, fitness for life with the new sexual identity); international aspects (place where the operation is performed); the legal consequences, retrospective or otherwise, of such a change (rectification of civil status documents); the opportunity to choose a different forename; the confidentiality of documents and information mentioning the change; effects of a family nature (right to marry, fate of an existing marriage, filiation) and so on. On these various points there is as yet no sufficiently broad consensus between the Member States of the Council of Europe to persuade the court to reach opposite conclusions to those in its *Rees* and *Cossey* judgments.[68]

The Court nevertheless agreed with the Commission (by a majority of 15 votes to 6) that the situation under the French legal system differed significantly from that in the United Kingdom, and was not compatible with the respect due to the applicant's private life. France had several means to choose from for remedying this state of affairs, and the court did not regard it as its function to indicate the most appropriate. The dissenting judges differed from the majority essentially on the question of whether the Court ought to impose on France a duty to recognise a new sexual identity in the face of the complex and varied issues which would then arise in other areas of the law. As several judges pointed out, a person's civil status (including his or her sexual identity) has an effect which goes beyond the individual interest, as it may affect the rights of others, and cannot be regarded as no more than an aspect of his or her right to self-determination. Some judges raised the question of how one defines a transsexual, and whether one should insist on full reconstructive surgery, or should grant recognition merely on the basis of psychological beliefs and hormone treatment (which might be reversible). Questions were asked about the situation where the transsexual is married or wishes to marry, or has children or may have children or wishes to adopt some or become the father of a child by means of A.I.D. It was pointed out that the International Commission on Civil Status, which has as its object the drawing up of recommendations on draft conventions with a view to harmonising the provisions in force in its member states relating to the status of the individual, the family and nationality, had concerned itself for some time with the position of transsexuals, and had not yet reached the stage of drawing up a recommendation or draft convention.

The possibility of the rights of others impacting upon the position of transsexuals was demonstrated by the next relevant case to come before the court, *X, Y and Z* v *The United Kingdom*.[69] X was a female-to-male transsexual. Y was a woman with whom X lived. Z was a child born to Y as the result of artificial insemination by donor (A.I.D.). X had been present throughout the A.I.D. treatment. Their complaint concerned the fact that, following Z's birth, X was not permitted to be registered as the child's father. The Human Fertility and Embryology Act 1990 provided that, where an unmarried woman gave birth as a result of A.I.D. with the involvement of her male partner, the latter, rather than the donor of the sperm, should be treated for legal purposes as the father of the child. Following the general approach of *Corbett* v *Corbett*, however, the Registrar General was of the view that only a biological male could be regarded as a man, and therefore as a father, for the purposes of registration. Although X was not permitted to be registered as Z's father, Z bore X's surname, and it was possible for X to apply for a residence order relating to Z, which would have the effect of giving him parental responsibility in respect of Z. X, Y and Z complained that they were denied respect for their family and private life, contrary to Article 8, as a result of the lack of recognition of X's role as father to Z, and also of discrimination contrary to Article 14 of the Convention. They pointed to prejudicial legal consequences for Z, in that she could not inherit from X on intestacy (although she could under the law of testate succession), would have no right to financial support from him and could not benefit through him from the transmission of tenancies or from nationality and immigration measures. They also pointed to possible social and psychological consequences for the child:

> It is submitted *inter alia*, that the law has a powerful symbolic as well as legal function in affirming an individual's status and value in society. The failure to give a transsexual legal recognition of his change in gender and role in the family has the effect of stigmatising him or her and those related to them are obliged to share the stigma and discredit. This places a strain on individuals in the family group: for example, exerting pressure on members to distance themselves from the stigmatised person, distorting family behaviour to cope with the "spoiled identity" and concealing the information from others. In the case of a child which has grown up close to a transsexual parent, it will come into conflict with society's view of the parent figure and find the validity of its family unit challenged by society. Children, it is postulated, require a secure family situation and this cannot be separated from the acceptance of the family unit in the society and law.[70]

The Commission accepted that the applicants enjoyed "family life" within the meaning of Article 8; and the majority of the Commission was of the opinion that, having regard in particular to the welfare of the child and her security within the family unit, the absence of a legal regime reflecting the applicants' family ties disclosed a failure to respect their family life. The majority were influenced by the fact that United Kingdom law had permitted the A.I.D. procedure on the condition that X would acknowledge himself to be the father of the child, and had thereby enabled the *de facto* family relationship between the applicants to come into being. In other words, it was the relationship between X and Y, and X's willingness to be treated as Z's father, that had led to the authorisation of the A.I.D. and Z's subsequent birth. This was reflected in the cautious terms in which the Commission's reasoning was expressed:

> It finds that in the case of a transsexual who has undergone *irreversible* gender re-assignment *in a contracting State* and lives *there* with a partner *of his former sex* and child in a family relationship, there must be a presumption in favour of legal recognition of that relationship, the denial of which requires specific justification.[71]

The majority did not consider it necessary to examine the complaint under Article 14. The minority, on the other hand, noted that, on the basis of the psychiatric material submitted, adverse effects on the personality and development of children due to their upbringing in atypical families such as that of the applicants could not be excluded. In such a sensitive and controversial area, the minority considered that the Member States must enjoy a wide margin of appreciation.

Before the Court, the applicants made another attempt to have the Court re-examine the principles underlying the *Rees* and *Cossey* judgments. Particular reliance was placed on scientific research suggesting that transsexuality might have a physiological basis in the structure of the brain, as mentioned above. The applicants further argued that the case in any event raised a different issue from *Rees* and *Cossey*, having regard to the interests of the child in having her social father recognised as such by law. The Government on the other hand pointed out that the essential nature of transsexualism remained uncertain.

The Court, like the Commission, treated the case as raising an issue relating to family life, rather than private life. The Court noted that there was no common European standard with regard to the granting of parental rights to transsexuals, nor any generally shared approach to the legal treatment of a relationship between a child conceived by A.I.D. and a person performing the social role of the child's father. The Court observed that the community as a whole had an interest in maintaining a coherent system of family law which placed the best interests of the child at the forefront. It was not clear that the amendment to the law sought by the applicants would necessarily be to the advantage of children in Z's position:

> In these circumstances, the Court considers that the State may justifiably be cautious in changing the law, since it is possible that the amendment sought might have undesirable or unforeseen ramifications for children in Z's position. Furthermore, such an amendment might have implications in other areas of family law. For example, the law might be open to criticism on the ground of in-

consistency if a female-to-male transsexual were granted the possibility of becoming a 'father' in law while still being treated for other legal purposes as female and capable of contracting marriage to a man.[72]

The Court concluded (by 14 votes to 6):

> In conclusion, given that transsexuality raises complex scientific, legal, moral and social issues, in respect of which there is no generally shared approach among the Contracting States, the Court is of the opinion that Article 8 cannot, in this context, be taken to imply an obligation for the respondent State formally to recognise as the father of a child a person who is not the biological father. That being so, the fact that the law of the United Kingdom does not allow special legal recognition of the relationship between X and Z does not amount to a failure to respect family life within the meaning of that provision.

No separate issue was said to arise under Article 14. An aspect of the case which appears somewhat surprising, to British eyes at least, is that the child was not separately represented for any distinct interest which she might have.

The most recent of the Court's decisions on transsexualism, *Sheffield and Horsham v The United Kingdom*,[73] concerned two post-operative male-to-female transsexuals. Both applicants had been married to women prior to undergoing gender re-assignment treatment, and the first applicant had fathered a child. She complained that she had been coerced into obtaining a divorce from her wife as a pre-condition to surgery being carried out, but that complaint was held to be inadmissible for failure to comply with the time limit imposed by the Convention. Her complaint, so far as admissible, concerned her continued treatment under English law as a male, the necessity to disclose her former sexual identity in certain contexts, including the obtaining of motor insurance, and her inability to marry a man. The second applicant's complaints were mostly of a similar nature. The complaints were brought under Articles 8, 12 and 14.

The Commission, under reference to the judgment in the case of *X, Y and Z*[74] observed that, even where a person appeared to suffer no immediate or direct consequences from an existing state of the law, a disparity between an individual's private life and the law might, where it related to an important element of personal identity, result in internal conflict or stigmatisation which in itself impinged on the enjoyment of rights guaranteed under the Convention. The Commission accepted that there might be a legitimate interest in a person's disclosing details of his or her medical history in certain contexts, such as the obtaining of life assurance. The Commission accordingly focused not on the law relating to the recording of gender, or on the confidentiality of any change of gender, but rather on the inability of the applicants to obtain legal recognition of their gender re-assignment, by reason of the principle, derived from *Corbett*, that sex is determined by biological factors. In that regard, the Commission noted that the medical profession had reached a consensus that transsexualism was an identifiable medical condition, in respect of which gender re-assignment treatment could be recommended for the purpose of improving the quality of life. In these circumstances the Commission declined to regard as decisive either a social reluctance to accept the phenomenon of transsexualism or difficulties in assimilating it into existing legal frameworks. Unsurprisingly, the Commission considered that there had been a failure to respect the applicants' private lives, contrary to Article 8. The Commission also concluded, by a bare majority, and without giving any clear reasons, that no separate issue arose under Article 12 or Article 14. In a partly dissenting opinion, Mr. Loucaides pointed out the differences between the issues arising under Articles 8 and 12, and put forward some reasons for treating the complaint under Article 12 differently from that under Article 8:

> It is true that the lack of recognition of the applicant's gender re-assignment is a legal impediment to the exercise of the applicant's right to marry. However, in the case of transsexuals the right to marry does not entirely depend on legal recognition of an individual's gender. The gender re-assignment of a person like the applicant may be legally recognised under the national laws of a State and yet she may not be able to exercise the right to marry under the same laws insofar as they may adopt biological criteria for determining a person's sex for the purpose of marriage. In fact this is the position in the United Kingdom. . . . It may be useful to stress here that "private life" and "marriage" are two different concepts, the scope and protection of which are governed by different factors and considerations. The right to respect for private life does not automatically coincide with the right to marry. The right to marry also has consequences for the other party to the marriage whose legitimate interests the law may be expected to protect. A transsexual may have a right to have his gender re-assignment le-

gally recognised as part of his private life but when it comes to his right to marry the biologically based definition of his sexual identity may have to be maintained. This is not only because it is in accordance with the concept of marriage in the context of Article 12 of the Convention, but also in order to protect the legitimate expectations of the other party to the marriage to know the gender status of his partner on the basis of biological criteria. This status is interwoven with the sexual life of the couple and their capacity to have children which are significant elements in a relationship of marriage.

Before the Court, it was common ground that the complaints under Article 8 fell to be considered from the standpoint of whether the United Kingdom had failed to comply with a positive obligation, by failing to take positive steps to modify the existing system of law. In the Court's view, the applicants had not shown that there had been conclusive scientific developments concerning either the causes of the condition of transsexualism or the effects of gender re-assignment treatment. The causes remained in doubt, and the treatment did not result in the acquisition of all the biological characteristics of the other sex. Nor had there been any decisive legal developments. Although most Member States permitted some sort of change to be made to a person's birth certificate to reflect gender re-assignment, there was no common European approach to the problems created by the recognition in law of post-operative gender status. In particular, there was not as yet any common approach to the repercussions which the legal recognition of a change of sex might entail for other areas of law such as marriage, filiation, privacy or data protection, or the circumstances in which a transsexual might be compelled by law to reveal his or her pre-operative gender. In relation to the latter point, the Court observed:

> [I]t must be acknowledged that an individual may with justification be required on occasion to provide proof of gender as well as medical history. This is certainly the case of life assurance contracts which are *uberrimae fidei*. It may possibly be true of motor insurance where the insurer may need to have regard to the sex of the driver in order to make an actuarial assessment of the risk.[75]

The Court accordingly concluded, by a bare majority, that the applicants had not established that the United Kingdom had a positive obligation to recognise in law their post-operative gender. But the court added:

> Having reached those conclusions, the Court cannot but note that despite its statements in the *Rees* and *Cossey* cases on the importance of keeping the need for appropriate legal measures in this area under review having regard in particular to scientific and societal developments, it would appear that the respondent State has not taken any steps to do so. . . . Even if there have been no significant scientific developments since the date of the *Cossey* judgment which make it possible to reach a firm conclusion on the aetiology of transsexualism, it is nevertheless the case that there is an increased social acceptance of transsexualism and an increased recognition of the problems which post-operative transsexuals encounter. Even if it finds no breach of Article 8 in this case, the Court reiterates that this area needs to be kept under review by contracting States.[76]

The British judge on the Court, Sir John Freeland, expressed his dismay at the United Kingdom's failure to undertake any review of the legal situation of transsexuals, and warned that "continued inaction on the part of the respondent State, taken together with further developments elsewhere, could well tilt the balance in the other direction." In relation to Article 12, the Court repeated the reasoning of the *Rees* and *Cossey* judgments. In relation to Article 14, the Court held that the considerations which led to its finding of there being no violation of Article 8 also constituted a justification, for the purposes of Article 14, of the differences in treatment between male-to-female transsexuals and men who were not transsexuals.

There might be thought to be considerable force in the points made in the dissenting opinion of Judges Bernhardt, Thor Vilhjalmsson, Spielmann, Palm, Wildhaber, Makarczyk and Voicu. In the first place, they argued that the complexity of the issues raised by transsexualism did not entail that a failure to attempt to address those issues could be consistent with respect for the private life of transsexuals:

> We accept, as the Court observes in paragraph 58 of its judgment, that transsexualism raises complex scientific, legal, moral and social issues, in respect of which there is no generally shared approach among the contracting States. However, what this means is that the legal recognition of a change of sex–or its repercussions in

areas of law such as marriage, filiation, privacy, adoption, etc.–takes diverse forms in the different countries. But how can we expect uniformity in such a complex area where legal change will necessarily take place against the background of the States' traditions and culture? However, the essential point is that in these countries, unlike in the United Kingdom, change has taken place–whatever its precise form is–in an attempt to alleviate the distress and suffering of the post-operative transsexual and that there exists in Europe a general trend which seeks in differing ways to confer recognition on the altered sexual identity.

Secondly, the minority emphasised the developing medical and societal acceptance of the phenomenon of transsexualism, and argued that the inability of science to ascertain the aetiology of transsexualism or to achieve a change in biological sex was of secondary importance:

It is not a sufficient answer to this important development that the scientific community cannot agree on the explanation of the causes of transsexualism or that surgery cannot–and perhaps will never be able to–lead to a change in the biological sex. Respect for privacy rights should not, as the legislative and societal trends referred to above demonstrate, depend on exact science.

In a separate dissenting opinion, Judge Van Dijk echoed the opinion of his predecessor as Dutch judge, Judge Martens, in the *Cossey* case:

What is at stake here is the fundamental right to self-determination: if a person feels that he belongs to a sex other than the one originally registered and has undergone treatment to obtain the features of that other sex to the extent medically possible, he is entitled to legal recognition of the sex that in his conviction best responds to his identity. The right to self-determination has not been separately and expressly included in the Convention, but is at the basis of several of the rights laid down therein, especially the right to liberty under Article 5 and the right to respect for private life under Article 8. Moreover, it is a vital element of the "inherent dignity" which, according to the Preamble to the Universal Declaration of Human Rights, constitutes the foundation of freedom, justice and peace in the world.

Judge Van Dijk also considered that a violation of Article 12 followed automatically from a violation of Article 8, on the basis that recognition of gender re-assignment had to apply in all legal contexts. This opinion was however shared by only one other judge out of the 20 on the Court.

Sheffield and Horsham is plainly not the Court's last word on the subject. Other British cases have been ruled admissible by the Commission but have not come before the Court.[77] Some of the points raised in the British cases may in any event be addressed by the Government. At a late stage during the proceedings of *Sheffield and Horsham*, the Government indicated its willingness to seek a solution within the framework of a friendly settlement. In April 1999 the Government appointed a Working Group to consider the need for reform: the Working Group reported in April 2000, and its report has been published as a discussion document.[78] Nor do British cases exhaust the issues which may arise. A case from Germany, for example, raised the question whether a pre-operative male transsexual, who was married and the father of children, and remained capable of fathering further children, was entitled to have his birth certificate rectified so as to record that he was female, notwithstanding the requirements of German law that he must first be divorced and sterile and have undergone gender-re-assignment surgery. The Commission dismissed the application, but in guarded terms.[79]

DISCUSSION

Most Western societies now permit gender re-assignment surgery and some allow such surgery to be performed by the State health service. In those societies which do permit it, it seems to me to be difficult to justify a refusal to recognise that successful gender re-assignment treatment has had any legal consequences for the patient's sexual identity, although the contexts in which, and conditions under which, a change of sexual identity should be recognised is a complex question. But for the law to ignore transsexualism, either on the basis that it is an aberration which should be disregarded, or on the basis that sex roles should be regarded as legally irrelevant, is not an option. The law needs to respond to society as it is and allow transgender persons to function as fully as possible in their new gender. The key words are "as fully as possible": what is possible has to be decided having regard to the interests of others (so far as they are affected) and of society as a whole (so far as that is engaged), and considering whether there are compelling reasons, in the particular context in question, for setting limits to the legal recognition of the new gender.

At the European level, it must be questionable whether the European Court of Human Rights case law on Article 8 in the *Rees*, *Cossey* and *Sheffield and Horsham* judgments can be upheld for much longer. Whether the case law on Article 12 will be upheld over the long term may also be questionable, but will depend on intervening developments in the law of the Member States. The Convention law concerning transsexualism appears to be in a transitional stage, reflecting the fact that some legal systems have gone much further than others in accepting transsexuals as members of the gender which they have adopted. The Court has correctly acknowledged that the legal and social issues are complex, and that there is a general interest in proceeding on the basis of research and considered debate, especially where the development of children is liable to be affected. Nor can the values prevailing in a society be disregarded, if the law is to be accepted and respected; but at the same time by adhering to the Convention, Member States have committed themselves to the values of a tolerant and inclusive society. Subject to respect for the fundamental rights guaranteed by the Convention, however, each Member State has a legitimate right to regulate its affairs according to the (reasonable) aspirations of its citizens. In these circumstances, while the Convention law is bound to develop, and such development is likely to be in the direction of requiring Member States to treat post-operative transsexuals as belonging to their new gender, the Court is also likely to continue to proceed on the basis that Member States must enjoy a wide margin of appreciation in this area.

As is apparent from the European case law, and that of other jurisdictions, the context of marriage is especially sensitive. This is unsurprising. Marriage remains one of the central institutions of most Western societies, and it is an especially sensitive area for the expression of ethical and social values, not least because it is an institution with religious as well as legal aspects. Although it has been subjected to a great deal of criticism, the judgment in *Corbett* is nevertheless an impressive analysis of the medical evidence and of the legal issues in the light of the family law and prevailing social attitudes of its time. The judgment in the New Zealand case of *Att.-Gen. v Otahuhu Family Court*,[80] twenty-four years later, is equally impressive, but to the contrary effect. The differences between the two judgments are essentially a reflection of the evolution of social attitudes, which the law properly reflects, over the intervening period. There does not appear to me to have been any critical development in medical knowledge since *Corbett*, but social attitudes have undoubtedly evolved, and that has been reflected to some extent in changes in family law. Gender re-assignment treatment is more generally accepted as an appropriate response to transsexuality. Feelings of intolerance towards transsexuals have lessened to some extent. At the same time, notions that marriage is necessarily based upon the ability to have sexual intercourse or to procreate appear to be waning, with greater emphasis being placed on psychological and social aspects of the companionship of the sexes. To base the legal concept of marriage on the Christian concept[81] might also be thought more questionable, in European societies at least, in current times than in 1970. The question of whether transsexuals should be allowed to marry thus involves an assessment of the nature and purpose of marriage in contemporary society, and in particular whether there continues to be a valid presupposition that only persons of opposite biological sex, rather than opposite gender, can fulfil the roles and obligations arising from the status. In the New Zealand case, Ellis J. concluded:

> I can see no socially adverse effects from allowing such transsexuals [i.e., post-operative transsexuals] to marry in their adopted sex. I cannot see any harm to others, children in particular, that is not properly proscribed and manageable in accordance with the existing framework of the law.[82]

So far as other areas of law are concerned, it seems to me to be important to recognise that different branches of the law raise different questions. Although the relevant considerations may have much in common, they are unlikely to be identical, and they may not necessarily lead to the same conclusion. Birth certificate and registration systems, for example, are creatures of statute: the recognition of gender re-assignment in that context does not necessarily have wider legal implications, but it raises technical questions concerning the design of the system, prospective or retrospective alterations, the form of any certificate, and the openness or confidentiality of the register. In contexts such as employment and economic activity, it may be appropriate to acknowledge gender re-assignment in some contexts but not in others: for example, whether a professional tennis player who was a male-to-female transsexual should be allowed to compete in a women's tennis tournament[83] raises a different issue from the question whether a nurse who is a male-to-female transsexual should be allowed to work on a women's ward. The problem in the former situation is the competitive advantage which the transsexual may enjoy by reason of a more powerful physique, whereas the problem in the latter situation (if any) may be the sensitivity of patients dealing in an intimate manner with a nurse who is biologically male. Different situations raise different issues.

Four major issues emerge from the cases discussed. One concerns the stage at which a change of gender should be recognised: whether legal recognition should be given to post-operative transsexuals only, or extended to transsexuals who have undergone partial surgery or none at all. There is no single moment when a change of gender can incontestably be said to occur. It appears that there is a continuum between, at one end, the transsexual who identifies with the opposite gender but has not received any hormonal or surgical treatment, to the transsexual who has successfully undergone full reconstructive surgery and is socially accepted as a member of the desired gender. If legal recognition is granted to the latter group, the question may be asked—as it has been, in some of the United States and European cases—why it is necessary that a transsexual should have to go through drastic, and possibly painful and expensive, surgery in order to be legally recognised as belonging to his or her chosen gender. The question may be thought to be particularly relevant in the case of female-to-male transsexuals, where complete reconstructive surgery is especially difficult and uncertain of success, and will not in any event result in full sexual function.

A second issue concerns any other pre-conditions to which the legal recognition of a change of gender should be made subject, such as the sterilisation of the transsexual and the dissolution of any existing marriage. As discussed above, some jurisdictions impose such conditions, but others do not. Such conditions raise sensitive issues.

A third issue is whether legal recognition should be granted for all purposes or should be confined to specific areas of the law. The latter course would enable the law to reflect fully any relevant differences between particular areas of the law, such as have been discussed above, but at the same time a case-by-case approach could result in confusion and uncertainty. The European case law and some of the domestic European systems, however, indicate that an intermediate position may be a practical solution, at least during a transitional period, if a total refusal to acknowledge a change of gender is unacceptable.

A fourth major issue which arises, if a transsexual is recognised as belonging to the chosen gender, concerns the confidentiality of the transsexual's previous sexual identity. Circumstances in which a transsexual may be bound to disclose his or her previous gender, or is unable to prevent its being discovered or disclosed, are bound to arise. Examples are criminal records and life insurance. Such circumstances will have to be assessed on their particular merits.

Generally, what emerges is the need, if a change of gender is to be legally recognised, for the issues to be addressed with sensitivity to the different questions arising in particular circumstances, but also with a general commitment to resolving those issues in a manner which treats transsexuals with compassion and with respect for their dignity. Human rights law expresses, and underpins, that commitment.

POSTSCRIPT

Since the foregoing paper was presented, in September 2000, there have been significant developments both in the United Kingdom and in the case-law of the European Court of Human Rights. The most important of these can be briefly summarised as follows.

In *Bellinger* v *Bellinger*[84] proceedings were brought by a post-operative male-to-female transsexual for a declaration that she had contracted a valid marriage with a man. The declaration was refused at first instance, and that decision was affirmed by a majority of the Court of Appeal, after a comprehensive consideration of medical evidence and of the case-law of the European Court of Human Rights and a variety of national jurisdictions. The majority of the Court of Appeal however added:[85]

> We would add however, with the strictness of the European Court of Human Rights well in mind, that there is no doubt that the profoundly unsatisfactory nature of the present position and the plight of transsexuals requires careful consideration. The recommendation of the interdepartmental Working Group for public consultation merits action by the government departments involved in these issues. The problems will not go away and may well come again before the European Court sooner rather than later.

Leave to appeal to the House of Lords was granted.[86]

In July 2002, a Grand Chamber of the European Court of Human Rights unanimously upheld a post-operative transsexual's rights to legal recognition of her new gender, under Articles 8 and 12 of the Convention, in the case of *Goodwin* v *United Kingdom*.[87] In relation to Article 8, the Court said:[88]

> In the twenty first century the right of transsexuals to personal development and to physical and moral security in the full sense enjoyed by others in society cannot be regarded as a matter of controversy requiring the lapse of time to cast clearer light on the issues involved. In short, the unsatisfactory situation in which post-operative transsexuals live in an intermediate zone as not quite one gender or the other is no longer sustainable... any "spectral difficulties," particularly in the field of family law, are both manageable and acceptable if confined to the case of fully achieved and post-operative transsexuals ... the respondent Government can no longer claim that the matter falls within their margin of appreciation save as regards the appropriate means of achieving recognition of the rights protected under the Convention.

In relation to Article 12, the Court said:[89]

> Article 12 secures the fundamental right of a man and a woman to marry and to found a family. The second aspect is not however a condition of the first and the inability of any couple to conceive or parent a child cannot be regarded as *per se* removing their right to enjoy the first limb of this provision ... it is true that the first sentence refers in express terms to the right of a man and a woman to marry. The Court is not persuaded that at the date of this case it can still be assumed that these terms must refer to a determination of gender by purely biological criteria. ... While it is for the Contracting State to determine *inter alia* the conditions under which a person claiming recognition as a transsexual establishes that gender re-assignment has been properly effected or under which past marriages cease to be valid and the formalities applicable to future marriages (including, for example, the information to be furnished to intended spouses), the Court finds no justification for barring a transsexual from enjoying the right to marry under any circumstances.

In response to the decision in *Goodwin*, the Government announced on 13 December 2002 its intention to introduce legislation to give legal recognition in their acquired gender to transsexual people who can demonstrate that they have taken decisive steps towards living fully and permanently in the gender acquired since they were registered at birth, making it possible for them to marry in their acquired gender.[90] It is proposed that (subject to exceptions) formal recognition in the acquired gender will bring with it the rights and responsibilities appropriate to that gender, normally from the date that when change is recognised. Registration in the new gender will not cancel out rights and obligations previously incurred. There will be provision for disclosure in certain circumstances, such as possibly to insurance and pension companies, and the Criminal Records Bureau. It is proposed that applications for recognition should be scrutinised by an authorising body, given powers to assess medical evidence. The medical criteria may include medical treatments to modify the person's sexual characteristics, but the Government will not require surgery as a condition of registration. In addition to meeting medical criteria, the transsexual person will have to have lived successfully in the acquired gender for at least two years. A new certificate will be issued by the Registrar General stating the required name and gender, which will be in addition to the original birth records, but indistinguishable from a birth certificate. It was undecided, as at the date of the announcement, whether the legislation would cover the whole of the United Kingdom, in view of the inter-relationship between devolved and reserved policy aspects.

NOTES

1. Case C-13/94, P v S and Cornwall County Council (1996) E.C.R.I.-2143,2157.

2. What follows is based primarily on the *Oxford Textbook of Medicine* (3rd Edition, 1996) section 12.9.1, and the *Diagnostic and Statistical Manual of Mental Disorders* (4th Edition, 1994), pp 532-8.

3. e.g., *Sheffield and Horsham* v *The United Kingdom*, (1999) 27 E.H.R.R. 163; App No 31177/96, *Roetzheim* v *Germany*, 23 October 1997 (European Commission on Human Rights, unreported); App No 6699/74, *X.* v *Federal Republic of Germany* (1979) 17 D.&R. 21.

4. e.g., *Sheffield and Horsham* (n. 4); *Roetzheim* (n. 4); *X* v *Federal Republic of Germany* (n 4).

5. *Roetzheim* (n. 4).

6. *S-T (formerly J)* v *J* [1998] Fam. 103.

7. Costa-Santos and Madeira, "Transsexualism in Portugal: the legal framework and procedure, and its consequences for transsexuals" (1996) 36 *Medicine, Science and the Law*, 221.

8. *Digest*, I.v. 10, recording Ulpian's opinion that hermaphrodites should be treated as belonging to the sex which predominates in them.

9. For example, in the film *The Crying Game*.

10. As I write, the tabloid press is running a humorous story about a transsexual vicar, and transsexualism is being used as the theme of humorous advertisements for lemonade and for a television comedy series.

11. A Private Members Bill on Gender Identity (Registration and Civil Status) proceeded as far as a Second Reading Debate on 2 February 1996.
12. "All-women Newnham split on don who had sex change," *The Times*, 24 June 1997.
13. e.g., *B v France*, (1992) 16 E.H.R.R.1.
14. See, e.g., Gooren, "Biological aspects of transsexualism," Council of Europe document No. CJ-DE/XXIII (93)5 and Zhon, Hofman, Gooren and Swaab, "A sex difference in the human brain and its relation to transsexuality," *Nature*, 1995, vol. 378 p. 68.
15. See, e.g., Report of the Proceedings of the XXIII and Colloquy on European Law, "Transsexuals, Medicine and the Law," Council of Europe, 1993: Breedlove, "Another Important Organ," *Nature* 1995, vol. 378, p. 15.
16. The definition of "gender" is itself a matter of debate, on which there is an extensive literature.
17. The refusal of a health authority to pay for gender re-assignment treatment was successfully challenged in *North West Lancashire Health Authority v A, D & G* [1999] Lloyd's Rep. Med. 399.
18. See *Report of the Interdepartmental Working Group on Transsexual People*, Home Office, 2000, p. 14.
19. *X, Petitioner*, 1957 S.L.T.(Sh.Ct.) 1. A similar view was reached in *Anonymous v Weiner* 270 N.Y.S. 2d 319 (1966).
20. *R. v Registrar General of Births, Deaths and Marriages for England and Wales, ex parte P and G, The Independent*, 22 February 1996.
21. *B v B* [1955] P. 42.
22. *S Y v S Y* [1963] P. 37.
23. [1971] P. 83.
24. At 107.
25. [1983] Q.B. 1053.
26. *R.(P.)1 and R.(P.)2*, (1980) National Insurance Commissioners Decisions.
27. *White v British Sugar Corporation Ltd* [1977] I.R.L.R. 121.
28. *S-T (formerly J) v J* (n. 7), at 123, per Ward L.J.
29. At 124.
30. *P v S* (n. 2). The United States case law (generally to the contrary effect) is discussed in the Advocate-General's Opinion.
31. e.g., *Chessington World of Adventures Ltd v Reed* [1998] I.C.R. 97, contrast *Bavin v NHS Trust Pensions Agency* [1999] I.C.R. 1192. See now the Sex Discrimination (Gender Reassignment) Regulations 1999, S.I. 1999 No. 1102. These prohibit discrimination against transsexuals, but subject to exceptions, where being "a man" or "a woman" is a genuine occupational qualification in view of specified circumstances: reg. 4.
32. *M v Chief Constable of the West Midlands Police* (1996) I.T. case 08964/96.
33. See the Report of the Interdepartmental Working Group (n. 21), pp. 58-67.
34. The case law of the Cour de Cassation between 1975 and 1990 is summarised in *B v France* (n. 15).
35. B.G.H. 21 September 1971, 13 G.H.Z. 57,63.
36. BVerfGE, 11 October 1978, N.J.W. 1979, p. 595.
37. *Sheffield and Horsham* (n. 4), Joint Partly Dissenting Opinion of Judges Bernhardt, Thor Vilhjalmsson, Spielmann, Palm, Wildhaber, Makarczyk and Voicu.
38. *Ibid.*

39. See, e.g., *Roetzheim* (n. 4), *Sheffield and Horsham* v *The United Kingdom*, Reports of Judgments and Decisions, No. 84, 1998-V, p. 2011 (Commission decision on admissibility), and the discussion in the *Working Group Report* (n. 21), pp. 36-7 and 45-52.

40. Being unmarried is required by the laws of Austria, Belgium, Finland and the Netherlands. In France, Italy and Portugal it is not a requirement, but a change of gender would constitute grounds for annulment or divorce. Sterility is required by the laws of the Netherlands and Sweden, but not in the other European countries mentioned. Full re-assignment surgery is required in Austria, Belgium, Denmark and France, but not in Finland, Italy, the Netherlands or Sweden. The Italian legislation of 1982 has been described by the Constitutional Court, in language reminiscent of the German case, as "inspired by the values of the freedom and dignity of the individuals": see the *Report of the Interdepartmental Working Group* (n. 21), p. 65.

41. *W* v *W* (1976) 2 W.L.D. 308.

42. *R.* v *Harris and McGuinness* (1988) 17 N.S.W.L.R. 158A. The approach of an Australian court was different in a case concerned with the marriage of a hermaphrodite: *In the Marriage of C and D* (1979) 35 F.L.R. 340, 28 A.L.R. 524.

43. *R.* v *Cogley* (1989) V.R.799, *obiter* (the charge being one of assault with intent to rape). The Crown Court in England has also held that a male-to-female transsexual can be raped, in a judgment of 28 October 1996: see App. No. 25680/94, *I.* v *The United Kingdom*, (1997) 23 E.H.R.R. C.D. 66.

44. The Australian Capital Territory, South Australia and New South Wales.

45. *M T* v *J T* (1976) 355A 2d 204, (1976) 2 F.L.R. 2247, Superior Court of New Jersey, Appellate Division. A different view was taken in respect of transsexuals who had not undergone full re-constructive surgery, in *Anonymous* v *Anonymous* 325 N.Y.S. 2d. 499 (1971) and *B* v *B* N.Y.S. 2d. 712 (1974). A marriage licence was also refused in *Re Ladrach* 513 N.E. 2d. 828 (Ohio, 1987). The Supreme Court has held that the imprisonment of a transsexual (who had undergone limited surgical and other treatment, but not full reconstructive surgery) in a male penitentiary did not constitute cruel and unusual punishment: *Farmer* v *Brennan*, 511 U.S. 825 (1994). As to whether he was entitled to further gender re-assignment treatment while in prison, see *Farmer* v *Moritsugu*, U.S. Court of Appeals, 2nd Cir., 2 April 1999; cf. *Schuler* v *The McGraw-Hill Companies Inc.* U.S. Court of Appeals, 10th Cir., 22 April 1998. See also n. 33.

46. M v *M* [1991] N.Z.F.L.R. 337, Family Court; *Att.-Gen.* v *Otahuhu Family Court* [1995] 1 N.Z.L.R. 603.

47. (1980) 3 E.H.R.R. 557.

48. Series B No. 36.

49. para. 45.

50. para. 50.

51. paras. 51-2.

52. para. 60.

53. *X* v *Federal Republic of Germany* (n. 4).

54. (1987) 9 E.H.R.R. 56.

55. App. No. 9420/81, *38 Transsexuals* v *Italy*, 5 October 1982, unpublished.

56. para 43.

57. para. 49.

58. para. 50.

59. *Marckx* v *Belgium*, (1979) 2 E.H.R.R 330

60. (1990) 13 E.H.R.R. 622.
61. Following the approach taken in App. No. 10622/83, *James* v *The United Kingdom*, 15 December 1988, and App. No. 11095/84, *W.* v *The United Kingdom*, 17 March 1989.
62. para. 42; similarly *Rees*, para. 47.
63. para. 46.
64. para. 2.7.
65. *B* v *France* (n. 15).
66. As translated. The original French does not distinguish between sex and gender, but uses the word "sexe" throughout.
67. para. 71. The French text does not speak of "gender identity" but of "l'identité sexuelle."
68. para. 48.
69. (1997) 24 E.H.R.R. 143
70. Opinion of the Commission, para. 45.
71. para. 67 (emphasis added).
72. para. 47.
73. n.4.
74. And also the case of *Dudgeon* v *The United Kingdom*, (1981) 4 E.H.R.R. 149, concerning the criminalisation of homosexual activities.
75. para. 59.
76. para. 60.
77. *I* v *The United Kingdom* (1997) 23 E.H.R.R. C.D. 66; App. No. 28957/95, *Goodwin* v *The United Kingdom*, 1 December 1997.
78. *Report of the Interdepartmental Working Group on Transsexual People* (n. 21).
79. *Roetzheim* (n. 4).
80. [1995] 1 N.Z.L.R. 603
81. *Hyde* v *Hyde* (1861-73) All.E.R. Rep 175.
82. At 607. One other possible approach would be the legal recognition of forms of cohabitation other than marriage, as exists in French law and in some Scandinavian countries. This possibility does not foreclose the question whether marriage should be open to transsexuals.
83. *Richards* v *United States Tennis Association* 400 N.Y.S. 2d. 267 (1997). Hence the gender specification tests applied by the International Olympic Committee since 1968: see the Report of the Interdepartmental Working Group on Transsexual People (Home Office, 2000), pp. 53-57.
84. [2002] Fam. 150
85. At p. 178
86. The appeal was due to be heard on 20-21 January 2003.
87. (2002) 35 E.H.R.R. 18
88. At paras. 90-93.
89. At paras. 98-103.
90. The text of the announcement is available at www.lcd.gov.uk/constitution/transsex/statement.

Sexual Orientation and Gender Identity in North America: Legal Trends, Legal Contrasts

R. Douglas Elliott

McGowan Elliott & Kim LLP, Toronto, Ontario, Canada

Mary Bonauto

Gay and Lesbian Advocates & Defenders of Boston, Massachusetts

SUMMARY. The article provides a comparative analysis of recent legal developments with regard to LGBT rights in Canada and the United States of America. Both countries have made great progress towards better protection and full recognition of LGBT rights. Despite this progress, Canada appears to be ahead of the United States, as illustrated by two most recent court decisions (e.g. *Halpern*, legalizing same-sex marriage in Ontario, and *Lawrence v. Texas*, decriminalizing consensual sodomy in the United States). *[Article copies available for a fee from The Haworth Document Delivery Service: 1-800-HAWORTH. E-mail address:*

R. Douglas Elliott is a partner with McGowan Elliott & Kim LLP, Toronto, Ontario, Canada. He is also the male Director for North America and President of the International Lesbian and Gay Law Association (ILGLaw; Website: www.ilglaw.org). Correspondence may be addressed: 10 Bay Street, Suite 1400, Toronto, Ontario, M5J 2R8, Canada. Mary Bonauto is Civil Rights Director of Gay and Lesbian Advocates & Defenders of Boston, Massachusetts, USA. She is also the female Director for North America of ILGLaw. Correspondence may be addressed: 294 Washington St., Suite 740, Boston, MA 02108, USA.

[Haworth co-indexing entry note]: "Sexual Orientation and Gender Identity in North America: Legal Trends, Legal Contrasts." Elliott, R. Douglas, and Mary Bonauto. Co-published simultaneously in *Journal of Homosexuality* (Harrington Park Press, an imprint of The Haworth Press, Inc.) Vol. 48, No. 3/4, 2005, pp. 91-106; and: *Sexuality and Human Rights: A Global Overview* (ed: Helmut Graupner, and Phillip Tahmindjis) Harrington Park Press, an imprint of The Haworth Press, Inc., 2005, pp. 91-106. Single or multiple copies of this article are available for a fee from The Haworth Document Delivery Service [1-800-HAWORTH, 9:00 a.m. - 5:00 p.m. (EST). E-mail address: docdelivery@haworthpress.com].

http://www.haworthpress.com/web/JH
© 2005 by The Haworth Press, Inc. All rights reserved.
Digital Object Identifier: 10.1300/J082v48n03_06

<docdelivery@haworthpress.com> Website: <http://www.HaworthPress.com>
© 2005 by The Haworth Press, Inc. All rights reserved.]

KEYWORDS. Homosexuality, gay rights, equality rights, privacy rights, (non)-discrimination, religion, Canada: history, United States of America (U.S.A.): history, progress, Canada: Supreme Court, United States of America (U.S.A.): Supreme Court, Canada: Charter of Rights, constitution, sodomy laws, recognition: same-sex relationships, marriage, common law, Feder-ation/-al, Ontario, Halpern

INTRODUCTION

The United States of America and Canada are two nations who share the longest undefended border in the world. As prosperous Western democracies that departed from their roots in the British parliamentary system with constitutional equality guarantees, they share many political and cultural values. Both countries are home to thriving lesbian and gay communities with considerable visibility. To the casual observer, the two societies might be difficult to distinguish. However, there are differences. The United States was the birthplace of Stonewall, and has made remarkable progress since then on the road to equality under the law. However, surprisingly it is Canada that has advanced further.

In this brief overview, we discuss some of the recent trends in the relevant law in each country. The issues and trends are clearly shared, but the state of progress is different. The authors are committed to equality for all sexual minorities. In the interest of economy of language, the acronym "LGBT" for "lesbian, gay, bisexual and transgendered" will generally be used in this article. However, on occasion it will be appropriate to speak of transgendered persons or same-sex couples. This is not intended to minimize the importance of equality for all sexual minorities.

UNITED STATES OF AMERICA

As the most powerful nation on earth with a culture that has global reach, developments in the USA naturally are of great importance to lawyers everywhere. The USA has a long tradition of constitutional equality and was the birthplace of the modern LGBT equality movement at Stonewall. It is a nation blessed with a rich network of local and national legal and community advocacy groups, lawyers, academics and some prominent openly lesbian and gay politicians. The modern American LGBT movement for equality drew significant inspiration from the African-American and women's movements. Like those groups, the LGBT community has found the goal of full equality an elusive one.

The history of the legal struggle for equality before the United States ("U.S.") Supreme Court is older than Stonewall and dates back to the 1950s, as has been well documented in the recent book *Courting Justice*.[2] The US *Bill of Rights* is one of the most important documents in the world history of the quest for equality under the law.[3] However, it is an eighteenth century document, created at a time when the word "homosexual" had not yet been coined. Earlier LGBT cases relied on traditional constitutional rights or freedoms such as freedom of speech, due process and privacy to advance equality without forcefully engaging the scope of the constitutional equal protection guarantee.

To some extent this also reflected the unhelpful jurisprudence that had grown up around the equal protection guarantee in other circumstances. The jurisprudence became more robust in cases like *Brown* at a time when the LGBT movement in the USA was in its infancy.[4] More recent cases seeking LGBT equality have more directly engaged equal protection arguments, stressing that the constitution contains enduring principles and is not a rulebook based on 18th century conditions. An excellent example of this shift in emphasis can be seen in criminal cases.

Criminal law is primarily, although not exclusively, a state responsibility under the American federal system. One of the great impediments to progress in the USA has been the continuing existence of sodomy laws in 13 states. Although most of these statutes are rarely enforced, they have been used by our opponents as a legal justification for denying other rights, although not always with success.

The most serious judicial setback for the American LGBT communities in modern times was the US Supreme Court's notorious decision in *Bowers* v. *Hardwick*.[5] Counsel for the gay man, as a tactical matter, chose not to emphasize equal protection arguments but privacy concepts. Notwithstanding this conservative approach, the majority of the Court upheld Georgia's sodomy law with express reference to Judeo-Christian teaching about homosexuality. The decision has been widely criticized. Following this ruling, many lawyers turned to state constitutions to attack sodomy laws with considerable albeit imperfect success. Remarkably, Georgia's sodomy law was one of those subsequently declared unconstitutional based on the state constitution.

The Supreme Court was recently called upon to re-visit its earlier decision in the case of *Lawrence* v. *Texas*.[6] This time, equal protection arguments and privacy arguments were both central to the case for the gay men seeking to strike down the law. Fortunately *Bowers* is now consigned to history as Justice Kennedy for the majority expressly overruled the case, finding that it was wrongly decided. The Court's rationale turned on the privacy and liberty arguments that had been rejected previously, while also characterizing the equal protection arguments as "tenable." While the five-member majority opinion is infused with powerful language about the dignity of same-sex relationships, Justice O'Connor's separate concurring opinion would have let Bowers stand, and focused instead on the equal protection violation. There were two dissents. Justice Thomas was scornful of the Texas sodomy law, but found that the state had the right to enact the prohibition. Justice Scalia wrote a spirited and bitter dissent, contrasting his colleagues' reluctance to overrule *Roe* v. *Wade* on grounds of preserving precedent when subsequently considered in *Casey*, with their willingness to sweep aside *Bowers* in the present case.

Lawrence is undoubtedly the greatest victory to date for the LGBT community in the American courts. It will form a firm foundation for further advances. As a general matter, by so thoroughly repudiating *Bowers* as wrong now and wrong when decided, the Court abolished the notion that there is a "gay exception" to the United States Constitution or that gay people must surmount additional hurdles in asserting constitutional protections enjoyed by others. This is powerful enough, but there are also other aspects of *Lawrence* that bode well for future jurisprudence. First, while the Court took the broader approach of privacy in *Lawrence* and directly rejected the rationale and result in *Bowers*, there is every reason to believe that equal protection claims are also on firmer ground, such as have been successfully advanced in Canada. Second, the case gives a tremendous boost to the struggle for equal marriage, including, ironically, Justice Scalia's dissent, where he identified discriminatory marriage laws as threatened by the majority's ruling. Finally, the case is noteworthy for its consideration of international legal developments. Once again, even Justice Scalia was moved to comment on the recent opening up of marriage by the Canadian courts, which he characterized as "imposing homosexual marriage." Given the worldwide trend to lesbian and gay equality, this greater willingness by the U.S. Supreme Court to consider the context of international legal advances bodes well for future cases.

Since the American system facilitates grassroots democracy, one of the challenges in the USA has been efforts to repeal or curtail our victories through the use of referenda, commonly called "initiatives." The extreme right organizes well-funded and well-organized campaigns to back these efforts. The first high profile initiative was in the late 1970s in Dade County, Florida, in a campaign that featured Anita Bryant. While these efforts continue and have hindered progress, the US Supreme Court drew a line in the sand in the landmark 1996 case of *Romer v. Evans*.[7] The majority struck down an anti-gay amendment to Colorado's constitution that was passed by a referendum as it made an entire class of persons "strangers to the law." *Romer* gave renewed hope to a community still struggling with the loss in *Bowers v. Hardwick*. The Court's reliance on equal protection concepts gives some further cause for optimism in future cases.

Considerable progress has been made in securing anti-discrimination ordinances from municipalities, state laws and executive orders forbidding discrimination, as well as workplace anti-discrimination protection secured by contract. Efforts to obtain a federal *Employment Non-discrimination Act* have so far failed.[8] Although difficult to achieve, such measures have proved to be generally robust. In fact, a number of states have gone even further and passed hate crimes legislation. President Clinton's executive order forbidding discrimination in the federal civil service was not repealed by President Bush. However, there have been sectors where achieving such measure has proved very challenging. Two of the most prominent are the military and the Boy Scouts.

There have been a number of high profile cases in the United States where excellent service men and women have lost their positions or even their lives due to their sexual orientation. President Clinton's executive order imposing an outright ban on discrimination in the military was superceded by the law passed by Congress in 1993 that enshrines the concept of "Don't Ask, Don't Tell."[9] Being gay or lesbian will still lead to a discharge, and the statute is the only American law specifically authorizing an employee's termination on the grounds of sexual orientation. However, theoretically there are no investigations initiated to uncover gay and lesbian service personnel in the absence of a confession or credible evidence of homosexual activity. According to the Servicemembers Legal Defense Network, pursuing and harassing LGBT service members has continued in violation of these limited protections. There seems little chance that the policy will change under the current administration, even though many of America's allies forbid such discrimination in their own militaries, including the UK, Israel, and, of course, Canada.

The case of *Dale* put a beloved American institution under the microscope: the Boy Scouts of America.[10] In the result, the US Supreme Court ruled that as a private organization the Boy Scouts was permitted to interpret its "morally straight" code so as to exclude gay scouts and scout leaders. However, the Scouts were forced to admit that they had such a policy as a result of the case. This put them in violation of many laws, policies and ordinances of organizations such as municipalities that assisted them by such measures as providing free or low cost facilities for meetings or deducting charitable contributions from employees' wages. It caused a vigorous debate on the issue in American society, and, for example, caused Steven Spielberg to publicly dissociate himself from scouting. While Congress passed a statute that purported to protect the Scouts,[11] in fact this statute did little more than provide a cosmetic restatement of constitutional rights the Scouts likely already enjoyed.

Transgendered persons have had some success in achieving express inclusion in anti-discrimination laws or executive orders, with six states and over fifty cities and counties offering protection. However, there has been a mixed record in the courts. Some courts have found that transgendered persons can rely on laws barring sex discrimination. However, in two prominent cases, *Littleton* and *Gardiner*, the courts insisted on a chromosomal approach to determining gender.[12]

Perhaps the most prominent feature of the struggle for LGBT equality in the USA has been the fight for equal access to marriage. The battle has not been without its critics, not only from the religious right but from within the community. For many gay and lesbian Americans, equal access to marriage remains an important goal. Denying them their right to choose their marriage partner strikes at the heart of their dignity and humanity. Our struggle has been inspired by the previous efforts to end the ban on inter-racial marriage that culminated in the US Supreme Court's striking down of Virginia's anti-miscegenation law in *Loving*.[13]

A spectacular breakthrough was achieved in *Baehr* v. *Miike* when the Hawaiian courts ruled that same-sex couples might have a constitutional right to equal access to marriage.[14] That victory was short lived when a constitutional referendum again retracted the gains made in court. However, the case did establish a helpful judicial precedent. Hawaii introduced some protections for same-sex partners by statute, a process Evan Wolfson has dubbed "losing forward " or "winning by losing."[15] Even an unsuccessful court case can advance public education and legal rights, provided that the litigation is part of a process of engaging the public.

Another incomplete victory followed in the case *Baker* v. *Vermont*.[16] The Court stopped short of insisting on equal access to marriage, simply insisting on equal access to the same range of benefits and obligations. Despite vocal opposition, Vermont, under the leadership of Governor Dean, passed a civil union law similar to the Scandinavian style registered partnership laws. Unfortunately, it only extends to matters within the jurisdiction of the state and is not recognized under federal law.

The response to these developments from legislatures has been decidedly mixed, and sometimes discouraging. Congress in 1996 passed the ironically named *Defense of Marriage Act* or DOMA restricting legal respect for marriages under federal law to opposite sex couples.[17] Many states passed similar laws respecting matters under their jurisdiction, so-called "mini-DOMAs." However, the Assembly of California, the most populous state in the union, has recently passed a civil union law similar to that of Vermont.[18] A bill has been introduced to the same effect in New Jersey.

One of the most interesting developments in the legislative arena came in the wake of the tragic events of September 11, 2001. The *Mychal Judge Act*, named for a popular gay Catholic priest killed that day, ensured that some same-sex partners received survivor benefits of a type that ordinarily would be reserved for the surviving spouse of a married couple.[19]

The struggle continues unabated in the courts. A case in New Jersey is under way seeking legal recognition. A Massachusetts case, *Goodridge*, has been argued before the states' highest Court. A decision is expected soon.[20]

A boon to the struggle was a recent publication regarding family law from the highly respected American Law Institute or ALI.[21] The ALI has suggested unmarried same-sex couples should be given some recognition in American family law, including division of assets on dissolution and parenting rights and obligations. The report has outraged conservative commentators.

One of the looming issues for the United States in light of Vermont civil unions and the legal recognition of same-sex marriage in Canada, the Netherlands and Belgium is the interstate validation of such civil unions and marriages. The Connecticut Appellate Court in *Rosengarten*, as well as the Georgia Court of Appeals, have declined to extend respect to Vermont civil unions.[22] However, a gleam of hope has been offered from the judiciary with the well-reasoned decision by a trial level court in *Langan v. St. Vincent's Hospital*.[23] The Court in that case permitted a wrongful death action, brought by a surviving same-sex partner, to proceed. The Court noted that there had been a Vermont civil union, and that New York lacked a mini-DOMA and had introduced some measures to afford recognition to same-sex couples.

CANADA

Although Canada is overshadowed by its enormously powerful southern neighbour on the world stage, it has nonetheless been a world leader in human rights at least since John Humphrey drafted the *Universal Declaration of Human Rights*.[24] Since the 1982 entrenchment of its own domestic *Charter of Rights and Freedoms*, Canada increasingly has established itself as one of the global pacesetters in equality for gays, lesbians, bisexuals and transgendered persons.[25] The general trend is extremely positive, although there have been some rulings and legislative responses that have not been completely satisfactory.[26]

Canada is a constitutional monarchy based on the British system. It is also a federation, with the criminal law power at the federal level. The first obstacle on the path to equality was removed in Canada in the wake of the worldwide wave of reforms triggered by the Wolfenden Report.[27] In contrast to the American situation, consensual homosexual acts in private have not been criminal in Canada for over 30 years. Although there have been issues in Canada with respect to the antiquated bawdyhouse laws and their occasional use against gay and lesbian bathhouses, criminal law reform in Canada has meant prohibiting and punishing hate crimes against gays and lesbians. Although the Canadian Parliament has enacted increased penalties for crimes motivated by homophobia, the offence of promoting hatred against an identifiable group does not yet include the LGBT community in the scope of its protection.[28]

Canada began to have local anti-discrimination laws in the 1970s, and they are now virtually universal throughout the nation. However, Canada had no constitutionally entrenched equality rights until the *Constitution Act, 1982* established the *Charter of Rights and Freedoms* as the supreme law of the land. Section 15(1) of the *Charter* guarantees all Canadians equality, subject to the limitation in section 1 of such reasonable limits as are demonstrably justified in a free and democratic society. Although the equality guarantee does not expressly include sexual orientation as an enumerated ground, in a series of rulings including *Egan, Vriend* and *M. v. H.*, Canada's Supreme Court has made it clear that the equality guarantee protects gays and lesbians and their relationships.[29]

The ban on gays and lesbians in the military ended with the court rulings in *Douglas* and *Haig*, and the issue is simply no longer controversial in Canada.[30] There has been no *Dale* case because the Canadian Boy Scouts do not have an anti-gay policy like their American equivalent. *Vriend* makes clear that discrimination on the basis of sexual orientation must be prohibited by all state actors in Canada.

Canada, unlike the United States, has had laws that have increasingly recognized the rights of unmarried heterosexual couples, so-called "common law" relationships. As a result, LGBT activists decided to defer attempts to achieve equal access to marriage to efforts to achieve equal status with heterosexual common law couples. The landmark ruling of the Supreme Court of Canada in *M. v. H.*, which determined that a lesbian was entitled to seek financial support from her former same-sex common law partner under Ontario's law, sent a clear message that the battle had been won on this issue. It has triggered a wave of statutory reforms.[31] At the federal level, *The Modernization of Benefits and Obligations Act*, commonly known as *Bill C-23* or *MOBA*, has dramatically changed the landscape by comprehensively amending federal statutes to generally equalize the treatment of married couples, common law couples and same-sex common law couples.[32] This important achievement was subject to what Kees Waaldijk has called the "law of small change," as it included an interpretive provision reaffirming Parliament's view that marriage is between one man and one woman.[33]

There are some additional problems that persist at the federal level. Parliament has also deferred the logistical problems associated with insisting on a one-year cohabitation requirement for same-sex couples in the immigration context, although regulations are expected very shortly to deal with that problem. There are also problems due to limited or nonexistent retroactive benefits. Finally, Parliament has not yet addressed the problem of the discriminatory age of consent that has been ruled unconstitutional by the courts but which has not been officially changed pending a review aimed at increasing the age of consent for all.[34]

The federal legislation was also of limited benefit to our communities because most family law matters are within the control of provincial governments under the Canadian system. At the provincial level, the response to the Supreme Court's decision has varied. Ontario itself, the province that was the subject of the ruling in *M. v. H.*, introduced omnibus legislation, but insisted on creating a third category for same-sex couples.[35] Ontario also only granted access to the less comprehensive regime of rights and obligations afforded to heterosexual common law couples. This distinction gained added significance when the Canadian Supreme Court ruled recently that some distinctions between the legal regime governing common law and married heterosexual couples are constitutionally valid.[36] Some provinces have done nothing to respond, and New Brunswick has changed only the spousal support law that was directly in issue in the case. Many provinces, such as Alberta, have changed legislation in a piecemeal fashion, often in response to lawsuits or other pressures. For example, Alberta has recently agreed to pay same-sex pensions to the survivors of deceased civil servants because of union demands and threats of litigation.[37]

An entirely different approach has been taken by Nova Scotia, which has introduced a European style system of registered domestic partnerships.[38] Quebec has followed suit. Given the widespread recognition of common law relationships in most provinces other than Quebec, and the progress regarding marriage, it is questionable whether this model will gain in popularity. There are doubts about the status of these types of relationships when the partners move to neighboring provinces, such as New Brunswick, where there is neither such a system nor much recognition of common law rights.

The Canadian courts have continued to lead the way in reform. The Supreme Court of Canada itself has made important rulings in two cases since 1999, although neither dealt with relationships and families *per se*. While neither decision was a setback to our cause, neither delivered a clear victory. *Little Sisters Bookstore* involved a gay and lesbian bookstore in Vancouver that was targeted by Canada Customs and subjected to repeated seizures of materials said to be obscene, even though many of the same materials were imported by mainstream bookstores without incident.[39] The Supreme Court condemned the harassment in strong language, but ordered only partial change to the Customs regulation, upholding the right of the Canadian government to conduct seizures at the border of gay and lesbian pornography that was believed to be obscene.

In *British Columbia College of Teachers v. Trinity Western University*, the Supreme Court dealt with the increasingly important questions of balancing the rights of religious conservatives and the rights of gays and lesbians to equality.[40] The Court held that a private conservative

Christian university was entitled to have its education graduates licensed as teachers in the public system, but that the province could insist that they not act on their homophobic religious beliefs in public schools.

Transgender issues have rarely been litigated in Canada. However, the Ontario Human Rights Commission recently issued an important report stressing the importance of protecting transgendered persons from discrimination. In British Columbia, the provincial Human Rights Tribunal ruled that a rape crisis centre had discriminated against a male to female transsexual when she was refused permission to volunteer at the centre, a decision affirmed by the Court.[41] Given that Canada's laws generally treat opposite sex and same-sex couples equally, there is less likelihood of a matter like *Littleton* reaching the courts. Given Canadian jurisprudence, one would expect a different result if such a case was advanced.

The lower courts saw a number of important rulings, mostly positive, but one clearly negative. However, the sole negative ruling was soon overturned.

In conservative Alberta, the Court of Queen's Bench ruled that same-sex couples must be allowed to adopt children, following earlier Ontario case law.[42] The Alberta government has changed the statute in light of the Court's ruling.

Three of the significant lower court rulings relate to matters that remain very much in progress through the Canadian courts. Canada has two government pension plans that provide benefits to surviving partners, the Quebec and Canada Pension Plans.[43] The governing statutes of both plans have been amended to include same-sex couples, but with limited or no retrospective effect. The Quebec Court of Appeal in *Bleau v. Quebec*, relying on *M. v. H.*, held recently that the failure to include same-sex couples retrospectively violated the Quebec *Charter of Rights*.[44] The Quebec government has decided not to appeal this decision. A national class action lawsuit is underway in Ontario, scheduled to be tried in September 2003, that challenges the lack of benefits under the Canada Pension Plan during the 1985-1998 period that was excluded under *MOBA*.[45] In earlier rulings, the case had survived efforts by the Canadian government to have it dismissed.

A case that has captured the imagination of the Canadian public, and to a certain extent the world, was the recent case of Marc Hall. Hall was a 17-year-old student at a Catholic high school in suburban Toronto who was denied permission to attend his high school graduation dance, known as the "prom," with a same-sex date.[46] The school denied permission on the basis that homosexual acts are prohibited by the Catholic Church and on their view that same-sex dancing is sexual activity. Backed by a coalition of unions, students, liberal Catholics and gay and lesbian community organizations, Hall sought an injunction against the Board.[47] The Board relied on its entrenched rights under the Canadian constitution as a publicly funded Catholic school to enforce their religious views. The Court ruled against the Board, and issued an injunction. The case established a remarkable precedent in employing an injunction to prevent an act of discrimination, rather than seeking redress after the discrimination occurred. It also is a blow to religious conservatives who for the first time have been forced to respect the rights of gays and lesbians to equality within religious schools. Finally, it marks the first time in recent memory that the Catholic Church has lost a case in the Canadian courts where it sought to enforce its conservative views on people within the Catholic school system.

Sadly, the Catholic School Board has decided that the case must proceed to trial although Marc has already been to his prom. There is concern by the Board that a dangerous precedent has been set. The trial has not yet been scheduled.[48]

Legal challenges were launched in British Columbia, Quebec and Ontario challenging the exclusion of same-sex couples from marriage.[49] The most negative Canadian Court ruling in recent memory was the British Columbia trial level marriage decision of Justice Pitfield.[50] Justice Pitfield held that the restriction on same sex marriage was discriminatory under section 15(1) of the *Charter*, but justified under the reasonable limits exemption of section 1 of the *Charter*. More remarkably, the Court also held that same-sex marriage was legally impossible in Canada in the absence of a constitutional amendment. Fortunately, an appeal from that decision was granted and this regressive decision has been overturned. In a strongly worded and unanimous decision, the British Columbia Court of Appeal found the exclusion of same-sex couples from marriage to violate the equality guarantee and found that there was no constitutionally valid alternative to marriage. Governments were given until July 12, 2004, to amend incidental legislation to give effect to this ruling.[51] The Canadian Government has until June 30, 2003, to seek leave to appeal this decision.

A similar result had been achieved at the lower court level in Quebec.[52] The lower court in Ontario had also found the bar to same-sex marriage unconstitutional, but opined that there might be constitutional alternatives. The majority would have given the Canadian Government until July 12, 2004, to resolve the problem, failing which same-sex marriage would become a legal reality.[53]

The Ontario Court of Appeal recently released its ruling which upheld the Ontario's lower court ruling that the bar was unconstitutional, but ordered a much more dramatic remedy.[54] The definition of marriage was immediately changed. The authorities were ordered to begin licensing and registering same-sex marriages. No delay was to be permitted, sending governments scrambling to respond. Perhaps most importantly, the Court ruled that two same-sex marriages that had taken place at the Metropolitan Community Church of Toronto in January 2001 were valid, making them the first legal same-sex marriages in the world. Canada also becomes the first jurisdiction to offer same-sex marriage to non-residents. Many American couples have taken advantage of the ruling, including Rev. Tory Perry, the founder of Metropolitan Community Churches worldwide.

The Quebec Court of Appeal is scheduled to hear an appeal in September of 2003. The Federal Government has abandoned their appeal, but the religious conservative interveners plan to carry on with the case.

The Federal Government has announced that it will not appeal the Ontario decision, although some interveners from the case are attempting to do so. A draft Bill confirming the new definition of marriage will be referred for an advisory opinion from the Canadian Supreme Court. Three questions will be posed that aim to ensure the constitutional validity of the new definition and the legal protection of clergy who object to marrying same sex couples. The Bill will then be submitted to Parliament for a free vote. However, as the opposition has noted, the legal definition of marriage has already changed so the Bill is somewhat superfluous. The only hope for the opponents of equality lies with the invocation of section 33 of the Canadian constitution, which allows Parliament to exempt laws from the equality guarantee. However, this constitutional "weapon of mass destruction" has never been invoked by the Federal Parliament in the history of the *Charter*.

CONCLUSIONS

Important advances toward equality have been made in both the USA and Canada for gays and lesbians. The struggle for equal access to marriage has been a particularly prominent legal issue in both nations in recent years. Although its constitutional equality guarantees are much younger, Canada has managed to eclipse the USA for the moment in advancing toward equality. While the factors responsible are complex, some features are likely Canada's longer history of freedom from archaic and intrusive sodomy laws, its newer and broader equality guarantee, the widespread legal recognition of heterosexual common law relationships and the weaker influence of the religious right.

Closer cooperation between legal activists on both sides of the border has been a feature of the battle for equality in recent years, especially around marriage. The gains achieved demonstrate the importance of international cooperation in this area.

Since Canada has now legally recognized same-sex marriage, it will be interesting to see in light of cases like *Langan* v. *St. Vincent's Hospital* what an American court will make of a request for legal recognition in the USA of a same-sex marriage lawfully contracted in Canada. It is interesting to note that Canada imposes neither residency nor citizenship requirement for couples wishing to marry there, and some prominent US activists have married in Canada in a process that has echoes of a kind of gay Gretna Green.[55] The impact of Canada's bold move forward has been described as the "Canadian earthquake" in the U.S.A.

Niagara Falls, the honeymoon capital of North America, straddles the border between the USA and Canada. It is a place that is at once a symbol of the friendship between two nations, and of the love between two persons that is embodied in marriage. As a result of the Canadian earthquake, Niagara Falls may have additional symbolic significance for gays and lesbians in North America in the years ahead.

NOTES

1. The authors would like to thank Sasha Dmitrenko and Peter Basso for their assistance with this article. All errors remain the responsibility of the authors alone.

2. Joyce Murdoch, *Courting Justice: Gay Men and Lesbians v. the Supreme Court* (Basic Book, 2001).

3. U.S. Const. amend. I-X.

4. *Brown* v. *Board of Education*, 349 U.S. 294 (1955).

5. *Bowers* v. *Hardwick*, 478 U.S. 186 (1986).

6. *Lawrence & Garner* v. *Texas* (U.S.S.C. decision pending).

7. *Romer* v. *Evans*, 517 U.S. 620 (1996).

8. See, e.g., http://www.hrc.org/issues/federal_leg/enda/index.asp.

9. 10 U.S.C. sec. 654. For more information, please visit <www.sldn.org>.

10. *Boy Scouts of America* v. *Dale*, 530 U.S. 640 (2000).

11. *Boy Scouts of America Equal Access Act*, 20 USCS § 7905 (2003).

12. *Littleton* v. *Prang*, 9 S.W.3d 223 (1999) (C.A. Texas), *In re Estate of Gardiner*, 273 Kan. 191 (2002).

13. *Loving* v. *Virginia*, 388 U.S. 1, 18 L. Ed. 2nd 1010, 87 S.Ct.1817 (1967).
14. 80 Haw. 341 (1996).
15. From personal communication between Evan Wolfson and Douglas Elliott with permission to use it.
16. *Baker* v. *Vermont*, 170 Vt. 194, 744 A.2d 864 (Vt. 1999); *Vermont Civil Union Act*, Vermont Acts 1999, Act 91.
17. 1 U.S.C.S. sec. 7.
18. See 15 V.S.A. § 1201 (2003) (Vermont, as amended in 1999, No. 91 (Adj. Sess.), § 41.
19. *The Police and Fire Chaplains Public Safety Officer's Benefit Act*, 42 USCS § 3711 (2003).
20. *Goodridge* v. *Department of Public Health*, SCJ No. 08860 (2003). Ms. Bonauto is counsel in the case. See <www.glad.org> for details about this case.
21. American Law Institute, *Principles of the Law of Family Dissolution: Analysis and Recommendations* (2002) <www.ali.org>.
22. *Rosengarten* v. *Downes*, 71 Conn. App. 372 (2002), *Burns* v. *Burns*, 253 Ga. App. 600 (2002).
23. *Langan* v. *St. Vincent's Hospital* (2003) N.Y. Misc. LEXIS 673.
24. GA Res. 217 (III), UN GAOR, 3d Sess., Supp. No. 13, UN Doc. A/810 (1948) 71.
25. *Canadian Charter of Rights and Freedoms*, Part I of the *Constitution Act*, 1982, being Schedule B to the *Canada Act* 1982 (U.K.), 1982, c. 11. (hereinafter "the Charter")
26. A more general discussion on various developments towards/against gay equality in Canada can be found at Bruce MacDougall, "The Celebration of Same-Sex Marriage" (2000-2001) 32 Ottawa L. Rev. 235-267 (2000-2001) 32 R.D. Ottawa 235-267, or D.G. Casswell, "Moving Toward Same-Sex Marriage" (2001), 80 Can. Bar Rev. 810. In these articles, the authors argue that the debate around same-sex marriage signifies that Canada is at the forefront of the global gay rights movement.
27. During the 1950s, Sir John Wolfenden was asked by the British government to study law reform around sexuality. His landmark report decried British laws prohibiting male homosexuality as "the Blackmailer's Charter." He urged decriminalization of male homosexual acts between consenting adults in private. However, it would take over ten years before Parliament would act on this recommendation in England. See Wolfenden, *Report of the Committee on Homosexual Offences and Prostitution* (London: Her Majesty's Stationary Office, 1957).
28. There is an ongoing effort to include the LGBT community in the legislation.
29. *Egan* v. *Canada*, [1995] 2 S.C.R. 513, *Vriend* v. *Alberta*, [1998] 1 S.C.R. 493, *M.* v. *H.*, [1999] 2 S.C.R. 3.
30. See, e.g., *Haig* v. *Canada* (1992), 9 O.R. (3d) 495 (C.A.).
31. *M.* v. *H.*, [1999] 2 S.C.R. 3.
32. S.C. 2000, c. 12.
33. Please see 'Small Change': How the Road to Same-Sex Marriage Got Paved in the Netherlands,' in Robert Wintemute and Mads Andenaes (eds.), *Legal Recognition of Same-Sex Partnership. A Study of National, European and International Law*, Oxford: Hart Publishing 2001, p. 437-464.
34. *R* v. *Carmen M.*, [1995] 23 O.R. (3d) 629 (C.A.).
35. Bill 5: *An Act to Amend Certain Statutes Because of the Supreme Court Decision in M. v. H*, S.O. 1999, c/6 (or referred to by Canadian activists as *"The Devil Made Me Do It!"* Act).

36. *Nova Scotia* v. *Walsh*, [2002] S.C.J. No. 84
37. For the discussion on the response to *M. v. H* by various provinces, see Jason Murphy, "Dialogic Responses to M. v. H.: From Compliance to Defiance" (2001) 59(2) U.T. Fac. L. Rev 299-317.
38. *Visual Statistics Act*, RS 1989, c.494 as amended in 2001, c.5, ss. 40-49; c.45.
39. *Little Sisters Book and Art Emporium* v. *Canada*, [2000] 2 S.C.R. 1120. Mr. Elliott acted as counsel for the intervener *Canadian AIDS Society*.
40. *Trinity Western University* v. *British Columbia College of Teachers*, [2001] 1 S.C.R. 772. Mr Elliott acted as co-counsel for the intervener, *EGALE Canada*.
41. *Vancouver Rape Relief Society* v. *British Columbia*, [2000] B.C.J. No. 1143.
42. *A (Re)*, [1999] A.J. No. 1349.
43. *E.g., Canada Pension Plan Act*, R.S.C. 1985, c. C-8.
44. *Bleau* c. *Quebec*, [2002] J.Q. no 362 (judgment available in French only).
45. *Hislop* v. *Canada*, [2002] O.J. No. 2799 (S.C.J.). Please note that the author is the leading counsel for the plaintiffs in this case.
46. *Hall* v. *Powers*, [2002] O.J. No. 1803.
47. The Coalition in Support of Marc Hall was composed of the Canadian AIDS Society, Canadian Auto Workers Union, Canadian Federation of Students, Canadian Gay and Lesbian Archives, Canadian Unitarian Council, Catholics for a Free Choice, Challenge the Church, Coalition for Lesbian and Gay Rights in Ontario, EGALE Canada, Equal Marriage for Same-Sex Couples, Foundation for Equal Families, Liberals for Equality Rights, Metropolitan Community Church of Toronto, Ontario Division of the Canadian Union of Public Employees, Ontario Federation Of Labour, Parents Family & Friends of Lesbians and Gays (PFLAG), PRIDE York Region, Public Service Alliance of Canada, and Windsor Pride Committee. Mr. Elliott acted as counsel for the Coalition together with Victoria Paris.
48. Mr. Hall's counsel, David Corbett, was recently appointed the Ontario Superior Court, the first openly gay man so appointed.
49. For a comprehensive coverage of these cases and surrounding circumstances, please refer to <http://www.samesexmarriage.ca>. Mr. Elliott is counsel for the Metropolitan Community Church of Toronto.
50. *EGALE Canada Inc.* v. *Canada*, [2001] B.C.J. No. 1995, rev'd [2003] B.C.C.A. No. 251.
51. *EGALE Canada Inc.* v. *Canada*, [2003] B.C.C.A. No. 251.
52. *Hendricks* v. *Québec*, [2002] J.Q. no 3816 (C.S.).
53. *Halpern and MCCT* v. *Canada (A.G.)*, [2002] 60 O.R. (3d) 321 (Div. Ct.), aff'd [2003] O.J. No. 2268 (C.A.).
54. See *supra*.
55. For background on the historical significance of Gretna Green, please see http://www.gretnaweddings.com.

Sexuality and Human Rights in Europe

Helmut Graupner, JD

Australian Society for Sex Research

SUMMARY. Written human rights law in Europe is as scanty as in the rest of the world. Case-law however provides considerable protection of sexual rights. It guarantees comprehensive protection of autonomy in sexual life, also for minors, and provides protection against discrimina-

---

Helmut Graupner (www.graupner.at), Doctor in Law (University of Vienna), is Rechtsanwalt (attorney-at-law), admitted to the bar in Austria and in the Czech Republic. He is Vice President of the Austrian Society for Sex Research (ÖGS) (www.oegs.net; www.courage-beratung.at) and President of the Austrian lesbian and gay rights organisation Rechtskomitee LAMBDA (RKL) (www.RKLambda.at); Vice President for Europe, International Lesbian and Gay Law Association (ILGLaw) (www.ILGLaw.org); Austrian member, European Group of Experts on Combating Sexual Orientation Discrimination working for the Commission of the European Union (http://www.meijers.leidenuniv.nl/index.php3?m=10&c=98); member, Scientific Committee of the Center for Research and Comparative Legal Studies on Sexual Orientation and Gender Identity (CERSGOSIG), Turin (www.cersgosig.informagay.it); member, Editorial Board of the *Journal of Homosexuality*; member, World Association for Sexology (WAS) (www.worldsexology.org); member, Expert Committee for the Revision of the Law on Sexual Offences, appointed by the Austrian Minister of Justice in 1996; 1996 and 2003, expert, Justice Committee of the Austrian Federal Parliament; 2002 and 2004, lecturer, University of Innsbruck ("Sexuality & the Law"); 2001, Gay and Lesbian Award (G.A.L.A.) of the Austrian Lesbian and Gay Movement (http://www.hosilinz.at/presse/2001/011013_gala2001.html). This essay is based upon a paper of same title presented at the International Bar Association (IBA) 2000 Annual Conference (Amsterdam, September 17th-22nd 2000). Last update: 11.01.2004. Correspondence may be addressed: Rechtskomitee LAMBDA, Linke Wienzeile 102, A-1160 Vienna, Austria (E-mail: hg@graupner.at).

[Haworth co-indexing entry note]: "Sexuality and Human Rights in Europe." Graupner, Helmut. Co-published simultaneously in *Journal of Homosexuality* (Harrington Park Press, an imprint of The Haworth Press, Inc.) Vol. 48, No. 3/4, 2005, pp. 107-139; and: *Sexuality and Human Rights: A Global Overview* (ed: Helmut Graupner, and Phillip Tahmindjis) Harrington Park Press, an imprint of The Haworth Press, Inc., 2005, pp. 107-139. Single or multiple copies of this article are available for a fee from The Haworth Document Delivery Service [1-800-HAWORTH, 9:00 a.m. - 5:00 p.m. (EST). E-mail address: docdelivery@haworthpress.com].

http://www.haworthpress.com/web/JH
© 2005 by The Haworth Press, Inc. All rights reserved.
Digital Object Identifier: 10.1300/J082v48n03_07

tion based on sexual orientation. Negative attitudes of a majority may not justify interferences with the sexual rights of a minority and society could be expected to tolerate a certain inconvenience to enable individuals to live in dignity and worth in accordance with the sexual identity chosen by them. Compensation for interference with sexual autonomy and freedom is awarded. This high-level protection (as compared to other parts of the world) is however limited. It seems to be granted only in areas where it corresponds with public attitudes and social developments. And it is seldom secured on the national level but nearly exclusively by the European Court of Human Rights, whose case-law is often weakened by inconsistency. *[Article copies available for a fee from The Haworth Document Delivery Service: 1-800-HAWORTH. E-mail address: <docdelivery@haworthpress.com> Website: <http://www.HaworthPress.com> © 2005 by The Haworth Press, Inc. All rights reserved.]*

KEYWORDS. Human rights, sexual rights, youth rights, sexual autonomy, sexuality, sexual freedom, sexual abuse, homosexuality, pornography, prostitution, marriage, sado-masochism, transsexuality, sex-education, European Court of Human Rights

HISTORY

Enlightenment and the French Revolution gave birth to the idea of human rights. And it was the French Revolution which did away with all the prior criminal bans on consensual sexual relations. The *"Declaration of the Rights of Man and the Citizen" of 1789* established the principle that "liberty consists in being able to do all that does not harm others" (Art. 4).[1] Accordingly the offences, which in part were even capital offences, of "lewdness committed with one-self" (masturbation), "fornication" (non-marital cohabitation), "leading a lewd life," intercourse between Christians and Non-Christians (often called a "particular abomination"), "lewdness against the order of nature" (anal and oral intercourse, hetero- and homosexual), prostitution, incest and adultery had been done away with. As a matter of course sexual violence and abuse of prepuberal children remained serious offences.[2]

All the countries which took over the French Criminal Code (the "Code Napoléon") or which modelled their Criminal Code after it did the same. And with time also other European countries followed suit, so that today in most of Europe–as a principle–consensual sexual relations, contacts and acts with consenting partners are no longer criminal offences.[3]

Given this historic development and the common origin of the idea of human rights and sexual freedom one would expect that sexuality or "sexual rights," as we can call it, are at the very core of human rights protection. Are they?

WRITTEN LAW

Written human rights law is scanty when it comes to sexuality. There is nothing explicit on sexuality or sexual rights in the *Universal Declaration of Human Rights 1948*.[4] The same is true of the global and regional human rights treaties elaborated on the basis of this Declaration, the *International Covenant on Civil and Political Rights*[5] (ICCPR), the *International Covenant on Economic, Social and Cultural Rights*,[6] the *European Convention on Human Rights (ECHR)*,[7] the *American Convention on Human Rights* and the *African Charter on Human and Peoples' Rights*.[8] Only the *Convention on the Rights of the Child of 1989*[9] contains a limited reference to sexual rights when it obliges states to combat sexual exploitation.[10]

Until recently the situation at the national level was no different. Four state constitutions in *Germany*–and *South-Africa*,[11] *Ecuador*[12] and *Fiji*[13] outside of Europe–now expressly ban discrimination and inequality on the basis of "sexual orientation" or "sexual identity."[14] And the constitution of *Switzerland* of 1999 bans discrimination on the basis of a person's "form of life," which term is intended to include sexual life.[15] Since 1998 Art. 13 of the *Treaty on the Foundation of the European Community (EC-Treaty)*, as amended by the Treaty of Amsterdam,[16] expressly empowers the Council of Ministers of the European Union to act against discrimination on the basis of "sexual orientation."[17] In 2000 the Council of Ministers availed itself of this power by issuing a directive obliging the member states of the European Union to comprehensively ban sexual-orientation-based (direct and indirect) discrimination in employment and occupation.[18] By now eighteen states in Europe have included "sexual orientation" as a protected category into their (non-constitutional) anti-discrimination legislation[19] and also Art. 21 of the *Charter of Fundamental Rights of the European Union*, adopted in 2000, bans sexual orientation discrimination.[20]

All these new references to sexual rights however are rather narrow and limited. The term "sexual orientation" or "sexual identity" usually is intended to refer to homo- and heterosexual orientation only.[21] In addition those references are made in the context of equality-rights. That means that these constitutional provisions do guarantee equal treatment of homo- and heterosexual persons and behavior; but they do not say anything about the regulation of sexuality and sexual behavior that can legitimately be made in general. In other words: those rights do not protect against undue inference with sexual life as such, they just guarantee that such inferences burden heterosexuals and homosexuals alike and to the same degree. They usually also do not include gender identity issues.

This scantiness of written human rights law however does not mean that it excludes from its protection the sexual sphere. As a matter of course fundamental rights do cover sexual life. The fact is that this is not expressly emphasized. But the general right to privacy and respect for private life,[22] the right to equality and non-discrimination,[23] the right to freedom of expression and information,[24] the right to freely assemble and to form associations,[25] and, not least, the right to life[26] and the right not to be treated in a cruel, inhuman or degrading manner,[27] can also be used to protect sexuality and sexual rights.

SEXUAL RIGHTS

But are human rights in fact used to protect sexual life by the bodies called to enforce human rights? To give an answer to that question it has first to be made clear what sexual rights are.[28] Since "sexual rights" essentially are human rights in the field of sexuality and sexual behavior the answer can be found by referring to the central idea of human rights: uniqueness and autonomy of the individual. Or as the German Constitutional Court[29] put it in the words of the German philosopher Immanuel Kant: a human being never has to be used as a means to an end, but always has to be the end in itself! An old Jewish saying is: if you are destroying a single person you are destroying a world and if you are saving a single person you are saving a world. That is exactly what human rights are about: human dignity, consisting in uniqueness, autonomy and self-determination of the individual.[30]

Following that suit "sexual rights," being fundamental rights in the area of sexuality, would be understood to guard human sexual dignity, as manifestations of a basic principle of sexual autonomy and sexual self-determination. This basic right to sexual self-determination does encompass two sides. Correctly understood it enshrines both the right to engage in wanted sexuality and the right to be free and protected from unwanted sexuality, from sexual abuse and sexual violence. Both sides of the "coin" have to be given due weight and neither one neglected. Only then can human sexual dignity be fully and comprehensively respected.

CASE-LAW

It is exactly that conception of sexual rights which appears in the case-law of the *European Court of Human Rights* (ECHR).[31] According to the Court the very essence of the Convention[32] is respect for human dignity and freedom,[33] and the notion of personal autonomy is an important principle underlying the interpretation of the right to respect for private life.[34] Safeguarding that respect has to be based upon present-day conditions and obligations arising from it have to be met at any time.[35] Attitudes of former times therefore may not serve as justification for lack of such respect today; moreover, states have to actively remove the negative effects which may materialize today as a result of such former attitudes.[36]

Analysis of European case-law in the area of sexuality and sexual rights demonstrates that the Court in fact does protect both aspects of sexual autonomy; it also shows that such protection provided by national courts is poor.

Freedom from Sexual Abuse or Violence

With regard to the right to freedom *from* unwanted sexual abuse and violence the Court's conception of the Convention rights is central. The Court construes those rights as not only including the negative right to be left alone from state intervention but also the positive right to (active) protection of those rights, against the State as well as against other private individuals.[37] In addition, the Court does not restrict the right to "respect for private life" (Art. 8 ECHR) to the classical right to do what you want, but sees this right as a comprehensive personality right, including the right to physical and moral (psychological) integrity and security.[38]

On that basis the Court held that, under Art. 8 ECHR, a State has to offer adequate protection against sexual abuse and violence; and that in grave cases it is even under a human rights obligation to use the criminal law for the purpose of deterrence.[39] The obligation under Article 6

ECHR to secure fair trial for persons accused of sexual abuse has to be balanced against the obligation to protect victims of abuse; defense rights may (and in some circumstances must) be reasonably limited in the interests of persons who are, or who are presumed to be, victims of sexual abuse.[40] The duty to protect however does not bar states from establishing a reasonable time-limit for bringing criminal charges and civil claims on the basis of sexual abuse (prescription).[41]

The obligation to protect extends not just to the criminal justice system but to the whole State, including the social welfare system. Measures should provide effective protection, in particular, of children and other vulnerable people. While acknowledging the difficult and sensitive decisions facing social services and the important countervailing principle of respecting and preserving family life, the Court obliges states to take reasonable and effective steps to prevent ill-treatment as soon as the authorities have or ought to have knowledge of the transgression.[42] If authorities fail to do so, states are under a human rights obligation to acknowledge the failure and to compensate the victims. Compensation should in principle include redress for non-pecuniary damage.[43] The positive obligation to protect a person's private life also requires social services to grant a person access to her/his personal files if this person suspects having been abused as a child, even if this person is considering the possibility of suing the authority.[44]

Abuse reaching the intensity of cruel, inhuman or degrading treatment[45] or even affecting life calls for particularly strong protection, as the Court classifies the rights to life and the prohibition of cruel, inhuman or degrading treatment as one of the most fundamental values of a democratic society[46] and ranks Arts. 2 and 3 ECHR as the most fundamental provisions of the Convention.[47] In addition the prohibition of cruel, inhuman or degrading treatment (Art. 3 ECHR) is absolute and does not allow for any exception. The test under Article 3 does not require it to be shown that "but for" the failure of the authorities ill-treatment would not have occurred; a failure to take reasonably available measures which could have had a real prospect of altering the outcome or mitigating the harm is sufficient to engage the responsibility of the State.[48] If a condition of probation on a person convicted of sexual abuse of the child daughter of his cohabitee is to cease to reside with the family, the Court has held that the social services authorities are under the obligation to monitor the offender's conduct, i.e., compliance with the order.[49]

As States are under the obligation to secure the Convention rights in all their actions (Art. 1 ECHR), they are barred under the Convention from deporting or extraditing someone to another country if there is a real risk that this person will be subjected there to treatment contrary to the Convention (such as sexual abuse)–be it by the foreign State or by private individuals against whom this State does not afford adequate protection, even if that country is not bound by the Convention.[50]

Recently the Court rejected the notion that a person under the age of consent was always incapable of consent and that therefore sexual contact with such a person would be violent in each and every case.[51] Not to equate sexual offences against children with crimes of violence in all circumstances does not deprive of protection of physical and moral integrity.[52] The Court accepted that the applicant in question, at the age of 13, had been a willing, active participant in the sexual acts with a 53 year old man and sought to make money out of them. It was therefore not inconsistent with the acknowledgement of the applicant's vulnerable and damaged[53] character to find that he was not a victim of violence.[54]

Freedom to Engage in Sexual Activity

With regard to the other side of the coin, the freedom *to* engage in consensual sexual activity, the case-law of the *European Court of Human Rights* and the *European Commission of Human Rights* is based on the understanding that the right to respect for private life (Art. 8 ECHR) enshrines the right to personal development,[55] to free expression and the development of one's personality,[56] and to establish and develop relationships with other human beings[57] especially in the emotional field for the development and fulfillment of one's own personality.[58] The purpose of the protection of private life lies in safeguarding an area for individuals in which they can develop and fulfill their personality,[59] and in securing the right to choose the way in which to lead sexual life.[60] Sexuality and sexual life for the Commission and the Court always has been at the core of private life and its protection.[61] Also the *German Federal Constitutional Court* includes in the protection of the right to privacy the right of the individual to decide on his/her own views on sexuality.[62]

State regulation of sexual behavior interferes with this right, and accords with the Convention only if justified under par. 2 of Art. 8 ECHR.[63] Also, regulations set by an employer are seen as such an interference if the State by its labour laws allows for such regulations.[64]

The Court also indicated that public sexual behavior falls under the protection of par. 1 of Art. 8 ECHR.[65] This would be consistent with the concept of sexuality and sexual behavior as essentially private manifestations of personality. Sexuality is so central to one's personality that, as a general principle, it should come under the notion of "private life."[66] The decision whether private life is affected or not should not depend on whether the behavior takes place in public or in private. Examination of norms regulating sexual behavior in public, for instance to avoid annoyance, should always be done under par. 2 of Art. 8 ECHR, thereby avoiding major problems arising from the otherwise necessary decision of whether certain conduct in fact took place in private or in public.[67]

Under the concept of positive obligations arising from the Convention rights[68] States must also protect against interferences from other private individuals. A State always comes under such an obligation when there is a direct and immediate link between the protection sought and private life. In the case of violence or abuse on the basis of someone's sexuality or sexual life this link is obvious. When it comes to refusal of access to premises, however, the State, under Art. 8 ECHR, is under an obligation to act only if that lack of access interferes with the victim's right to personal development and the right to establish and maintain relations with other human beings.[69] So, if there are other places where the person discriminated against could turn for the same purpose the state is not under a duty to act.[70] Applying these criteria in the area of employment would mean that if an employee is dismissed on the basis his/her sexuality, the State will have to act if the loss of employment seriously impairs the person in his/her intimate relations with other people (for instance as a result of lack of funds, or as a result of psychological problems); it will not be so if the measure has not such a detrimental effect.

The right to non-discrimination (Art. 14 ECHR)[71] prohibits States, on non-objective and unreasonable grounds, to refuse social benefits on the basis of one's sexuality, particularly one's sexual orientation.[72]

It is interesting to draw comparisons with the United States. It was there that courts for the first time used human rights law to secure sexual rights. At the beginning of the seventies several state courts invalidated the sodomy laws of their states. Based on privacy and equality arguments, they declared general bans on hetero- and/or homosexual oral and anal intercourse to be unconstitutional. This development suddenly stopped with the rise of the AIDS epidemic. Between 1983 and 1992 no sodomy statute has been declared unconstitutional by a court or repealed by the legislature. The courts started to act again in 1992 and the legislatures in 1993.[73] And in 1986 the US Supreme Court expressly decided that the states have a right to criminalize homosexual anal and oral intercourse since such a ban accorded with millennia of moral teaching.[74]

AIDS did not have such a devastating effect on sexual rights in Europe. The organs of the European Convention on Human Rights, while consistently declaring total bans of homosexual acts to be compatible with the Convention until then,[75] changed their minds at the beginning of the eighties and hitherto repeatedly ruled that a total ban violates the right to respect for private life.[76] They changed their minds according to changing public opinion throughout Europe and according to the changing state of the law in the several member States. Fewer and fewer States criminalized homosexuality and the Court regarded this as decisive in its decision to depart from the earlier case law of the Commission.[77]

As the Convention organs constantly in their case law refer to the legal consensus among the member States,[78] it is not surprising that it took them a lot more time to find a violation of human rights in regulations that do not generally ban homosexual relations but "only" establish a higher minimum age limit for them than for heterosexual acts. It was not until 1997 that the European Commission on Human Rights declared such unequal age limits to be in violation of the Convention,[79] and it took the Court until 2003 to do so.[80] On the national level the Constitutional Courts of Austria and Hungary, in 2002, struck down higher minimum age limits for homosexual contact as compared to heterosexual contact.[81] While the Hungarian Constitutional Court based its decision on the view that the distinction between hetero- and homosexual conduct was not justified,[82] the Austrian Constitutional Court struck down the law on a completely different basis. It did so on the ground that the offence was construed in a way that allowed for legal relationships (for instance between a 18 year old and a 16 year old) to become a criminal offence (for example, when the older partner turned 19), which the Court considered unreasonable and therefore a violation of the right to equality.[83]

Also in the area of age-of-consent laws a look over the Atlantic seems to be instructive. While in Canada in the nineties of the past century the courts also found the special higher age limit of 18 for anal intercourse as compared to 14 for all other sexual acts a violation of human rights,[84] in the USA that issue is still more than controversial. The Florida Supreme Court in 1995 invalidated a statute criminalizing consensual sexual relations of adolescents of "previous chaste character," arguing that law violated the right of young people to privacy,[85] while the California Court of Appeals in 1998 ruled not only that such interferences are justified but also that minors do not "have a constitutionally protected interest in engaging in sexual intercourse" at all, thus exempting the legislature from the necessity of giving any reason for a ban on juvenile sexuality.[86] In this case the Court thus confirmed the conviction of a 16 year old adolescent for engaging in consensual sexual intercourse with his 14 year old girlfriend.[87]

In Europe no such human rights cases on general age-of-consent laws are known,[88] most probably due to the fact that in Europe the general minimum age limits for sexual relations are much lower than in the USA. While in several US states minimum age limits for sexual contact often go as high as 17 or 18,[89] in one-half of the European jurisdictions, consensual sexual relations of and with 14 year old adolescents are legal, and in three-quarters with 15 year olds.[90] Just one European jurisdiction (Northern Ireland) outlaws consensual sexual relations of 16 year olds.[91] In only one case the European Commission on Human Rights had to decide on the issue. In 1997 it upheld a general age of consent of 14 years,[92] in spite of the fact that in the country in question–as opposed to nearly all other jurisdictions in Europe[93]–there was no power of discretion granted to the authorities or any other means which would enable the screening out of cases where the age limit was violated but where it is established that there was no abuse.[94] The Court however recently acknowledged the right of adolescents over the age of 14 years to sexual self-determination when it awarded an applicant compensation for having been prevented, between the ages of 14 and 18, from entering into relations corresponding to his disposition (for homosexual contact with older, adult men).[95,96]

It was not until recently that the Court issued a judgement dealing with group sexual activity. In 2000 it held that the British ban on group sex including gay male sexual activity violates the Convention.[97] What makes this judgment particularly remarkable is that the Court did not refer to the non-discrimination clause of the Convention (Art. 14) but to the right to respect for private life (Art. 8), thus establishing a fundamental right to consensual group sex, which now cannot be banned even if such a ban would cover heterosexual and homosexual group sex equally.

European human rights case law has also begun to step beyond the area of criminal law. In November 1998 the European Commission of Human Rights and the old European Court of Human Rights were replaced by a new permanent European Court of Human Rights.[98] This new Court has already issued major gay rights decisions beyond the criminal law. In September 1999 it declared the exclusion of lesbians and gays from armed forces to be in violation of the right to respect for private life.[99] And in December 1999 it ruled custody decisions (in part) based on the homosexuality of one parent constituted unjustified discrimination on the basis of "sexual orientation."[100] In 2003 the Court declared unacceptable the eviction of a gay man from the flat he had shared with his deceased partner for years, while surviving partners of an opposite-sex couple enjoy a right of succession of the tenancy.[101]

So, with respect to homosexuality, remarkable progress has occurred in human rights case law. After constant rejection in the nineteen-fifties, sixties and seventies, human rights claims of homosexuals are now more and more heard by the courts. The Court today explicitly considers discrimination on the basis of sexual orientation as unacceptable[102] and as serious as discrimination on the basis of race, colour, religion and sex.[103] In the case of distinctions based upon sex or sexual orientation the margin of appreciation is narrow and the Court requires particularly serious reasons for such distinctions to be justified.[104] Measures involving a difference in treatment based upon sex or sexual orientation can only be justified if they are *necessary* for the fulfillment of a legitimate aim; mere reasonableness is not enough.[105]

Predisposed bias on the part of a heterosexual majority against a homosexual minority cannot, as the Court has repeatedly held, amount to sufficient justification for interference with the rights of homo- and bisexual women and men, any more than similar negative attitudes towards those of a different race, origin or colour.[106] Society could be expected to tolerate a certain inconvenience to enable individuals to live in dignity and worth "in accordance with the sexual identity chosen by them."[107]

Today not having discriminatory legislation against homosexuals, especially a criminal ban on homosexual relations, is a pre-condition for admission to the European Union[108] and to the Council of Europe.[109] The Parliamentary Assembly of the Council of Europe repeatedly condemned discrimination on the basis of sexual orientation as "especially odious" and "one of the most odious forms of discrimination."[110,111]

As States are under the obligation to secure the Convention rights in all their actions (Art. 1 ECHR), they also have to safeguard those rights in deciding issues of deportation or extradition, even if the other country is not bound by the Convention.[112] If there is a real risk that the life of the person to be deported or extradited is endangered or that this person would be subjected to torture, or to inhuman or degrading treatment or punishment,[113] deportation and extradition are always inadmissible, because the rights to life (Art. 2 ECHR, Art. 1 Protocol No. 6) and the prohibition of torture and inhuman or degrading treatment or punishment (Art. 3 ECHR) do not allow for exceptions.[114]

If there is a real risk of treatment contrary to the Convention which does not reach such an intensity (as for instance simple imprisonment, limited in time, for consensual homosexual acts), and therefore such treatment "just" would affect other (not absolute) Convention rights, deportation and extradition is, in principle, also not admissible, but it could be justified. For such justification to be successfully invoked a government would have to show that all the conditions for dispense from the (negative or positive) obligations arising from the Convention right in question are met. In the case of threatening simple imprisonment, limited in time, for consensual homosexual acts (which interferes with the right to respect for private life, Art. 8 ECHR) for instance, justification affords that deportation or extradition, despite those conditions, is necessary for the achievement of one of the legitimate aims listed in par. 2 of Art. 8.[115] Whereby "necessity" in this context is linked to a "democratic society," whose hallmarks are "tolerance, pluralism, broadmindedness,"[116] those hallmarks requiring that there is a pressing social need for the measure and that the measure is proportional to the aim sought to achieve.[117] Unless a state could establish that deportation or extradition is so justified, for instance on public security grounds in the case of a seriously dangerous person, the threat of imprisonment for consensual homosexual acts should render deportation and extradition inadmissible.

The Court recently issued two important decisions on the right of freedom of religion (Art. 9 ECHR) when balanced against sexuality and sexual freedom. In 2000 it ruled that parents cannot object to sex education lessons in public schools on religious grounds, if such sex education is aimed at giving the pupils objective and scientific information about human sexual behaviour, sexually transmitted diseases and AIDS and if they were not a source of indoctrination in favour of a specific form of sexual behaviour.[118] In 2001 the Court held that pharmacists could not rely on their religious beliefs or impose them on others to justify refusing to sell contraceptive pills, which are legally available for sale and, by law, can be sold only on prescription in pharmacies; there were many ways in which the applicants could manifest their beliefs outside the professional sphere, the Court emphasized.[119]

The Force of Public Opinion

Progress in human rights protection of the freedom to express one's sexuality, however, is based upon changing public attitudes towards the sexual behavior in question.[120] In the case of a total ban on homosexual relations, for instance, it took the repeal of laws in nearly all European states, triggered by three revolutions, the French, the Russian and the Sexual,[121] before the Convention organs declared it a human rights violation; just a handful of countries still kept such a ban. The same is true for discriminatory age-of-consent regulations.[122] If we consider areas involving less public acceptance, the situation seems much worse, with the case law less positive.

When it comes to *transsexualism*, for instance, the Court ruled in 1992 that under Art. 8 a State has to issue personal identification documents referring to the "new" sex of the person to protect that person's right to withhold from others the fact of gender reassignment.[123] But it constantly held that a State need not change the birth certificate itself, in spite of the fact that this document also must often be presented to other persons and that nearly all European states allow(ed) for such alteration of the certificate.[124] The Court disregarded its own often practised referral to legal consensus in the member States of the Council of Europe. It took until 2003 for the Court[125] to acknowledge that, in the 21st century, the right of transsexuals to personal development and to physical and moral security in the full sense enjoyed by others in society could no longer be regarded as a matter of controversy requiring the further passage of time to cast clearer light on the issue. It obliged States to change birth certificates after gender-reassignment (under Art. 8 ECHR) and to allow for marriage with a person of the former sex (Art. 12 ECHR: right to marry).[126]

Even more striking is the situation in the area of *sado-masochism (S & M)* where the Court in 1997 did not find a violation of the Convention despite the fact that the plaintiffs have been convicted for totally consensual homosexual S&M acts without lasting negative effects or wounding, while the courts in their home country have declared heterosexual S&M acts legal, even when they involved acts as grave as branding of the buttocks. The Court, under Art. 8, merely referred to the legitimacy of outlawing even consensually inflicted injuries if they are more than just transient, and did not address the equality arguments under Art. 14, nor did it refer to sports events regularly inflicting more than transient injuries, such as boxing.[127]

With regard to *pornography* there is only one case where the Convention organs found a violation. In 1993 the European Commission of Human Rights decided that the right to freedom of information (Art. 10 ECHR) includes the right of adults to view (gay) pornography in the backroom of a sex-shop where no one else can be annoyed.[128] However, this decision is rather narrow: it confines the right to view and show pornography in very limited circumstances: adults in a backroom where no one else has access. This decision seems to endorse a concept of sexuality that is tolerable only if kept behind closed doors, and a view that sexually explicit material should be withheld even from sexually mature minors simply because they are a few months short of their majority.[129]

Prostitution has been considered a human rights issue only by the Federal Court of Switzerland. It held prostitution to fall under the basic right to pursue a profession and to make earnings; as a consequence the legislature can regulate, but not totally ban, prostitution.[130] The Constitutional Court of Austria did not follow that approach and considered professional sexual acts outside the scope of human rights protection; but it did hold that sexual acts for remuneration (which are not yet commercial) do fall under the protection of the constitutional right to respect for private life and therefore cannot be banned.[131] No other courts so far have recognized the right to sexual self-determination in the form of sex for remuneration.

The controversial issue of *adoption of minors by homo- or bisexual persons* was before the Court in 2002. All but two jurisdictions in Europe allowed single adoption by a homosexual person.[132] Despite the fact that the applicant, who had been refused single adoption solely on the basis of his homosexuality, relied on that consensus, the Court alleged that domestic laws on adoption were very diverse and therefore States would enjoy a wide margin of appreciation, allowing them to ban single adoption by homo- and bisexual persons solely on the basis of their sexual orientation. That the question at issue before it was single adoption, and not other aspects of adoption. That there was the highest possible legal consensus among member States on that issue did not matter.[133]

Same-sex marriage has constantly been considered not to be a human rights issue by the *Court* since 1986[134] and by the national courts so addressed.[135] Under Art. 12 ECHR "men and women of marriageable age have the right to marry and to found a family, according to the national laws governing the exercise of this right." So the right to marry is secured only "according to the national laws"; but this clause empowers States merely to establish the conditions and formalities for entering, and dissolution of, marriage. They are not allowed to interfere with the very essence of the right, to bar people from marriage under any circumstances.[136] The Court did not see this essence of the right affected by a total ban on same-sex or transsexual marriage.[137] But recently it changed its position.

In 2002 the Court ruled the essence of the right to marry was impaired when a transsexual person, after gender reassignment, is not allowed to marry a member of her/his former sex.[138] The Court in this judgment acknowledged the human right to marry a person of biologically the same sex. It is only a very small step to also grant the right to marry a person who is not only biologically, but also genitally and socially, of the same sex, as the reasoning of the judgment equally applies to such cases as well.

The Court stressed the major social changes in the institution of marriage since the adoption of the Convention as well as dramatic changes brought about by developments in medicine and science;[139] and it rejected as artificial the argument that post-operative transsexuals had not been deprived of the right to marry because they remained able to marry a person of their former opposite sex. The Court emphasized that the applicant lived as a woman and would only wish to marry a man but had no possibility of doing so and could therefore claim that the very essence of her right to marry had been infringed.[140] Also as regards (fully) same-sex marriage, the institution of marriage has undergone major social changes and medicine and science have brought about dramatic changes. Equally artificial is the (often heard) argument that homosexuals are not deprived of the right to marry because they remain able to marry a person of the opposite sex. Homosexuals, using the line of argument established by the Court in the transsexual marriage cases, live with same sex partners and would only wish to marry a person of the same sex; when they have no possibility of doing so, the very essence of their right to marry is infringed. The Court also stressed that the inability of any couple to conceive or be a parent to a child cannot be regarded *per se* as removing their right to marry.[141] Finally the Court noted that Article 9 of the recently adopted Charter of Fundamental Rights of the European Union departs, no doubt deliberately, from the wording of Article 12 of the Convention in removing the reference to men and women.[142]

The Dutch Supreme Court and the German Supreme Court in their judgments of 1990 and 1993, while restricting the concept of marriage to opposite-sex couples, emphasized that not to recognize same-sex partnerships in any way in law would violate human rights.[143] As a result both States later introduced registered partnership for same-sex couples. The Netherlands in the meantime also opened up civil marriage for same-sex partners.[144]

The Curse of Inconsistency

The protection the Court affords to sexual rights is considerably impaired by inconsistency in the Court's case law. Leading cases and constant case law are often ignored by the three-judges-committees ruling on *a limine* inadmissibility of an application.[145]

Such a Committee in May 2000 *a limine* rejected the application of a *lesbian and gay association* which was *denied registration* on the basis that it did not exclude persons under 18 years of age from membership, while for heterosexual associations no such restriction was established. The Court denied examination of the application on the basis that the restriction was prescribed by law, pursued the legitimate aim of the protection of morals and the rights and freedoms of others and was proportionate to the aims pursued.[146] No more reasoning was provided despite the fact that the Commission three years before had found no justification for a minimum age limit of 18 for homosexual acts as opposed to 16 years for heterosexual acts.[147] And this was despite the fact that the Court itself at that time had already found that discrimination on the basis of sexual orientation is unacceptable[148] and as serious as discrimination on the basis of race, colour, religion and sex,[149] and that predisposed bias on the part of a heterosexual majority against a homosexual minority cannot amount to sufficient justification for the interferences with the rights of homo- and bisexual women and men, any more than similar negative attitudes towards those of a different race, origin or colour.[150] Shortly afterwards the Court declared admissible three complaints against a minimum age limit of 18 for homosexual acts as opposed to 14 years for heterosexual acts,[151] found a violation[152] and awarded an adolescent a considerable amount of compensation for having been prevented, between the ages of 14 and 18, from entering into relations corresponding to his disposition for homosexual contact with older, adult men.[153]

In 2002 a Committee *a limine* rejected the application of a 16-year-old *gay adolescent*, who was diagnosed as sustaining a contusion of the head after he refused to name his sex partners during hours of interrogation by police detectives on the basis of an anti-homosexual criminal law.[154] The fact that the detention of the juvenile had been decided by a police official was also no problem for the Committee. According to the case law of the Court a human rights violation is established if someone incurs injuries while with the (police) authority, unless the authority provides a plausible different explanation for the injuries.[155] In addition the Court requires independent inquiries into such allegations and considers a lack of such independent inquiries to be a violation of the Convention as well.[156] The applicant proved that the contusion was sustained during his stay at the police department. Nevertheless the

Committee decided not to deal with the application, merely stating that it did not find "any appearance" of a violation of the Convention.[157]

Also in 2002 a Committee *a limine* rejected the case of a *gay man* who had proven his innocence regarding an anti-homosexual age of consent offence. Despite the proof of his innocence authorities refused to delete his data from the rogue's gallery (photos, finger prints, genetic data, etc.) in the nation- and European-wide police databanks.[158] The man had been found sitting in a car chatting with two adolescents and therefore he would have to be considered a potentially "dangerous offender." The man complained to the Court in 1998 and before the Court dealt with the case, the data had been deleted due to the repeal of the anti-homosexual legislation in the home-country of the man. The Committee used this deletion (3 1/2 years after the filing of the application and 7 years after storage of the data) to refuse to deal with the application. The applicant would already have been afforded relief on the domestic level, the Committee argued, so that he no longer could allege to be a victim of a violation of the Convention.[159]

Again this decision goes against the constant case law of the Court, which established that a matter before the Court is only resolved (Art. 34, 37 par. 1 lit. b ECHR) when (a) the alleged violations of the Convention have been clearly acknowledged by the member State and (b) the victim has been afforded adequate redress for the violation.[160] If a matter can be resolved only on the basis that a human rights violation has ceased (here, by the deletion of the data), it would mean that an illegally detained person, for instance, could not file an application once s/he has been released; and a victim of torture could not complain because the torturer ceased to torture. The applicant expressly relied on the case law of the Court and the absurd consequences a different opinion would cause. He pointed to the fact that the member State never acknowledged that the storage of the data was in violation of the Convention and that he never received redress; even the costs and expenses of the applications to the national courts and to the Court he had to pay himself. Nevertheless the Committee decided not to deal with the application without addressing the arguments of the applicant.

In 2003 a Committee again *a limine* rejected the application of a *gay man*. The man, under anti-homosexual legislation, had been sentenced to one year imprisonment for consensual caressing of the genitals of a 14-year-old male adolescent, conduct which was (and is) completely legal if the actions are heterosexual or lesbian. The man was referred to an institution for mentally abnormal offenders and had been released five months after the expiry of his one-year prison term. The national court, in 2001, released him upon 5-year probation, which period of probation was clearly prescribed by law. As the national court had no power of discretion, an appeal against the condition was futile. In addition, if the man appealed the decision, such an appeal would have had suspensive effect, causing him to spend even more months in the institution, solely due to his futile appeal. The applicant therefore decided not to appeal and applied to the Court complaining that he has not been released unconditionally. He relied on the consistent case law of the Court establishing the principle that remedies which have no prospect of success need not to be exhausted;[161] he pointed out that the Court had held that the rule of exhaustion of domestic remedies must be applied with some degree of flexibility and without excessive formalism and that it has further recognised that the rule is neither absolute nor capable of being applied automatically; in reviewing whether it has been observed it is essential to have regard to the particular circumstances of each individual case. This, according to the Court means amongst other things that it must take realistic account not only of the existence of formal remedies in the legal system of the Contracting Party concerned, but also of the general legal and political context in which they operate as well as the personal circumstances of the applicants.[162] The applicant noted that according to the Court the Convention generally, as a treaty for the collective enforcement of human rights and fundamental freedoms, must be interpreted and applied so as to make its safeguards practical and effective.[163] He also pointed out that the Court held that the burden of proof for non-exhaustion of domestic remedies is on the government.[164] The Committee nevertheless, without addressing his arguments, rejected his application, merely stating that he failed to exhaust domestic remedies, without any further explanation.[165]

In a further decision of 2003 a Committee *a limine* again rejected a gay rights application in contradiction to the case law of the Court. The applicant had been arrested and prosecuted under the discriminatory age of consent law in Austria, later held to be in violation of the Convention by the Court.[166] He had finally been acquitted on the basis of having thought that his partner was already 18. The Court repeatedly has decided that an acquittal, without acknowledgment of the violation and adequate redress, does not resolve a matter.[167] Both never took place in the case of the applicant. The applicant stressed that the violation has never been acknowledged and that he never got redress, and he expressly relied on the case law of the Court. Nevertheless the Committee rejected the application, merely stating that the application of the man, who had been arrested and prosecuted under the anti-homosexual statute already found to be in violation of the Convention by the Court at that time, did not disclose any appearance of a violation.[168]

Protection by the Court of victims of human rights violations is also remarkably weakened by the fact that the Court regularly does not award to (successful) applicants all of the *costs and expenses* the application procedure incurred.[169] In the leading cases on discriminatory age of consent regulations for gay sex, for instance, the Court awarded EUR 10.000,–and EUR 5.000,–for legal costs in the procedure before it, while the applicants, according to their national tariffs for attorney-fees, had to pay EUR 58.302,28 and EUR 30.305,34.[170] It seems obvious that victims who are not wealthy can be seriously barred from applying to the Court if, even in the case of success, they have to pay such considerable amounts by themselves.

CONCLUSION

To sum it up, human rights law in practice currently seems to protect sexual rights to a considerable degree; but, when it comes to freedom *to express one's* sexuality, the protection arises predominantly in areas where it accords with public attitudes and does not exceed social developments. It seems that human rights tribunals more often follow the attitudes of the majority rather than apply the core task of human rights which is to protect the individual and minorities against unjustified interference by the majority, no matter–as John Stuart Mill put it[171]–how big the majority and how strong its moral rejection and repulsion of the acts, attitudes and values of the minority or the individual might be. Interferences solely based on the views of the majority Mill called a "betrayal of the most fundamental values of the political theory of democracy."[172] One could formulate it provocatively by saying that the most noble task of human rights, namely to protect the weak against the strong, minorities and the individual against a majority, is fulfilled only if an even bigger majority of member States is perceived by the Court to regard restrictions imposed on sexual minorities as being contrary to human rights. And even then not it does not do so consistently.

While, as compared to other parts of the world, there is relatively well established liberty and equality in sexual affairs in Europe, human rights law seems to provide limited protection of this freedom; and as can be seen from this overview this protection is nearly exclusively on the European, not the national, level.

In that sense one may indeed be anxious about developments in future case law in this area. The controversial issues are manifold.

Sweden in 1999 reintroduced the total criminal ban on *sex for remuneration* (this time not punishing the sex-workers but their clients),[173] and upcoming EC-legislation[174] obliges all member States of the European Union to create extensive offences of *"child"-pornography* and *"child"-prostitution*,[175] defining as "child" every person under 18, without differentiating between five-year-old children and 17-year-old juveniles. These offences go far beyond combating child pornography and child prostitution, thus making a wide variety of adolescent sexual behaviour, hitherto completely legal in the overwhelming majority of jurisdictions in Europe, serious crimes. For instance: pictures made by a 16-year-old girl of herself in "lascivious" poses, which this girl shows to her 17-year-old boyfriend; photographs of a 17-year-old girl in her bikinis "lasciviously" exposing her pubic area, taken by her 15-year-old boyfriend (for his bedside table); standard pornography involving younger looking 20-year-old adults; "lascivious" pictures of one's own spouse which is under 18 or even (just) looks younger than 18; a virtual animation showing a 17-year-old beauty "lasciviously" posing created by a 14-year-old boy on his home computer, if he does not protect the file with a password; or "Webcam-sex" between adolescents, who legally could have "real" sex with each other. The heavy criticism this equation of adolescents with children caused among experts highlights the major human rights problems these offences will cause.[176,177]

In December 2002 the Court declared admissible the application of an HIV-positive man who has been held in isolation detention for years on the basis of prevention of spreading disease.[178] The Court has also held that medical treatment without consent of the person treated violates the right to respect for private life,[179] which should also outlaw HIV-testing without the consent of the person tested.[180]

In Austria the discriminatory age of consent for gay men has been substituted in 2002 by a general offence criminalizing sexual contacts with adolescents under certain circumstances.[181] This new, gender-neutral, provision however is used disproportionate with respect to male homosexual relations.[182] Such (indirect) discrimination comes into conflict with the right to non-discrimination[183] and the European Parliament already has called on Austria to end this discrimination in enforcement.[184]

Finally in 2001 the Court ruled that television authorities cannot refuse to broadcast advertisements of political NGOs.[185] This indicates that also sexual minorities have a human right to adequate media presentation of their political agenda.

NOTES

1. The French constitution of 1795 in its preamble called this principle "by nature engraved in all hearts."

2. For details see Helmut Graupner, *Sexualität, Jugendschutz und Menschenrechte: Über das Recht von Kindern und Jugendlichen auf sexuelle Selbstbestimmung* (Frankfurt/M., Peter Lang, 1997a), Vol. 1, 126ff, Vol. 2, 361ff; Helmut Graupner, "Von 'Widernatürlicher Unzucht' zu 'Sexueller Orientierung': Homosexualität und Recht" in Hey, Pallier & Roth (eds.), *Que(e)rdenken: Weibliche/männliche Homosexualität und Wissenschaft* (Innsbruck, Studienverlag, 1997b) 198ff.

3. For details see Graupner (1997a), *supra*, Vol. 1, 126ff, Vol. 2, 361ff; Graupner (1997b), *supra*, 198ff

4. UNGAOR 962 (1948), Res. 217 III (C), *www.unhchr.ch*

5. (1966) UNTS Vol.999 p. 171, *www.unhchr.ch*

6. (1966) UNTS Vol. 993 p. 3, *www.unhchr.ch*

7. (1950) ETS No. 005, *http://conventions.coe.int*

8. See for further details the chapter of Phillip Tahmindjis in this book.

9. (1989), *www.unhchr.ch*

10. Art. 34: "States Parties undertake to protect the child from all forms of sexual exploitation and sexual abuse. For these purposes, States Parties shall in particular take all appropriate national, bilateral and multilateral measures to prevent:
 a. The inducement or coercion of a child to engage in any unlawful sexual activity;
 b. The exploitative use of children in prostitution or other unlawful sexual practices;
 c. The exploitative use of children in pornographic performances and materials.

On the basis of this in 2000 an optional protocol "on the sale of children, child prostitution and child pornography" has been elaborated (*www.unhchr.ch*). It is striking that this protocol on sexual exploitation is much stricter than the optional protocol "on the involvement of children in armed conflicts" adopted by the General Assembly the same day (*www.unhchr.ch*). While the age limit for pornography and prostitution has been set at 18, without any exception, the age limit for recruitment into the armed forces can be as low as 15; only participation in hostile conflicts and compulsory recruitment are banned under the age of 18. In addition states must ban child pornography and child prostitution by criminal law, whereas with respect to child soldiers they are only obliged to "take all feasible measures to ensure" that persons under 18 do not participate in armed conflicts and are not subjected to compulsory recruitment; they are not under a duty to criminalize such practices. And only the optional protocol "on the sale of children, child prostitution and child pornography" obliges states to make breaches both criminal and grounds for extradition; the optional protocol "on the involvement of children in armed conflicts" does not contain such obligations.

11. Sec. 9 Bill of Rights ("sexual orientation"); for details see Helmut Graupner, *Keine Liebe zweiter Klasse–Diskriminierungsschutz & Partnerschaft für gleichgeschlechtlich L(i)ebende*, (Rechtskomitee LAMBDA, Vienna, 2002), 36, *www.RKLambda.at* (Publikationen).

12. Art. Art. 23 ("orientación sexual"); for details see Graupner (2002), *supra*, 40.

13. Art. Art. 38 ("sexual orientation"); for details see Graupner (2002), *supra*, 38.

14. Berlin (Art. 10: "sexuelle Identität"), Bremen (Art. 2: "sexuelle Identität"), Brandenburg (Art. 12: "sexuelle Identität"), Thuringia (Art. 2: "sexuelle Orientierung"), for details see Graupner (2002), *supra*, 32.

15. Art. 8 ("Lebensform"), for details see Graupner (2002), *supra*, 32.
16. CONF/4005/97 ADD 2, *http://europa.eu.int/eur-lex*
17. Art. 13 par. 1 EC: "Without prejudice to the other provisions of this Treaty and within the limits of the powers conferred by it upon the Community, the Council, acting unanimously on a proposal from the Commission and after consulting the European Parliament, may take appropriate action to combat discrimination based on sex, racial or ethnic origin, religion or belief, disability, age or sexual orientation."
18. Directive 2000/78/EC, *http://europa.eu.int/eur-lex*. The directive has to be implemented in all member states until December 2nd, 2003 at the latest (Art. 18).
19. *Austria* (just a ministerial decree on the federal level; statutory protection in the state of Vienna only); *Belgium, Czech Republic, Denmark, Finland, France, Germany, Iceland, Ireland, Lithuania, Luxemburg, Malta, Netherlands, Norway, Romania, Slovenia, Spain, Sweden*. For details including full text of the laws see Graupner (2004), *supra*, 32ff; see also the map at *www.RKLambda.at* (Rechtsvergleich)
20. OJ C 364/1-22 (18.12.2000), *http://europa.eu.int/eur-lex*; The Charter is not binding but it is used in interpretation of binding EU-law (see Court of First Instance, Case T-54/99 *max.mobil Telekommunikation Service GmbH*, 31.01.2002, par. 48)
21. The Dutch and the Swedish laws expressly so state, see Graupner (2002), *supra*.
22. See for instance Art. 8 ECHR
23. See for instance Art. 14 ECHR; Art. 1 Protocol No. 12 (not yet in force)
24. See for instance Art. 10 ECHR
25. See for instance Art. 11 ECHR
26. See for instance Art. 2 ECHR, Art. 1 Protocol No. 6 (ban on death penalty)
27. See for instance Art. 3 ECHR
28. For a charter of sexual rights see World Association of Sexology (WAS), Declaration of Sexual Rights (26.08.1999), *http://www.worldsexology.org/english/about_sexualrights.html*
29. BVerfGE 7, 198; 48, 127 [163]; 49, 286 [298]; Graupner (1997a), *supra*, Vol. 1, 39 (notes 11, 12), 55 (note 61).
30. For a further and detailed discussion of this concept see Graupner (1997a), *supra*, Vol. 1, 44ff.
31. *http://www.echr.coe.int*
32. The *European Convention of Human Right (ECHR)*
33. *Christine Goodwin vs. UK* (28957/95), judg. 11.07.2002 [GC] (par. 90); *I. vs. UK* (25680/94), judg. 11.07.2002 [GC] (par. 70)
34. *Christine Goodwin vs. UK* (28957/95), judg. 11.07.2002 [GC] (par. 90); *I. vs. UK* (25680/94), judg. 11.07.2002 [GC] (par. 70)
35. See for instance *L. & V. vs. Austria* (39392,98, 39829/98), judg. 09.01.2003 (par. 47); *S.L. vs. Austria* (45330/99), judg. 09.01.2003 (par. 39); *Wessels-Bergervoet vs. NL* (34462/97), judg. 04.06.2002 (par. 52f); for an analysis of the respective case-law of the *Court* see Graupner (1997a), *supra*, Vol. 1, 75ff.
36. *Wessels-Bergervoet vs. NL*(34462/97), judg. 04.06.2002 (par. 52f)
37. *Z. & Others vs. UK* (29392/95), judg. 10.05.2001 [GC] (par. 73); *E. & Others vs. UK* (33218/96), judg. 26.11.2002 (par. 88)
38. *Christine Goodwin vs. UK* (28957/95), judg. 11.07.2002 [GC] (par. 90: " physical and moral security"); *I. vs. UK* (25680/94), judg. 11.07.2002 [GC] (par. 70 : "physical and moral security"); *D.P. & J.C. vs. UK* (38719/97), judg. 10.10.2001 [GC] (par. 118: "physical and moral integrity"); *X. & Y. vs. NL* (8978/80), 26.03.1985 (par. 22:

"physical and moral integrity"); *Ilaria Salvetti vs. Italy* (42197/98), dec. 09.07.2002 ("physical and psychological integrity")

39. If effective deterrence, in a case where fundamental values and essential aspects of private life are at stake, cannot be achieved otherwise: *X. & Y. vs. NL* (8978/80), 26.03.1985 (par. 27); In *Carl Wade August vs. UK* (36505/02), judg. 21.01.2003, the Court held that the provision of an *ex gratia* award by the State to victims of abuse does not form part of the deterrent framework to protect children effectively against adult abusers (par. The Law, par. 1).

40. *S.N. vs. Sweden* (34209/96), judg. 02.07.2002 (par. 47); *Owen Oysten vs. UK* (42011/98), dec. 22.01.2002

41. *Stubbings & Others vs. UK* (22083/93 ; 22095/93), judg. 22.10.1996 (par. 66, 74)

42. *Z. & Others vs. UK* (29392/95), judg. 10.05.2001 [GC] (par. 73); *E. & Others vs. UK* (33218/96), judg. 26.11.2002 (par. 88)

43. *Z. & Others vs. UK* (29392/95), judg. 10.05.2001 [GC] (par. 109); *E. & Others vs. UK* (33218/96), judg. 26.11.2002 (par. 110)

44. *M.G. vs. UK* (39393/98), judg. 24.09.2002

45. In *E. & Others vs. UK* (33218/96), judg. 26.11.2002, the Court held that sexual and physical abuse on a regular basis over years in childhood, including (attempted) rape, "no doubt" qualifies as inhuman and degrading (par. 89).

46. *Z. & Others vs. UK* (29392/95), judg. 10.05.2001 [GC] (par. 73)

47. *Z. & Others vs. UK* (29392/95), judg. 10.05.2001 [GC] (par. 109)

48. *E. & Others vs. UK* (33218/96), judg. 26.11.2002 (par. 99)

49. *E. & Others vs. UK* (33218/96), judg. 26.11.2002 (par. 96); if there is a real and immediate risk of serious reoffending the *Court*, under Art. 2 ECHR (right to life), established the obligation of authorities not to grant prison leave if they know or should know of the risk: *Mastromatteo vs Italy* (37703/97), judg. 24.10.2002 [GC] (par. 68, 74)

50. *Ramdane Ammari vs. Sweden* (60959/00), dec. 22.10.2002 (The Law, B.)

51. *Carl Wade August vs. UK* (36505/02), judg. 21.01.2003

52. *Carl Wade August vs. UK* (36505/02), judg. 21.01.2003 (The Law, par. 1)

53. The applicant at the time of the contacts was placed in residential care on the basis of being a "disturbed child." His partner was not affiliated with the residential institution or in another way exercising authority over him.

54. *Carl Wade August vs. UK* (36505/02), judg. 21.01.2003 (The Law, B.); The man was imprisoned for infringing the age of consent and the applicant later on sought ex gratia award from the state on the basis of his being a victim of a violent offence. UK law provided for *ex gratia* awards by the State only to victims of violent offences and the applicant complained against the decision of the national courts that–on the basis of his willingness and active part in the sexual contacts–he was not the victim of *violent* offence. In 1979 a study of the British Home Office said: "Consent to a course of action does not imply a mature understanding of the consequences of that course of action but merely a willingness that it should take place" (R. Walmsley & K. White, *Sexual Offences, Consent and Sentencing*, Home Office Research Study 54 (London 1979). For a discussion of this problem see Graupner (1997a), Vol. 1, 253ff.

55. *Christine Goodwin vs. UK* (28957/95), judg. 11.07.2002 [GC] (par. 90); *I. vs. UK* (25680/94), judg. 11.07.2002 [GC] (par. 70); *Zehnalová & Zehnal vs. CZ* (38621/97), dec. 14.05.2002

56. *Fretté vs. France* (36515/97), judg. 26.02.2002 (par. 32)

57. The right does not extend to relations with animals: European Commission of Human Rights, *X. vs. Iceland* (6825/74), dec. 18.05.1976

58. *Zehnalová & Zehnal vs. CZ* (38621/97), dec. 14.05.2002; European Commission of Human Rights, *X. vs. Iceland* (6825/74), dec. 18.05.1976

59. European Commission of Human Rights, *Brüggemann & Scheuten vs. Germany* (6959/75), report 12.07.1977

60. *Fretté vs. France* (36515/97), judg. 26.02.2002 (par. 32)

61. *L. & V. v. Austria* (39392/98, 39829/98), judg. 09.01.2003, par. 36 ("most intimate aspect of private life"); *S.L. v. Austria* (45330/99), judg. 09.01.2003, par. 29 ("most intimate aspect of private life"); European Commission of Human Rights: *Sutherland vs. UK 1997* (25185/94), dec. 01.07.1997 (par. 57: "most intimate aspect of effected individuals 'private life'", also par. 36: "private life (which includes his sexual life)"; so also the *Court* in: *Dudgeon vs. UK* (7525/76), judg. 22.10.1981, par. 41, 52; *Norris vs. Ireland* (10581/83), judg. 26.10.1988 (par. 35ff); *Modinos vs. Cyprus* (15070/89), judg. 22.04.1993 (par. 17ff); *Laskey, Brown & Jaggard sv. UK* (21627/93; 21826/93; 21974/93) 19.02.1997, par. 36; *Lustig-Prean & Beckett vs. UK* (31417/96; 32377/96) (par. 82), 27.09. 1999; *Smith & Grady vs. UK* (33985/96; 33986/96), judg. 27.09.1999 (par. 90); *A.D.T. vs. UK* (35765/97), judg. 31.07.2000 (par. 21ff); *Fretté vs. France* (36515/97), judg. 26.02.2002 (par. 32)

62. BverfGE 47, 46 [73]

63. Art. 8 ECHR: (1) Everyone has the right to respect for his private and family life, his home and his correspondence. (2) There shall be no interference by a public authority with the exercise of this right except such as is in accordance with the law and is necessary in a democratic society in the interests of national security, public safety or the economic well-being of the country, for the prevention of disorder or crime, for the protection of health or morals, or for the protection of the rights and freedoms of others.

64. *Madsen vs DK (58341/00)*, dec. 07.11.2002 (urine testing)

65. *Dudgeon vs. UK* (7525/76), judg. 22.10.1981 (par. 49)

66. For that concept see Graupner (1997a), Vol. 1, 85f.

67. This problem arises for instance in the case of semi-public contacts, such as at publicly accessible places (beaches, parks) where no one is present who could perceive the acts (e.g., in the middle of the night); or in a locked and closed cubicle in a public lavatory. In *England & Wales* even sexual acts in a locked hotel room or in a sleeping train compartment have not been deemed "in private" as staff regularly have access with their keys.

68. For that concept see Graupner (1997a), Vol. 1, 85f

69. See *Zehnalová & Zehnal vs. CZ* (38621/97), dec. 14.05.2002

70. See *Zehnalová & Zehnal vs. CZ* (38621/97), dec. 14.05.2002

71. In connection with Art. 1 of the Protocol No. 1 to Convention (right to protection of property).

72. See mutatis mutandis *Willis vs. UK* (36042/97), judg. 11.06.2002 (par. 29ff)

73. For details see Graupner (1997a), Vol. 2, 324ff)M; Helmut Graupner, Sexual Consent–The Criminal Law in Europe and Overseas, *Archives of Sexual Behavior*, Vol. 29, No. 5, 415-461 (NY, Kluwer Academic/Plenum 2000); Helmut Graupner, *Sexual Consent–The Criminal Law in Europe and Overseas*, Keynote-Lecture at the 7th International Conference of the International Association for the Treatment of Sexual Offenders (IATSO) "Sexual Abuse and Sexual Violence–From Understanding to Protection and Prevention" (Vienna, September 11th-14th 2002), Friday, 13th September 2002, *http://members.aon.at/graupner/documents/Graupner-paper-kn-oFN.pdf*

74. *Hardwick vs. Bowers*, 106 S.Ct. 2841 (1986); This ruling has been overturned by the Supreme Court not before 2003 (*Lawrence et al. vs. Texas*, 02-102, dec. 26.06.2003, *www.supremecourtus.gov*)

75. See Graupner (1997a), Vol. 1, 476 (note 3)

76. *Dudgeon vs. UK* (7525/76), judg. 22.10.1981; *Norris vs. Ireland* (10581/83), judg. 26.10.1988; *Modinos vs. Cyprus* (15070/89), judg. 22.04.1993 ; European Commission of Human Rights, *Marangos vs. Cyprus* (31106/96), report 03.12.1997

77. *Dudgeon vs. UK* (7525/76), judg. 22.10.1981

78. For details see Graupner (1997a), Vol. 1, 75ff

79. European Commission of Human Rights: *Sutherland vs. UK 1997* (25185/94), dec. 01.07.1997

80. *L. & V. vs. Austria* (39392,98, 39829/98), judg. 09.01.2003; *S.L. vs. Austria* (45330/99), judg. 09.01.2003

81. In both countries the cases concerned age limits of 18 (Art. 209 Austrian Criminal Code, Art. 199 Hungarian Criminal Code), while the general age of consent for heterosexual contact is 14. In Hungary the discriminatory age of consent did cover also lesbian relations (Art. 199 CC).

82 Judg. 03.09.2002 (1040/B/1993/23), *www.mkab.hu*

83. Judg. 21.06.2002 (06/02). Under Austrian constitutional law the right to equality, as a general principle, prohibits the legislature from passing seriously unreasonable legislation (for details see Graupner, 1997a, Vol. 1, 104ff).

84. Federal Court of Canada, *Henry Halm vs. The Minister of Employment and Immigration*, dec. 24.02.1995; Ontario Court of Appeal, *R. v. C. M.*, dec. 24.05.1995; Quebec Court of Appeal, *R. v. Roy*, Decision 15.04.1998

85. *B.B. v. State* (1995)

86. *The People v. T.A.J.* (1998); see also *People v. Scott* [Cal. SC 1994])

87. *The People v. T.A.J.* (1998)

88. In the seventies the *European Commission of Human Rights* had to decide on the forcible return to their families of 14 year old girls who had run away to live with their partners. The *Commission* decided that it fell within the states' margin of appreciation to bring back the girls but that they were not under a positive obligation to do so (*X & Y vs. NL*, 6753/74; *X vs. DK*, 6854/74). The sexual relations of the girls with their partners and state interference with them, i.e., criminal liability of their partners, was not an issue before the *Commission*.

89. See Graupner (1997a), *supra*, Vol. 2, 324ff; Helmut Graupner, Sexual Consent–The Criminal Law in Europe and Overseas, *Archives of Sexual Behavior*, Vol. 29, No. 5, 415-461 (NY, Kluwer Academic/Plenum 2000); Helmut Graupner, *Sexual Consent–The Criminal Law in Europe and Overseas*, Keynote-Lecture at the 7th International Conference of the International Association for the Treatment of Sexual Offenders (IATSO) "Sexual Abuse and Sexual Violence–From Understanding to Protection and Prevention" (Vienna, September 11th-14th 2002), Friday, 13th September 2002, *http://members.aon.at/graupner/documents/Graupner-paper-kn-oFN.pdf*; In February 2002 the *Kansas Court of Appeals* confirmed a sentence of 17 years imprisonment for an 18 year old male who had consensual oral sex with a male school mate aged 14 years and 11 months; in addition the maximum sentence would have been 15 months if the couple would have been male-female. The *Kansas High Court* denied review and the case has been brought before the *Supreme Court (State v. Limon*, 41 P.3d 303, 2002 Kan. App. LEXIS 104, *http://www.geocities.com/WestHollywood/4810/Queerlaw/Limon.html* (Feb. 1, 2002), review denied (June 13,

2002), petition for certiorari filed, 71 U.S.L.W.3319 (Oct. 10, 2002) (No. 02-583), http://archive.aclu.org/court/limon_cert.pdf). The *Supreme Court* on 27.06.2003 vacated the appeals court judgment and remanded the case to the Court of Appeals of Kansas for further consideration in light of *Lawrence* v. *Texas* (*Limon, Matthew R.* v. *Kansas*, 02.583, 27.06.2003).

90. *ibid.*
91. *ibid.*
92. *M.K. vs Austria* (28867/95), dec. 02.07.1997
93. See Graupner (1997a), *supra*, Vol. 2, 245ff; Helmut Graupner, Sexual Consent–The Criminal Law in Europe and Overseas, *Archives of Sexual Behavior*, Vol. 29, No. 5, 415-461 (NY, Kluwer Academic/Plenum 2000); Helmut Graupner, *Sexual Consent–The Criminal Law in Europe and Overseas*, Keynote-Lecture at the 7th International Conference of the International Association for the Treatment of Sexual Offenders (IATSO) "Sexual Abuse and Sexual Violence–From Understanding to Protection and Prevention" (Vienna, September 11th-14th 2002), Friday, 13th September 2002, http://members.aon.at/graupner/documents/Graupner-paper-kn-oFN.pdf
94. For a further discussion of this problem see Graupner (1997a), *supra*, Vol. 1, 315ff; Helmut Graupner, Love vs. Abuse–Crossgenerational Sexual Relations of Minors: A Gay Rights Issue?, *Journal of Homosexuality*, Vol. 37 (4) 23-56, (NY, Haworth Press, 1999)
95. *S. L. vs Austria* (par. 52); The applicant, who submitted the application at the age of 17, began to be aware of his sexual orientation about the age of eleven or twelve. While other boys were attracted by women, he realised that he was emotionally and sexually attracted by men, in particular by men who are older than himself. At the age of fifteen he was sure of his homosexuality. He submitted that he lives in a rural area where homosexuality is still taboo. He suffered from the fact that he could not live his homosexuality openly and–until he reached the age of eighteen–could not enter into any fulfilling sexual relationship with an adult partner for fear of exposing that person to criminal prosecution under Article 209 of the Criminal Code (*Strafgesetzbuch*) (which criminalized male homosexual contacts of persons over the age of 19 with persons between 14 and 18). He asserted that he was hampered in his sexual development. He reiterated that he felt particularly attracted by men older than himself but that Article 209 of the Criminal Code made any consensual sexual relationship with men over nineteen years of age an offence. Moreover, Article 209 generally stigmatised his sexual orientation as being contemptible and immoral. Thus, he suffered feelings of distress and humiliation during all of his adolescence. The *Court* held that it "attaches weight to the fact that the applicant was prevented from entering into relations corresponding to his disposition until he reached the age of eighteen" and awarded the applicant EUR 5.000–for non-pecuniary damage (par. 9f, 49, 52).
96. While the *European Commission of Human Rights* constantly has been reluctant in the area of sexuality it, already in the seventies, felt inclined to acknowledge the right of adolescents to self-determination and the legal force of their consent in another area. A 15- and a 16-year-old adolescent who had voluntarily recruited into the British army wanted to leave the armed forces arguing that their obligations interfered with their family-lives (Art. 8 ECHR). The *Commission* held that the British army had the right to refuse the leave, on the basis that also minors could not set aside voluntarily entered obligations of military service (YB XI, 562f).

97. *A.D.T. vs. UK* (35765/97), judg. 31.07.2000. Contrast *Laskey, Brown & Jaggard v UK* (21627/93; 21826/93; 21974/93), judg 19.02.97 where convictions for group sado-masochistic sex involving injury were held not to violate the Convention.

98. Protocol No. 11; See http://www.echr.coe.int

99. *Lustig-Prean & Beckett vs. UK* (31417/96; 32377/96), judg. 27.09. 1999, 25.07.2000; *Smith & Grady vs. UK* (33985/96; 33986/96), judg. 27.09.1999, 25.07.2000; See also *Perkins & R. vs. UK*, (43208/98, 44875/98), judg. 22.10.2002; *Beck, Copp & Bazzeley vs. UK* (48535/99, N "48536/99 and N" 48537/99), judg. 22.10.2002

100. *Salgueiro da Silva Mouta vs. Portugal* (33290/96), judg. 21.12.1999. Cases concerning statutory exclusion of homosexuals from blood donations has been struck off the list after the law has been changed and the ban lifted (*Tosto vs. Italy* (49821/99), dec. 15.10.2002; *Crescimone vs. Italy*, 49824/99, dec. 15.10.2002; *Faranda vs. Italy*, 51467/99, dec. 15.10.2002)

101. *Karner vs. Austria* (40016/98), judg. 24.07.2003. Since the applicant himself had died after the filing of his application the *Court* had to decide whether to strike the case off its list or to continue the examination of the application; it continued examination qualifying the issue as an "important question of general interest not only for Austria but also for other Member States" (par. 27). The *Karner* case is about unequal treatment of non-married same-sex couples in relation to non-married opposite-sex couples. In *Saucedo Gomez v. Spain* (Appl. 37784/97), dec. 26.01.1999, and in *Nylynd v. Finland* (Application No. 27110/95), dec. 29.06.1999, the *Court* found unequal treatment of married vs. unmarried opposite-sex couples within the states' margin of appreciation. Still in 2001 the Court found even unequal treatment of same-sex couples in respect to those unmarried opposite-sex couples within the states' discretion, who (like same-sex couples) could not marry (*Mata Estevez vs. Spain*, Appl. 56501/00, dec. 10.05.2001).

102. *Salgueiro da Silva Mouta vs. Portugal* (33290/96), judg. 21.12.1999 (par. 36)

103. *Lustig-Prean & Beckett vs. UK* (31417/96; 32377/96), judg. 27.09. 1999 (par. 90); *Smith & Grady vs. UK* (33985/96; 33986/96), judg. 27.09.1999 (par. 97); *Salgueiro da Silva Mouta vs. Portugal* (33290/96), judg. 21.12.1999 (par. 36); *L. & V. v. Austria* (39392/98, 39829/98), judg. 09.01.2003 (par. 45, 52); *S.L. v. Austria* (45330/99), judg. 09.01.2003 (par. 37, 44)

104. *L. & V. v. Austria* (39392/98, 39829/98), judg. 09.01.2003 (par. 45); *S.L. v. Austria* (45330/99), judg. 09.01.2003 (par. 37); *Karner vs. Austria* (40016/98), judg. 24.07.2003 (par. 37)

105. *Karner vs. Austria* (40016/98), judg. 24.07.2003 (par. 41)

106. *Lustig-Prean & Beckett vs. UK* (31417/96; 32377/96), judg. 27.09. 1999 (par. 90); *Smith & Grady vs. UK* (33985/96; 33986/96), judg. 27.09.1999 (par. 97); *L. & V. v. Austria* (39392/98, 39829/98), judg. 09.01.2003 (par. 52); *S.L. v. Austria* (45330/99), judg. 09.01.2003 (par. 44)

107. *Christine Goodwin vs. UK* (28957/95), judg. 11.07.2002 [GC] (par. 91); *I. vs. UK* (25680/94), judg. 11.07.2002 [GC] (par. 71)

108. See *European Parliament*: Urgency Resolution on the Rights of Lesbians and Gays in the European Union (B4-0824, 0852/98; par. J), 17.09.1998; Resolution on the Respect of Human Rights within the European Union in 1997 ((A4-0468/98; par. 10), 17.12.1998; Resolution on the Respect of Human Rights within the European Union in 1998/99 (A5-0050/00; par. 76, 77), 16.03.2000; http://www.europarl.eu.int/plenary/default_en.htm

109. See *Parliamentary Assembly of the Council of Europe*: Written Declaration No. 227, Febr. 1993; Halonen-Resolution (Order 488 [1993]); Opinion No. 176 (1993); Opinion 221 (2000); *http://assembly.coe.int*

110. Opinion 216 (2000); Rec. 1474 (2000) (par. 7) ; In September 2001 the *Committee of Ministers of the Council of Europe* assured the Assembly "that it will continue to follow the issue of discrimination based on sexual orientation with close attention" (Doc 9217, 21.09.2001).

111. In 1994 the *UN-Human Rights Committee*, on a global level, on the basis of the International Covenant for Civil and Political Rights declared a total ban of homosexual contacts in violation of the right to privacy (*Toonen vs. Australia*, CCPR/C50/D/488/1992, 31.03.1994). And in 1998 the Committee in its review of the report of Austria under the Covenant called for the repeal of the discriminatory higher age of consent of 18 for gay men as compared to 14 for heterosexuals and lesbians (CPR/C/79/Add.103, 19.11.1998). The *Committee on the Rights of the Child* repeatedly called for the repeal of higher ages of consent for homosexual conduct (CRC/C/15/Add.134, 16.10.2000; CRC/C/15/Add.135, 16.10.2000) and expressed its concern "that homosexual and transsexual young people do not have access to the appropriate information, support and necessary protection to enable them to live their sexual orientation" (CRC/C/15/Add. 188, 09.10.2002); *www.unhchr.ch*

112. See for many others *Ramdane Ammari vs. Sweden* (60959/00), dec. 22.10.2002 (The Law, B.)

113. Which includes life imprisonment without possibility of release (*Nivette vs. France*, 44190/98, dec. 03.07.2001; *Einhorn vs. France*, 71555/01, dec. 16.10.2001)

114. The exceptions contained in Art. 2 ECHR are not relevant in extradition cases. The exception of times of war (or imminent threat of war) in Art. 2 of Protocol No. 6 seems to exempt the extraditing state from the prohibition of the death penalty only if itself is at war (or imminent threat of war) but not if the state to where a person shall be extradited is at war.

115. For the text of Art. 8 EVHR see above

116. *Dudgeon vs. UK* (7525/76), judg. 22.10.1981, par. 53; *Norris vs. Ireland* (10581/83), judg. 26.10.1988 (par. 44); *Modinos vs. Cyprus* (15070/89), judg. 22.04.1993 (par. 25); *Lustig-Prean & Beckett vs. UK* (31417/96; 32377/96) (par. 80), 27.09. 1999; *Smith & Grady vs. UK* (33985/96; 33986/96), judg. 27.09.1999 (par. 87)

117. *Dudgeon vs. UK* (7525/76), judg. 22.10.1981, par. 51; *Norris vs. Ireland* (10581/83), judg. 26.10.1988 (par. 41f); *Modinos vs. Cyprus* (15070/89), judg. 22.04.1993 (par. 25); *A.D.T. vs. UK* (35765/97), judg. 31.07.2000 (par. 32f); For a detailed discussion of the requirements for interferences being justified according to Art. 8 par. 2 ECHR see Graupner (1997a), *supra*, Vol. 1, 86ff

118. *Jimenez Alonso & Jimenez Merino vs. Spain* (51188/99), dec. 25.05.2000

119. *Pichon & Sajous vs. France* (49853/99), dec. 04.10.2001

120. Thereby the requirements on the finding of a legal consensus are stricter here than in other areas. While the Court in the 1980s let suffice mere legal trends in the member states of the Council of Europe when it decided issues regarding the status of illegitimate children or discrimination on the basis of sex (*Marckx vs. Belgium* (6833/74), judg. 13.06.1979, par. 41; *Abdulaziz & Others vs. UK*, (9214/80 et al.), judg. 28.05.1985, par. 78; *Inze vs. Austria* (8695/79), judg. 28.10.1987, par. 41), it took until 2003 for the Court for the first time to let a mere legal trend suffice in the sexual area (*Christine Goodwin vs. UK* (28957/95), judg. 11.07.2002 [GC], par. 85; *I. vs. UK* (25680/94), judg. 11.07.2002 [GC], par. 65).

121. For the effects of those three revolutions on the decriminalization of homosexuality see Graupner (1997b), *supra*.

122. When the Court issued its judgments in *L. & V. vs. Austria* and *S.L. vs. Austria* only seven of the 46 jurisdictions on the territory of the Council of Europe still kept higher minimum age limits for homosexual relations (see Helmut Graupner, *Sexual Consent–The Criminal Law in Europe and Overseas*, Keynote-Lecture at the 7th International Conference of the International Association for the Treatment of Sexual Offenders (IATSO) "Sexual Abuse and Sexual Violence–From Understanding to Protection and Prevention" (Vienna, September 11th-14th 2002), Friday, 13th September 2002, *http://members.aon.at/graupner/documents/Graupner-paper-kn-oFN.pdf* (Table II))

123. *B vs. France* (13343/87), judg. 25.03.1992

124. *Sheffield & Horsham vs. UK* (22985/93, 23390/94), judg. 30.07.1998; See also *Rees vs. UK (9532/81)*, judg. 17.10.1986;

125. The Commission in 1978 decided in favour of transsexuals (including the right to marry a member of the former sex), but the Court refused to follow that approach and declared the application inadmissible on formal grounds (*Van Oosterwijck vs. Belgium*, 7654/76, judg. 06.11.1980)

126. *Christine Goodwin vs. UK* (28957/95), judg. 11.07.2002 [GC] (par. 91); *I. vs. UK* (25680/94), judg. 11.07.2002 [GC] (par. 70); The *European Court of Justice* based its prohibition of discrimination of transsexuals in employment and occupation not on human rights arguments but on statutory interpretation of EC-legislation (*P. vs. S. & Cornwall County Council*, Case C-13/94, 1996; *http://europa.eu.int/eur-lex*).

127. *Laskey, Brown & Jaggard vs. UK* (21627/93; 21826/93; 21974/93) 19.02.1997

128. *Scherer vs. CH* (17116/90), dec. 14.01.1993; The *Court*, due to the death of the applicant, later struck the case off the list (judg. 25.03.1994)

129. The Court elaborates this concept also in *Mueller vs. Switzerland* (10737/84), judg. 24.05.1988

130. BGE 101 Ia (1975); EuGRZ 1976, 202

131. VfSlg. 8272/78; 8907/80; 11926/88

132. Joint adoption by a same-sex couple was not the issue before the Court.

133. *Fretté vs. France* (36515/97), judg. 26.02.2002. The significance of this judgment however is limited because it mirrors the opinion of only one of the seven judges on the panel. Four of the judges were of the opinion that there was no violation, but three of them (solely) on the basis that the application were not admissible on formal grounds.

134. *Rees vs. UK* (9532/81), judg. 17.10.1986; *Cossey vs. UK* (10843/84), judg. 27.09.1990; *Sheffield & Horsham vs. UK* (22985/93 ; 23390/94), judg. 30.07.1998

135. *German Constitutional Court* (BVerfGE 640/93), judg. 13.10.1993; *Supreme Court of the Netherlands* (Hoge Raad, RvdW 1990, 176), judg. 19.10.1990

136. *Rees vs. UK* (9532/81), judg. 17.10.1986; *Christine Goodwin vs. UK* (28957/95), judg. 11.07.2002 [GC] (par. 91); *I. vs. UK* (25680/94), judg. 11.07.2002 [GC]

137. *Rees vs. UK* (9532/81), judg. 17.10.1986 (par. 50); *Cossey vs. UK* (10843/84), judg. 27.09.1990 (par. 43ff); *Sheffield & Horsham vs. UK* (22985/93 ; 23390/94), judg. 30.07.1998 (par. 66)

138. *Christine Goodwin vs. UK* (28957/95), judg. 11.07.2002 [GC]; *I. vs. UK* (25680/94), judg. 11.07.2002 [GC]

139. *Christine Goodwin vs. UK* (28957/95), judg. 11.07.2002 [GC] (par. 100); *I. vs. UK* (25680/94), judg. 11.07.2002 [GC] (par. 80)

140. *Christine Goodwin vs. UK* (28957/95), judg. 11.07.2002 [GC] (par. 101); *I. vs. UK* (25680/94), judg. 11.07.2002 [GC] (par. 81)
141. *Christine Goodwin vs. UK* (28957/95), judg. 11.07.2002 [GC] (par. 100); *I. vs. UK* (25680/94), judg. 11.07.2002 [GC] (par. 80)
142. *Christine Goodwin vs. UK* (28957/95), judg. 11.07.2002 [GC] (par. 98); *I. vs. UK* (25680/94), judg. 11.07.2002 [GC] (par. 78)
143. *German Constitutional Court* (BVerfGE 640/93), judg. 13.10.1993; *Supreme Court of the Netherlands* (Hoge Raad, RvdW 1990, 176), judg. 19.10.1990
144. See Graupner (2002), *supra*.
145. Art. 27f ECHR
146. *SZIVÁRVANY Társulas a Melegek Jogaiért, Géza JUHÁSZ & Balázs PALFY vs. Hungary* (35419/97), dec. 12.05.2000
147. European Commission of Human Rights: *Sutherland vs. UK 1997* (25185/94), dec. 01.07.1997
148. *Salgueiro da Silva Mouta vs. Portugal* (33290/96), judg. 21.12.1999 (par. 36)
149. *Lustig-Prean & Beckett vs. UK* (31417/96; 32377/96), judg. 27.09. 1999 (par. 90); *Smith & Grady vs. UK* (33985/96; 33986/96), judg. 27.09.1999 (par. 97); *Salgueiro da Silva Mouta vs. Portugal* (33290/96), judg. 21.12.1999 (par. 36)
150. *Lustig-Prean & Beckett vs. UK* (31417/96; 32377/96), judg. 27.09. 1999 (par. 90); *Smith & Grady vs. UK* (33985/96; 33986/96), judg. 27.09.1999 (par. 97)
151. *L. & V. vs. Austria* (39392,98, 39829/98), dec. 22.11.2001; *S.L. vs. Austria* (45330/99), dec. 22.11.2001
152. *L. & V. vs. Austria* (39392,98, 39829/98), judg. 09.01.2003; *S.L. vs. Austria* (45330/99), judg. 09.01.2003
153. *S.L. vs. Austria* (45330/99), judg. 09.01.2003
154. For details see *http://www.rklambda.at/dokumente/news/News-PA-en-misshandlung-020805.pdf*
155. See for many others *Ribitsch vs. Austria* (18896/91), 04.12.1995; *Hugh Jordan vs. UK* (24746/94), *McKerr vs. UK* (28883/95), *Kelly and others vs UK* (30054/96) and *Shanaghan vs. UK* (37715/97), 04.05.2001; *Altay vs. Turkey* (22279/93), 22.05.2001; *Abdurrahman vs. Turkey* (31889/96), 14.02.2002
156. See for many others *Hugh Jordan vs. UK* (24746/94), *McKerr vs. UK* (28883/95), *Kelly and others vs. UK* (30054/96) and *Shanaghan vs. UK* (37715/97), 04.05.2001
157. *R.R. vs. Austria* (Appl. 46608/99), dec. 28.06.2002; for details see *http://www.rklambda.at/dokumente/news/News-PA-020805-Antwort.pdf* and *http://www.rklambda.at/dokumente/news/News-PA-020805-Beschwerde.pdf*
158. For details see *http://www.rklambda.at/dokumente/news/News-PA-021221.pdf*
159. *G.T. vs. Austria* (Appl. 46611/99), dec. 29.11.2002, *http://www.rklambda.at/dokumente/news/News-PA-021221-EGMR.pdf*
160. See, e.g., the decisions of the Court in *Mouisel vs. France* (67263/01), dec. 21.03.2002 ("une décision ou une mesure favorable au requérant ne suffit en principe à lui retirer la qualité de "victime" que si les autorités nationales ont reconnu, explicitement ou en substance, puis réparé la violation de la Convention . . . reconnaissance explicite d'une prétendue violation . . . au cours de la période dénoncée par le requérant . . . Par ailleurs, cette décision ne fournit pas une réparation adéquate); *Wejrup vs. Denmark* (49126/99), judg. 07.03.2002 (The Law, B.: "when . . . national authorities . . . acknowledged in a sufficiently clear way the failure . . . and have afforded redress"); *Association Ekin vs. France* (39288/98), judg. 17.07.2001 (par. 37f),

dec. 18.01.2000 ("reconnu, explicitement ou en substance, puis réparé la violation de la Convention"); *Ilascu and Others vs. Moldova & the Russian Federation* [GC] (48787/99), dec. 04.07.2001 (The Law, III. : "a decision or measure favourable to the applicant is not in principle sufficient to deprive him of his status as a 'victim' unless the national authorities have acknowledged, either expressly or in substance, and then afforded redress for, the breach of the Convention . . . firstly, . . . the applicant's conviction is still in existence . . . Furthermore, the Court has not been informed of any pardon or amnesty . . . secondly, . . . the applicant complained not only of his . . . sentence but also . . . of his detention, . . . of the proceedings which led to his conviction"); *Ihasniouan vs. Spain* (50755/99), dec. 28.06.2001 ("effacé les conséquences du grief"); *Constantinescu vs. Romania* (28871/95), dec. 27.06.2000 (par. 40: "a decision or measure favourable to the applicant is not in principle sufficient to deprive him of his status as a 'victim' unless the national authorities have acknowledged, either expressly or in substance, and then afforded redress for, the breach of the Convention"; even an acquittal, without acknowledgment of the violation and adequate redress, does not resolve a matter: par. 42ff!); *Beck vs. Norway* (26390/95), judg. 26.06.2001 (par. 27f: "acknowledged in a sufficiently clear way the failure," "adequate redress"); *Guisset vs. France* (33933/96), judg. 26.09.2000 (par. 66: "applicants will only cease to have standing as victims within the meaning of Article 34 of the Convention if the national authorities have acknowledged the alleged violations either expressly or in substance and then afforded redress," again the Court holds that even an acquittal, without acknowledgment of the violation and adequate redress, does not resolve a matter: par. 68ff); *Rotaru vs. Romania* [GC] (28341/95), judg. 04.05.2000 (par. 35f: "a decision or measure favourable to the applicant is not in principle sufficient to deprive him of his status as a 'victim' unless the national authorities have acknowledged, either expressly or in substance, and then afforded redress for, the breach of the Convention . . . Lastly, the . . . Court of Appeal . . . did not rule on the applicant's claim for compensation for non-pecuniary damage and for costs and expenses"); *Dalban vs. Romania* [GC] (28114/95), judg. 28.09.1999 (par. 44: "a decision or measure favourable to the applicant is not in principle sufficient to deprive him of his status as a 'victim' unless the national authorities have acknowledged, either expressly or in substance, and then afforded redress for, the breach of the Convention"; again the Court holds that even an acquittal, without acknowledgment of the violation and adequate redress, does not resolve a matter); *Amuur vs. France* (19776/92), judg. 25.06.1996 (par. 36: "a decision or measure favourable to the applicant is not in principle sufficient to deprive him of his status as a 'victim' unless the national authorities have acknowledged, either expressly or in substance, and then afforded redress for, the breach of the Convention"); *Heaney & Mc Guinness vs. Ireland* (34720/97), judg. 21.12.2000, (par. 45); *Quinn vs. Ireland* (36887/97), judg. 21.12.2000 (par. 45).

In that sense the Court in *Rotaru vs. Romania* declared that the standing as a victim did not cease with the deletion of the data, because (a) the domestic court did not give an opinion whether the storage was in violation of fundamental rights and (b) the applicant got no redress for non-pecuniary damage, pecuniary damage and his costs and expenses (*Rotaru vs. Romania* [GC], 04.05.2000, par. 36).

In *Paul and Audrey Edwards vs. UK* the Court held within the context of Art. 13 that the mere fact that a violation ceased to take effect pro futuro (there: the inability to use an effective remedy against violations) did not alter the fact that violations have been committed in the past (*Paul and Audrey Edwards vs. UK* (46477/99), judg. 14.03.2002,

par. 99). Also in this context the Court stresses the importance of adequate redress for violations of the Convention (par. 99ff).
In *Pisano vs. Italy* [GC] (36732/97), judg. 24.10.2002, the Court again held that even an acquittal, without acknowledgment of the violation and adequate redress, does not resolve a matter.

161. See *A.D.T. vs. UK* (35765/97), judg. 31.07.2000 (par. 11); *Cerin vs. Croatia* (54727/00), dec. 08.03.2001; *Dallos vs. Hungary* (29082/95), judg. 01.03.2001 (par. 39); *Vodenicarov vs. SK* (24530/94), judg. 21.12.2000 (par. 40, 42f); *Sabeur Ben Ali vs. Malta* (35892/97), 29.06. 2000 (par. 38-40)

162. *Cerin vs. Croatia* (54727/00), dec. 08.03.2001; *Ilhan vs. Turkey* (22277/93), judg. 27.06.2000 (par. 51)

163. *Ilhan vs. Turkey* (22277/93), judg. 27.06.2000 (par. 51)

164. *Cerin vs. Croatia* (54727/00), dec. 08.03.2001;

165. *August Sulzer vs. Austria* (72165/01), dec. 29.04.2003

166. *L. & V. vs. Austria* (39392,98, 39829/98), judg. 09.01.2003; *S.L. vs. Austria* (45330/99), judg. 09.01.2003

167. *Dalban vs. Romania* [GC], 28.09.1999 (par. 44); *Constantinescu vs. Romania*, 27.06.2000 (par. 40, 42ff); *Guisset vs. France* 26.09.2000 (par. 66, 68ff); *Pisano vs. Italy* [GC] (36732/97), judg. 24.10.2002

168. *F.J. vs. Austria* (Appl. 76600/01), dec. 16.05.2003; Only four months later another Committee did not *a limine* reject the application in a very similar case, where a gay man prosecuted under the same law as F.J. has been acquitted solely on the formal ground that the Constitutional Court had struck down the law before a final verdict in the case has been taken. Austria never acknowledged a violation of the applicant's human rights and never granted redress for pecuniary and non-pecuniary damage. The Court communicated the application to the Austrian government on 22.09.2003 (*Wolfmeyer v. Austria*, appl. 5263/03).

169. For criticism of this practice see Jochen Frowein & Wolfgang Peukert, *Europäische Menschenrechtskonvention, EMRK-Kommentar* (Kehl, N. P. Engel, 1996) (Art. 50 Rz 64 "bedenkliche Tendenz")

170. In other leading gay rights cases the *Court* awarded much higher sums for costs and expenses in proceedings before it: see *Lustig-Prean & Beckett vs. UK*, 31417/96; 32377/96, judg. 25.07.2000 (par. 39: EUR 31.000,–) and (*Smith & Grady vs. UK*, 33985/96; 33986/96, judg. 25.07.2000 (par. 32: EUR 32.000,–)

171. J. S. Mill, *On Liberty*

172. J. S. Mill, *On Liberty*

173. Chap. 35 §1 Criminal Code (as amended by law 98:393) (fine or jail up to six months). For the negative consequences of this legislation on the situation of sex-workers see Reinhard Wolff, Weniger Straßenstrich, mehr Elend, *tageszeitung (taz)*, (Berlin, January 2002).

174. "Framework-Directive on combating sexual exploitation of children and child-pornography" (COM [2000] 854, OJ C 62 E/327-330), *http://europa.eu.int/prelex/detail_dossier_real.cfm?CL=de&DosId=161008#311962*, *www.RKLambda.at* (News)

175. The original proposal by the Commission even obliged to criminalize "inducement" of "children" (under 18) into sexual contact. That would even have made it a criminal offence to proposition 17-and-a-half-year-old young men and women. In later versions this offence has been dropped (see *www.RKLambda.at* [News], *http://register.consilium.eu.int/scripts/utfregisterDir/WebDriver.exe?MIval=simple&MIlang=EN*).

176. For detailed criticism and the opinions of several sexological associations see *www.RKLambda.at* (News) and Helmut Graupner, *The 17-year-old Child–An Absur-*

dity of the Late 20th Century, Paper presented at the 7th International Conference of the International Association for the Treatment of Sexual Offenders (IATSO)–"Sexual Abuse and Sexual Violence–From Understanding to Protection and Prevention" (Vienna, September 11th-14th 2002), Symposion *"Sexuality, Adolescence & the Criminal Law,"* Friday, 13th September 2002, http://members.aon.at/graupner/documents/ Graupner-paper-symp.pdf; In 2002 the *U.S. Supreme Court* held a ban on virtual child pornography, not involving images of real persons under 18, as violating the right to freedom of speech (*Ashcroft vs. Free Speech Coalition*, opinion 16.04.2002, 535 U.S., No. 00-795; www.supremecourtus.gov).

177. The *Court* has already held that states can not set aside their obligations under the Convention by transferring competencies to supra-national bodies. So the *Court* claims its supervising power to also extent to acts of the European Union (or the EC) and to acts of member states determined by Union (or EC) law (see for instance *Matthews vs. UK* (24833/94), judg. 18.02.1999; *Segi & Others and Gestoras pro Amnistia & Others vs. 15 member states of the European Union*, 6422/02, 9916/02, dec. 23.05.2002).

178. *Enhorn vs. Sweden* (56529/00), dec. 10.12.2002

179. *Salvetti vs. Italy* (42197/98), dec. 09.07.2002

180. Mandatory testing for years now has been rejected by the Council of Europe and the World Health Organization (see *Committee of Ministers of the Council of Europe*, Rec. R [87] 25, 26.11.1987; *45th World Health Assembly*, resolution WHA 45.35, 14.05.1992; *Global Programme on Aids*, Statement from the Consultation on Testing and Counselling for Hiv-Infection, Geneva 16-18 November 1992)

181. The new Art. 207b Criminal Code contains three offences. *Paragraph 1* makes it an offence to engage in sexual contact with a person under 16 who for certain reasons is not mature enough to understand the meaning of what is going on or to act in accordance with such understanding provided that the offender practices upon the person's lacking maturity and his own superiority based on age. Paragraph 2 makes it an offence to engage in sexual contact with a person under 16 by practicing on a position of constraint. *Paragraph 3* makes it an offence to immediately induce a person under 18 against remuneration.

182. Reply of *Minister of Justice Dr. Dieter Böhmdorfer* to a parliamentary inquiry (2003), AB XXII. GP.-NR 91/AB, 03.04.2003 (100% of all court cases), http://www.parlament.gv.at/pd/pm/XXII/AB/his/000/AB00091_.html; Reply of *Minister of Justice Dr. Dieter Böhmdorfer* to a parliamentary inquiry (2003), AB XXII. GP.-NR 660/AB, 02.09.2003 (44,4% of all court cases, 100% of all incarcerations), http://www.parlament.gv.at/pd/pm/XXII/AB/his/006/AB00660_.html.

183. *Mc Shane vs. UK* (43290/98), judg. 28.05.2002 (par. 135)

184. *European Parliament*, Resolution on the Fundamental Rights in the EU (2002), A5-0281/2003 04.09.2003 (par. 79), www.europarl.eu.int.

185. *VgT Verein gegen Tierfabriken vs. Switzerland* (24699/94), 28.06.2001. The case concerned an animal protection NGO. In *Demuth vs. Switzerland* (38743/97), judg. 05.11.2002, the Court held that the states' margin of appreciation is wider in the case of commercial broadcasting and narrower in the case of political broadcasting (par. 42).

Advancing Human Rights Through Constitutional Protection for Gays and Lesbians in South Africa

Ronald Louw, B Proc, BA(Hons), LLM

University of Natal (Durban)

SUMMARY. As a consequence of the 1994 adoption of a justiciable Bill of Rights in South Africa, with an equality provision prohibiting discrimination on the ground of sexual orientation, a coalition of gay and lesbian organisations set about implementing a progressive agenda of gay and lesbian rights litigation. In striking down the offence of sodomy, the Constitutional Court established a jurisprudence of gay and lesbian rights to equality, dignity and privacy that proved to be the foundation for significant litigation around family law issues. Subsequent to the sodomy judgement, the Court has ruled that same-sex couples who are in permanent life partnerships should be entitled to the same rights as married couples to immigration, employment benefits, custody and adop-

---

Ronald Louw is Associate Professor of Law, University of Natal, South Africa, and Head of the School of Law. He is former Chairperson of the National Coalition for Gay and Lesbian Equality and a co-founder of the Durban Lesbian and Gay Community and Health Care, of which he is now a member of the Board of Trustees. He has published widely in the areas of Criminal Law, Prison Law and Constitutional Law (specifically in respect of gay and lesbian rights). Correspondence may be addressed: School of Law, University of Natal, Durban, 4041, South Africa (E-mail: Louw@nu.ac.za).

[Haworth co-indexing entry note]: "Advancing Human Rights Through Constitutional Protection for Gays and Lesbians in South Africa." Louw, Ronald. Co-published simultaneously in *Journal of Homosexuality* (Harrington Park Press, an imprint of The Haworth Press, Inc.) Vol. 48, No. 3/4, 2005, pp. 141-162; and: *Sexuality and Human Rights: A Global Overview* (ed: Helmut Graupner, and Phillip Tahmindjis) Harrington Park Press, an imprint of The Haworth Press, Inc., 2005, pp. 141-162. Single or multiple copies of this article are available for a fee from The Haworth Document Delivery Service [1-800-HAWORTH, 9:00 a.m. - 5:00 p.m. (EST). E-mail address: docdelivery@haworthpress.com].

http://www.haworthpress.com/web/JH
© 2005 by The Haworth Press, Inc. All rights reserved.
Digital Object Identifier: 10.1300/J082v48n03_08

tion of children. Despite the extensive equality jurisprudence of the Court, it is still uncertain whether it will rule in the future in favour of same-sex marriage or in favour of a civil union/domestic partnership model. *[Article copies available for a fee from The Haworth Document Delivery Service: 1-800-HAWORTH. E-mail address: <docdelivery@haworthpress.com> Website: <http://www.HaworthPress.com> © 2005 by The Haworth Press, Inc. All rights reserved.]*

KEYWORDS. Adoption, apartheid, Bill of Rights, child custody, equality, family law, same-sex domestic partnership, same-sex marriage, sodomy, South Africa

INTRODUCTION

After centuries of oppression and specifically four decades of apartheid and bitter struggle, South Africans drafted and almost unanimously adopted a democratic constitution[1] which has as its centre-piece a justiciable Bill of Rights.[2] It describes itself as the 'cornerstone of democracy'[3] enshrining the rights of all people and also affirming the values of dignity, equality and freedom. For so long a narrow minded white minority had established and enriched itself at the expense of the dignity, equality and freedom of so many of the majority of South Africans. Their bigoted form of Calvinism had led them not only to despise but also to outlaw all forms of difference. While the central theme of apartheid was racism, its reach was far wider in oppressing South Africans on a variety of grounds such as language, sex, ethnicity, culture, religion, and, not least of all, sexual orientation. With this history it is not surprising that the values of equality and dignity resonate throughout the Bill of Rights and also not surprising that its equality provision[4] seeks to be as inclusive as possible:

> The state [nor any person][5] may not unfairly discriminate directly or indirectly against anyone on one or more grounds, including race, gender, sex, pregnancy, marital status, ethnic or social origin, colour, sexual orientation, age, disability, religion, conscience, belief, culture, language and birth.[6]

In order to take forward the constitutional guarantees of equality and dignity, a number of gay and lesbian organisations and individuals established on 4 December 1994 the National Coalition for Gay and Lesbian Equality. It explicitly set about advancing gay and lesbian rights through a combination of advocacy, lobbying and litigation. This chapter focuses on the tactic of litigation.

INITIAL CHALLENGES

Although the Coalition had identified decriminalisation of sodomy as its first goal, the first constitutionally litigious issue that emerged dealt with the recognition of same-sex partners. While there was a risk in taking on this particular case, circumstances emerged beyond the control of the Coalition. Also the legal and social landscape had radically changed in the two years following the adoption of the Constitution.

The facts were simple: Ms. Yolande Langemaat, who was a captain in the South African Police Service, had, for more than a decade, lived with her partner Ms. Beverley Myburgh. In every respect they alleged, but for the law, their partnership was a marriage. One of the benefits accruing to employees of the SAPS was access to its South African Police Medical Scheme, Polmed, established in terms of the Police Act 7 of 1958 and governed by various Regulations and Rules. The latter extended the medical aid scheme benefit to certain categories of dependants of an employee. The Regulations defined dependant as 'the legal spouse or widow or widower or a dependant child' (at 314E). The Rules of the Scheme provided for a similar definition of dependant (at 314G-H). Ms. Langemaat's application to register her partner as her dependant with the scheme was refused by Polmed. She accordingly applied to the High Court to have the Regulations and Rules declared in conflict with the Constitution and thus invalid.[7]

In determining the application, the court was concerned primarily with the question of whether the nature of the relationship between the parties created a legal duty to maintain each other (at 315G-H). The court found that such a duty did exist and accordingly set aside the relevant Regulations and Rules as well as Polmed's refusal of Ms. Langemaat's application to register her partner. Until 4 February 1998, the date judgment was delivered, South African gays and lesbians had waited, sometimes impatiently, since 27 April 1994, for the first court pronouncement on the constitutional guarantee of equality. For decades, gays and lesbians had suffered discrimination. Virtually all sexual relations between gay men were criminalised either by the common law offences of sodomy and 'unnatural' acts[8] or by the infamous 'men at a party' provision contained in s 20A of the Sexual Offences Act 23 of 1957. Lesbian sexual relationships were criminalised only to the extent that they fell foul of the age of consent provision in s 14 of the same Act. But discrimination against gays and lesbians was far more pervasive than merely the discriminatory provisions of the criminal law. The latter, however, provided something of a spurious legal justification for other discriminatory provisions covering such diverse areas as family law, the military, education, and the workplace. The most infamous judicial pronouncement on lesbian relationships was the notorious pre-constitutional judgment of *Van Rooyen v Van Rooyen*[9] when the court held that a lesbian relationship would send out 'confusing signals' to children (at 328C-D), and that such relationships should be kept hidden from children. The court added that these 'signals' were 'contrary to what they [children] should be taught as normal or what they should be guided to as to be correct' (at 329I-J).[10]

Against this backdrop it was, therefore, much more than a breath of fresh air, but something akin to a judicial revolution, when a South African judge could say of Ms. Langamaat and Ms. Myburgh that:

> They are lesbians and cannot enter into a marriage. Despite this they own a house, operate joint finances, are financially co-dependant, make joint decisions and have named each other beneficiaries in their respective policies. On the undisputed facts I must conclude that theirs is an abiding and serious relationship. (at 314B-C)

The court went further, speaking passionately even for the rights of gays and lesbians:

> I would ignore my experience and knowledge of several same-sex couples who have lived together for years. The stability and permanence of their relationship is no different from the many married couples I know. Both unions are deserving of respect and protection. If our law does not accord protection to the type of union I am dealing with then I suggest it is time it does so. (at 316F-G)

Never before in the history of South Africa had a judge spoken so forthrightly and positively on gay and lesbian relationships. In this sense the court makes history and will be quoted, possibly lauded, by gay and lesbian activists for a long time to come. For a number of reasons, however, the judgment is poor in its constitutional analysis. While it was affirming in its support for gay and lesbian equality, it was only in the Constitutional Court's decriminalisation judgment that a sound sexual orientation jurisprudence was established.[11]

DECRIMINALISATION

The National Coalition for Gay and Lesbian Equality jointly with the South African Human Rights Commission[12] applied to the Witwatersrand High Court for an order declaring three crimes inconsistent with the Constitution of the Republic of South Africa, Act 108 of 1996. The three crimes were the two common law offences of sodomy and unnatural sexual acts and the statutory crime contained in section 20A of the Sexual Offences Act 23 of 1957. The crimes, it was argued by the applicants, discriminated against gay men and were therefore contrary to the equality provision in the Bill of Rights. Before commencing its analysis of the three offences, the court importantly affirmed the right of gays and lesbians not only to the full protection of the law but also to equal societal respect:

> Constitutionally we have reached a stage of maturity in which recognition of the dignity and innate worth of every member of society is not a matter of reluctant concession but one of easy acceptance.[13]

In respect of the offence of sodomy, defined as anal intercourse between men, the court found that even if the suppression of the conduct in the past might have been a necessary prop of both private and public morality, it was too tenuous a thread today to justify continued criminalisation. Neither religious belief nor popular opinion could constitute justification in the face of explicit constitutional protection. Furthermore the court specifically declined to draw a distinction between private and public acts and those with or without consent and the offence was struck down in its entirety. In respect of unnatural sexual acts, defined as any unnatural act by one person with another, the court noted that is was predominantly same-sex acts that had been prosecuted and accordingly it differentiated on the ground of sexual orientation. Although the court could find no legitimate governmental purpose for the differentiation, it did consider the question of whether certain forms of the offence might not be justified. The court held that: 'There are undoubtedly some acts which are so repugnant to and in conflict with human dignity as to amount to perversion of the natural order.'[14] The court concluded that there was a basis therefore for retaining the crime, but pruned of its homosexual content. Thirdly, the statutory offence challenged was one that criminalised any act which was 'calculated to stimulate sexual passion or give sexual gratification' between two men at a party, with a party being defined as any occasion where more than two persons were present. The court was again unable to find any rational purpose for the offence and accordingly found it to be inconsistent with the Constitution.

As the applicants had challenged a statutory provision, including the schedules of the Criminal Procedure and Security Officers Acts which listed sodomy as a prohibited act, the High Court decision had to be ratified by the Constitutional Court in terms of section 172(2)(a) of the Constitution.[15] Although the common law offence of sodomy was not directly before the Constitutional Court, in determining the constitutionality of the two schedules it was imperative that it dealt with the common law offence. It follows, therefore, that the offence of unnatural sexual acts was not considered by the Constitutional Court. With regard to section 20A the court rightly deal somewhat dismissively with the offence describing it as 'absurdly discriminatory.'

The court commenced its analysis of sodomy by defining the term 'sexual orientation.' This had given rise to some difficulties during constitutional negotiations in which some of the less liberal parties argued, without any international precedent, that it could lead to the legalisation of paedophilia and necrophilia. The court relied principally on an influential article written by Professor Edwin Cameron in which he defined sexual orientation as an erotic attraction to persons of either the opposite or same sex. The court expanded on this holding that the term should be given a generous interpretation so that it applied 'equally to the orientation of persons who are bi-sexual, or transsexual and . . . also . . . to the orientation of persons who might on a single occasion be erotically attracted to a member of their own sex.'[16]

Although the criminalisation of sodomy could be challenged on several constitutional rights, the court grounded its analysis on the right to equality, considered by commentators as a core value of the Constitution. The court noted that gay men are a permanent minority in society and have suffered from past disadvantage profoundly affecting their dignity, personhood and identity. The criminalisation of their sexual conduct, which caused no harm to anyone else, was done with no other purpose than to impose the moral and religious views of some on society generally.

Although the court found the criminalisation of sodomy to infringe the right to equality, it went further and found it to be inconsistent with the rights to dignity (section 10) and to privacy (section 14) as well. The court referred to the right to dignity as a cornerstone of the Constitution but acknowledged the difficulty of trying to capture the concept in precise terms. However, at its least, the court held that it was obliged to acknowledge the value and worth of all individuals in society. The symbolic effect of the offence was to state that in the eyes of the legal system all gay men were criminals which in turn exposed gay men to the risk of prosecution, adding that: 'Just as apartheid legislation rendered the lives of couples of different racial groups perpetually at risk, the sodomy offence builds insecurity and vulnerability into the daily lives of gay men.'[17] As the offence degraded and devalued gay men in the broader society, it constituted a 'palpable invasion' of their dignity.

The privacy argument is more complicated. In other jurisdictions the criminalisation of gay sex has been found to be inconsistent with the right to privacy. Contrary to international trends at the time, however, was the decision by the Supreme Court of the Unites States of America which found in its 1985 decision of *Bowers v Hardwick* 478 US 186 that the offence of sodomy did not infringe the right to privacy. Prior to the introduction of the Constitution, Cameron had criticised the privacy approach arguing that it suggested discrimination against gays and lesbians was confined to prohibiting conduct between adults in the privacy of the bedroom. Discrimination was in fact far more pervasive than that. It also had the potential to subtly reinforce the idea that homosexual intimacy was shameful or improper. A truly non-stigmatising society, Cameron argued, would have to go further than a privacy approach to protecting the rights of gays and lesbians. Judge Sachs in a separate but concurring judgment specifically criticised the above approach as treating privacy 'as a poor second prize to be offered and received only in the event of the Court declining to invalidate the laws because of a breach of equality.' While alleging an understanding of the applicants' concerns, he argued they were based on a set of flawed assumptions. Their approach created an 'inappropriate sequential ordering' of the rights to equality and to privacy, and, secondly, it undervalued the scope and significance of the right to privacy. The result, he argued, was to weaken the applicants' quest for human rights rather than strengthen it. Rights should rather be approached in an integrated fashion especially when several rights are violated simultaneously such as in the present case.

This makes it artificial to treat rights in the alternative rather than as interactive. According to Sachs J the applicants had misunderstood the concept of privacy by both restricting its protection to the bedroom and at the same time sealing off the bedroom from the reach of the law. Both were incorrect as the right to privacy did not protect places but people and promoted 'conditions in which personal self-realisation can take place.' Secondly, there are a number of justifiable restrictions that apply to private consensual intercourse such as 'inter-generational, intra-familial, and cross-species sex'[18] which the right to privacy will not protect.

While one cannot fault Sachs J on his integrated approach to rights and his criticism of an 'inappropriate sequential ordering' of rights, he misses some important points not least of all the nature of gay and lesbian politics in South Africa which goes back at least to the late 1960s. When the National Party government proposed amending the Immorality Act, the amendments were initially far more draconian than those that were eventually legislated. To a large degree this was the result of the intervention of the Law Reform Club which raised funds to engage counsel to assist in their representations to the parliamentary Select Committee. The Club, however, represented white, middle class, male interests and was firmly located within apartheid politics. In the 1980s gay and lesbian politics moved into the national arena partly as a result of anti-apartheid activist Simon Nkoli, who publicly came out as a gay man during his prosecution in the Delmas Treason Trial. The first mass-based black gay and lesbian organisation, the Gay and Lesbian Orgnaisation of the Witwatersrand (GLOW), was established by Nkoli after his acquittal. Signalling a major shift in gay and lesbian politics, GLOW committed itself to a 'Non-Racist, Non-Sexist, Non-Discriminatory Democratic Future.' This was followed by the affiliation of the Western Cape Organisation of Lesbian and Gay Activists (OLGA) to the United Democratic Front. OLGA, although predominantly white, located itself within the liberation struggle and was led by anti-apartheid activists. After the sexual orientation provision was included in the interim Constitution, extensive national lobbying was undertaken by the National Coalition for Gay and Lesbian Equality which was established in 1994 and represented the broadest range of gays and lesbians in South Africa to date. Through considerable political mobilisation the organisation contributed to securing the retention of the provision in the final Constitution. Thus over three decades gay and lesbian organisation in South Africa had relocated itself from a predominantly white, private and male preserve to a public, politicised and inclusivist movement. To advance gay and lesbian rights now on the basis of equality would be the logical development of this relocation, whereas to rely on the right to privacy would be to deny this history and to hark back to an era of reactionary gay and lesbian politics.[19]

The second problem in relying on a privacy argument is that it must necessarily raise the justifiable restrictions that Sachs J refers to. This has the effect referred to by Cameron of reinforcing the idea that homosexual intimacy might be shameful or improper, at least if not kept in check. No such stigma attaches to heterosexual intercourse even though the propensity for prohibited conduct is no different to that of gays and lesbians. It also has the effect of reducing, at least in respect of perception, sexual orientation to sexual intercourse. Sexual orientation is much more than that, relating to such diverse areas as employment, family law, immigration, and insurance. While the offences challenged here do indeed relate to sexual intercourse, the equality jurisprudence established created a convenient base from which to assert other, more important, rights to equality. The third problem with a privacy approach is more technical. It is only an enforceable right in respect of citizens' dealings with the State; in other words, it has only a vertical application, whereas the right to equality has not only vertical application but horizontal application as well as it is a right that is enforceable against anyone. Thus, for example, a restaurant owner need not respect a patron's constitutional right to privacy but is obliged to respect his or her right to equality.

Finally, the court had to consider whether it would restrict its judgment to private consensual sodomy as the offence was more extensive including so-called 'male rape' and sexual intercourse with a person below the age of consent. The court noted that in many countries that had decriminalised sodomy, they had simultaneously retained provisions, usually in statute form, that dealt with age, privacy and consent. But instead of conflating the offence with potentially emotive arguments the court rightly held:

> There can be no doubt that the existence of the common-law offence was not dictated by the objective of punishing "male rape." The sole reason for its existence was the perceived need to criminalise a particular form of gay sexual expression; motives and objectives which we have found to be flagrantly inconsistent with the Constitution. The fact that the ambit of the offence was extensive enough to include "male rape" was really coincidental. The core of the offence was to outlaw gay sexual expression of a particular kind.[20]

Furthermore, as under age and non-consensual anal intercourse can be prosecuted by other offences that already exist, the Court invalidated the offence in its entirety. This approach is to be welcomed as it shows an understanding not only that the offence is aimed principally at consensual same-sex intercourse, but it also provided a legal justification on which the whole edifice of gay and lesbian discrimination and stigma was built. Any retention of the offence, in whatever attenuated form, would have run the risk of retaining this foundation.

FAMILY LAW DEVELOPMENTS

The judgment is a major victory for gay an lesbian equality in South Africa. Far more important than decriminalising certain offences, which were in any event seldom prosecuted when consent was given, the judgment created a jurisprudential foundation on which to build far-reaching gay and lesbian rights to equality. The development of a progressive body of family law in South Africa has been slow. This is the result of a very conservative foundation laid by academic writers and the courts. Family law in South Africa has been traditionally defined as constituting that part of law that deals with married persons and their children.[21] In the early case of *W v W*[22] the court refused to recognise that a sex-change operation could legally change the sex of a person. In *Van Rooyen v Van Rooyen*[23] not only were stringent conditions placed on a lesbian mother who sought access to her children, but the court treated homosexuality particularly negatively. Since the enactment of the interim Constitution,[24] the legal definition of family has begun to widen. The most significant judicial break with the past has been that of *Langemaat v Minister of Safety and Security and Others.*[25]

With regard to custody of children by lesbian mothers, there have been significant shifts away from *Van Rooyen*. In *V v V*[26] the court found that the homosexuality of the mother was not necessarily a bar to joint custody.[27] There have been at least two unreported judgments where the courts have found in favour of lesbian mothers in custody matters.[28] In *Farr v Mutual & Federal*[29] the court explicitly held that two gay men living together in a domestic relationship constituted a family:

> I think that while society might not necessarily approve of homosexual relations, it does recognise that where such a relationship has a degree of permanency and the manner in which the partners live together resembles for all intents and purposes (save that their

sexual relations re homosexual and not heterosexual) a marriage between a husband and wife, they could be considered members of a family as would a husband and a wife.

A far-reaching understanding of family articulated by O'Regan J in the unanimous Constitutional Court judgment *Dawood v Minister of Home Affairs*[30] where she stated that 'families come in many shapes and sizes. The definition of family also changes as social practices change. In recognising the importance of the family, we must take care not to entrench particular forms of family at the expense of other forms.'[31] In *Du Toit v Minister of Population and Welfare Development* 2002 (10) BCLR 1006 (CC) the changing notion of family was again underscored when two women sought jointly to adopt two children. The court held that family care 'as contemplated in the Constitution can be provided for in different ways and that legal conception of family and what constitutes family life should change as social practices and traditions change' (at para 19).[32] While there have been considerable developments in broadening our conception of family law,[33] unquestionably the most significant issue remaining is that of gay and lesbian marriage. In this regard, the second NCGLE case, *National Coalition for Gay and Lesbian Equality v Minister of Home Affairs*[34] the court had to consider the residence application by a non-South African. Although the issue of marriage was raised, it was avoided by the court. Ironically the issue was raised by the government who argued that the matter brought by the Applicants was not ripe for constitutional determination.[35] It was argued that a regional committee of the department could interpret 'spouse,' as contained in the relevant provision, to include a same-sex life partner. It was, therefore, unnecessary to consider its constitutional validity. In dismissing this argument the court relied in the first instance on the definition of spouse in the *New Shorter Oxford Dictionary* where the it held that the ordinary meaning of the term connotes a 'married person; a wife, a husband.'[36] Nothing in the Act suggested a wider meaning. Secondly, the use of the term 'marriage' in the Act also indicated that the term 'spouse' was used for a partner in a marriage and that the term marriage extended no 'further than those marriages that are ordinarily recognised in our law.'[37] Finally, if the term 'spouse' could have been given a more extensive meaning, the court held that it would have been unnecessary to have made provision in the definition section of the Act to provide specifically that 'marriage' includes a customary union where the definition of customary union was based on an opposite-sex relationship.[38] To rely first of all on a dictionary definition, secondly, on the meaning of a word 'ordinarily recognised in our law,' and, thirdly, by applying a narrow legislative interpretation, the Court could not by its own restrictive parameters come to a conclusion any different to that of the current law. Such an avoidance of constitutional interpretation may prove to be an obstacle for future litigation of gay partnerships and the definition of marriage. It is not that we are bound by this narrow definition (in fact the Court's avoidance to deal with the issue might be a reason why it will require future constitutional analysis) but there are *indications* in the judgment, which if followed, could lead to an institution alternative to marriage in the recognition of gay and lesbian relationships.

Having come to the conclusion that it was not possible construe the term 'spouse' to include same-sex partners, the court nevertheless proceeded to affirm gay and lesbian relationships in the most positive way. The court commenced its discrimination analysis by building on the jurisprudence it had established in its *Sodomy* decision by stating:

> The denial of equal dignity and worth all too quickly and insidiously degenerates into a denial of humanity and leads to inhuman treatment by the rest of society in many ways. This is deeply demeaning and frequently has the cruel effect of undermining the confidence and sense of self-worth and self-respect of lesbians and gays.

The court went on to dismiss certain stereotypes discriminatory of gays and lesbians, most notably in respect of children. Although a gay and lesbian couple could not jointly adopt a child, an adopted child by one of the partners could be loved, cared and provided for jointly by both partners.[39] Most significantly the court held that in all respects a same-sex partnership resembled a marriage and that their family lives are indistinguishable from that of spouses:

> iv. Gays and lesbians in same-sex life partnerships are as capable as heterosexual spouses of expressing and sharing love in its manifold forms including affection, friendship, eros and charity;
> v. They are likewise as capable of forming intimate, permanent, committed, monogamous, loyal and enduring relationships; of furnishing emotional and spiritual support; and of providing physical care, financial support and assistance in running the common household;

vi. They are individually able to adopt children and in the case of lesbians to bear them;
vii. In short, they have the same ability to establish a *consortium omnis vitae*;
viii. Finally, and of particular importance for the purposes of this case, they are capable of constituting a family, whether nuclear or extended, and of establishing, enjoying and benefiting from family life which is not distinguishable in any significant respect from that of heterosexual spouses.[40]

Having established the extent of the discrimination against gays and lesbians, the court had no difficulty in concluding that section 25(5) of the Act constituted unfair discrimination and a limitation of the 'right of gays and lesbians who are permanent residents in the Republic and who are in permanent same-sex life partnerships with foreign nationals'[41] to equality. The court also concluded that the section constituted a 'severe limitation of the section 10 right to dignity enjoyed by gays and lesbians.'[42] The court found there to be no justification in the discrimination[43] and took the unusual and creative step in reading into the section, 'after the word "spouse," the following words: "or partner in a permanent same-sex life partnership."'[44]

SAME SEX MARRIAGE

These judgments of the Constitutional Court, all of which have been unanimous, constitute milestones for gay and lesbian legal equality in South Africa. Although the judgments have been positive and affirming, the strategic question that faces gay and lesbian activists is how to take forward the "Recognise our Relationships" campaign initiated by the National Coalition for Gay and Lesbian Equality.[45] It is arguable that the most important legal and jurisprudential development that gays and lesbians could achieve is that of the right to marry.[46] It is an important right for a number of reasons: first, it is a right that will be immediately accessible to all gays and lesbians. Secondly, it is important in that marriage constitutes the symbolic foundation upon which heterosexual society is built. Admission to the institution of marriage may constitute the most important test for determining the extent to which gays and lesbians will be treated equally. Thirdly, it will be a logical culmination of the Court's developing sexual orientation jurisprudence.

Marriage is much more than a union between two people: it constitutes a social endorsement of a relationship that if extended to gays and lesbians will enhance their social acceptance. There are significant consequences to marriage resulting not only in social but also economic stability. Marriage is thus much more than a legal entity and the extension of marriage to gays and lesbians will have ramifications far wider than the legal consequences of marriage. Marriage has a uniquely privileged status in society and to withhold that privilege from gays and lesbians will be to deny them equality, dignity and the freedom to choose with whom to associate and autonomy in making significant decisions about their personal lives. It is, therefore, a pity that the definition of marriage was raised in such an oblique manner and was dealt with perfunctorily at the beginning of the *National Coalition* judgment, for it is a decision that could have significant legal and social consequences for gays and lesbians. It is inevitable that the issue of gay and lesbian marriage will come before the court sometime in the future and it is regrettable that the Court has already expressed itself, albeit indirectly, in this regard. Although the *National Coalition* judgment is relevant specifically to the Aliens Control Act,[47] and dealt with the definition of 'spouse' rather than 'marriage,' it would need to be addressed in a future decision and so constitutes an obstacle to gay and lesbian equality activism. But far more importantly, and possibly constituting a more significant obstacle to gay and lesbian equality, is the creation of a new legal entity by the court, namely, that of a 'permanent same-sex life partner.'

Although the court specifically declined to comment on, or indicate to what extent, if at all, 'the law ought to give formal institutional recognition to same-sex life partners,'[48] the judgment does create a legal space for the statutory recognition for what has been variously termed domestic partnerships or civil unions. This is an option that has been followed in a number of north European jurisdictions and most recently in the US state of Vermont. The civil unions of the European jurisdictions are not equivalent to marriage as they typically restrict the right to adoption and other consequences of marriage such as donor insemination and adoption of a spouse's surname.[49] In April 2000[50] the state of Vermont enacted the most far-reaching legislation in respect of civil unions. Section 1, dealing with Findings of the General Assembly, stated that 'The state has a strong interest in promoting stable and lasting families, including families based upon a same-sex couple'[51] and 'Without the legal protections, benefits and responsibilities associated with civil marriage, same-sex couples suffer numerous obstacles and hardships.'[52] The Act proceeds to set out in detail the content of a civil union giving it the same content as marriage: 'Parties to a civil union shall have all the benefits, protections and responsibilities under law, whether they derive from statute, administrative or court rule, policy, common law or any other source of civil law, as are granted to spouses in a marriage.'[53]

While the Act must be acknowledged as a remarkable piece of legislation, I argue that it not only perpetuates but entrenches an inequality between gay and lesbian couples and heterosexual couples. The Act is explicit that marriage is a 'union between a man and a woman'[54] and a civil union is restricted to persons 'of the same sex and therefore excluded from the marriage laws of this state.'[55] The Act, therefore, recreates the discredited 'separate but equal' doctrine of racial legislation in the context of same-sex relations. By granting to gay and lesbian unions all the rights and obligations of marriages it would appear to be the granting of substantive equality. Denial of the name of marriage would appear to be a denial of formal equality only. However, I argue that the denial of the name of marriage to gays and lesbians denies more than the name and thus denies them substantive equality. Marriage remains a privileged social institution for heterosexual couples but most importantly retains the exclusivist traditional and religious content and the less tangible connotations of marriage. The Act states: 'Extending the benefits and protections of marriage to same-sex couples through a system of civil unions preserves the fundamental constitutional right of each of the multitude of religious faiths in Vermont to choose freely and without state interference to whom the religious status, sacrament or blessing of marriage under the rules, practices or traditions of such faiths.'[56] It is in this formulation that we see that the denial of the name of marriage amounts to a denial of substantive equality. The denial of the name was of course achieved through a complex statutory process which while retaining the appearance of marriage simultaneously denied gays and lesbians a spiritual and religious equality.[57] It is significantly the spiritual and religious content of marriage that accords marriage the socially privileged status that it has. When some gays and lesbians wish to marry it is not only the legal equality they desire but also the socially accepted status of *being married*. The Act's bracketing off of the religious, spiritual and less tangible content of marriage from civil unions seems to be paying undue deference to religious orthodoxy in the guise of religious freedom. This is done at the expense of gays and lesbians whose freedom of religion is instead violated. The Act fails to create an institution that upholds the equality of gays and lesbians as well as the freedom of religion of both heterosexuals and gay and lesbian couples.

POSSIBLE DEVELOPMENTS

There are many routes that we could go in South Africa in seeking to create an equality for gay and lesbian relationships. I argue that the retention of exclusivist marriage and the creation of a separate institution for gays and lesbians (even if it were an institution available to heterosexuals as well) would be by definition a violation of equality. Neither the Vermont model nor the north European models are satisfactory. However, the *National Coalition* case, in its recognition of 'permanent same-sex life partner' alongside 'spouse' has already laid the legal foundation for separate institutions. Furthermore the South African Law Commission is currently researching the legislative recognition of domestic partnerships. It is possible, therefore, that the Legislature will preempt any Constitutional Court decision in this regard and establish a civil union not unlike the Vermont model. Another option would be to strip ministers of religion of their state authority and grant no legal recognition to religious marriages. Although this would result in equality for all who wish to get married, it would simultaneously, and unnecessarily, infringe the freedom of religion of those persons whose religious marriages are recognised. If religious marriages continued to receive state sanction, then would an extension of marriage to gays and lesbians infringe on the religious freedom of others? No religious group can claim absolute right to define marriage. We have an unfortunate history in this regard where only Christian marriages once received state recognition. The extension of marriage to other religions and customary unions has not impinged on the right of Christians to marry. All it has removed is their absolute claim on marriage and such absolutism cannot be constitutionally acceptable.

In conclusion the only constitutionally acceptable solution is to extend to gays and lesbians the right to marry, and that they may then do so with the full religious blessing of whatever faith wishes to marry them. This extension could be achieved by legislation but such a controversial step by the Legislature is unlikely. Extension will in all probability only be achieved by the Constitutional Court. But will the Court uphold such a claim? Its jurisprudence in this regard is somewhat ambivalent. There are numerous grounds on which such a claim could be made, notably the right to equality, the right to privacy and the right to dignity.[58] The first indication of possible judicial acceptance of gay and lesbian marriage can be found in the *Sodomy* judgment where Ackermann J stated:

> The issues in this case touch on deep convictions and evoke strong emotions. It must not be thought that the view which holds that sexual expression should be limited to marriage between men and women with procreation as its dominant or sole purpose, is held by crude bigots only. On the contrary, it is also sincerely held, for considered and nuanced religious and other reasons, by persons who would not wish to have the physical expression of sexual orientation differing from their own proscribed by the law. *It is nevertheless equally important to point out, that such views, however honestly and sincerely held, cannot influence what the Constitution dictates in regard to discrimination on the grounds of sexual orientation.* (emphasis added)[59]

Yet in the *National Coalition* case Ackermann J seems to retreat from this position. Admittedly the issue of marriage was not directly before the court but only the definition of spouse, and the latter was not thoroughly canvassed. However, Ackermann J indicated a distinct reluctance to grapple with the constitutional interpretation of spouse. Secondly, the court's creation of a legal construct, 'permanent same-sex life partner,' suggests that it might already be considering an institution other than marriage with which to recognise gay and lesbian relationships. In contrast to this position is the recent judgment by O'Regan J in *Dawood*:[60]

> The decision to enter into a marriage relationship and to sustain such a relationship is a matter of defining significance for many if not most people and to prohibit the establishment of such a relationship impairs the ability of the individual to achieve personal fulfillment in an aspect of life that is of central significance. In my view, such legislation would clearly constitute an infringement of the right of dignity.[61]

The right to dignity here is given extensive content. Coupled with the equality protection for gays and lesbians, it would now be difficult for the Constitutional Court to refuse gays and lesbians the right to marry. If it did, such a decision by the Court would undermine its own equality and dignity jurisprudence which it has built not least of all upon the grounds of sexual orientation and marital status.

South African families are diverse in character and marriages can be contracted under several different legal regimes including African customary law, Islamic personal law and the civil or common law. However, full legal recognition has historically been afforded only to civil or common law marriages. Even if the legal implications of the marriage differ depending on the legal regime that governs it, the personal significance of the relationship for those entering it and the public character of the institution, remain profound. In addition, many of the core elements of the marriage relationship are common between different legal regimes.

Finally, in the light of the *possible* extension of marriage to different faiths and customs and the developing jurisprudence in *Dawood*, gay and lesbian activists should not narrowly call for *their* right to marry but instead for the equal right of *all* to marry whom had previously been excluded by apartheid laws.[62]

NOTES

1. Initially an 'interim' Constitution was passed into law, the Constitution of the Republic of South Africa Act 200 of 1993, which was then superseded by the 'final' Constitution, the Constitution of the Republic of South Africa Act 108 of 1996.

2. Contained in Chapter 2 of the 'final' Constitution.

3. Section 7(1) of the Bill of Rights.

4. Section 9 of the Bill of Rights.

5. Section 9(2) is effectively repeated in s 9(3) ensuring a horizontal application of the non-discrimination provision.

6. Section 9(2) of the Bill of Rights.

7. 1998 (3) SA 312 (T)

8. South African common law derives principally from Roman-Dutch Law, especially in respect of the criminal law, which was received upon colonization by the Dutch in 1652.

9. 1994 (2) SA 325 (W)

10. See Bonthuys E 'Awarding Custody and Access to Homosexual Parents of Minor Children: A discussion of *Van Rooyen v Van Rooyen* 1994 (2) SA 325 (W)' 1994 (3) *Stellenbosch Law Review* 298; De Vos P 'The Right of a Lesbian Mother to Have Access to Her Children: Some Constitutional Issues' (1994) 111 *SALJ* 687; Singh D 'Discrimination Against Lesbians in Family Law' in (1995) 11 *SAJHR* 571.

11. See R Louw 'Langemaat v Minister of Safety and Security: A gay and lesbian victory but a constitutional travesty' (1999) 15 *SAJHR* 393

12. The South African Human Rights Commission was established in terms of s 181 of the Constitution.

13. National Coalition for Gay and Lesbian Equality v Minister of Justice 1998 (6) BCLR 726 (W) at 112H

14. At 127E.

15. National Coalition for Gay and Lesbian Equality v Minister of Justice 1998 (12) BCLR 1517 (CC).

16. At para 21

17. At para 28

18. At para 118

19. See generally M Gevisser 'A Different Fight for Freedom: A History of South African Lesbian and Gay Organisations from the 1950s to 1990s' in M Gevisser and E Cameron (eds) *Defiant Desire: Gay and Lesbian Lives in South Africa* (1994).

20. At Para 69

21. See, for example, P J Visser & J M Potgieter (1998) *Introduction to Family Law*, 2nd Ed, Juta, 1 who not only define family law narrowly but display a hostile and bigoted attitude to homosexuality: 'It should be remembered that the prohibition on unfair discrimination against persons on account of their sexual orientation does not override the constitutional principle that the 'best interests of the child' are of paramount importance in every matter that concerns the child. And for as long as society does not see homosexuality and lesbianism as normal, it will frown upon any attempt to treat homosexual and lesbian parents as 'normal' for the purpose of access to young children. Moreover, the Constitution does not require that homosexualism must be actively promoted.' (170 note 108)

22. 1976 (2) SA 308 (W). For a fuller discussion of this see B Van Heerden, A Cockrell, R Keightly (Gen Eds) *Boberg's Law of Persons and the Family* 2 ed (1999) 209-261.

23. 1994 (2) SA 325 (W). See generally P De Vos 'The right of a lesbian mother to have access to her children: Some constitutional issues' (1994) 111 *SALJ* 687; E Bonthuys 'Awarding access and custody to homosexual parents of minor children: A discussion of *Van Rooyen v Van Rooyen* 1994 2 SA 325 (W)' (1994) 3 *Stell LR* 298; D Singh 'Discrimination against lesbians in family law' (1995) 11 *SAJHR* 571

24. Constitution of the Republic of South Africa Act 200 of 1993.

25. 1998 (3) SA 312 (T). See R Louw 'Langemaat v Minister of Safety and Security: A gay and lesbian victory but a constitutional travesty' (1999) 15 *SAJHR* 393.

26. 1998 (4) SA 169 (C).

27. The court had to decide whether an order for joint custody was appropriate. Although for the two years prior to the divorce the parents had in fact been exercising joint custody in practice, the plaintiff husband objected to such an order on two grounds and sought an order for sole custody. The two grounds were that the mother was suffering from borderline personality disorder and that she was lesbian. However, the evidence of the psychiatrist and psychologists for both parents did not consider the issue of sexual orientation to be a factor. Significantly the court quoted from one of the psychologists' reports that stated generally that the homosexual orientation and lifestyle per se of a parent does not constitute a moral or psychological threat to the wellbeing of children. The report continued that inappropriate sexual behaviour which impinges on children of whatever sexual orientation might be harmful. See also *EP Critchfield and Critchfield*, unreported case no 96/22531 (WLD) where the court viewed the homosexual encounters of the First Applicant during the marriage in 'no more serious a light than conventional adultery' (14 of the typed judgment).

28. In *Mohapi v Mohapi* (Unreported case, 1997 (WLD)) the applicant mother obtained an order of court for the father to return their minor daughter to her. In her papers, the mother acknowledged that she was lesbian and living in a relationship with another woman. She alleged that her daughter had 'an extremely good relationship' with her partner as well as her partner's daughter. The father had often vilified the mother in public regarding her sexual orientation and threatened to have her custody of their daughter removed by the court. Although the mother already had custody of her child and only sought an order for a return of her child, the court drew no adverse infer-

ence regarding her sexual orientation. In *Greyling v Minister of Welfare and Population Development and Others* (Unreported case no 8197/99, WLD) the applicant had been divorced three years prior to the matter and was granted custody of her daughter. After moving out of her parents' home a year later she formed a lesbian relationship with a co-worker. The applicants' parents objected to the relationship and obtained an order removing the daughter from her mother on the rather spurious grounds that the daughter did not wish to reside with her mother, that the mother and her partner 'do things which the minor child cannot or is afraid to speak of' and that the daughter was suffering psychological damage. After protracted delays largely at the hands of government officials, the applicant approached the High Court requesting the order of removal be set aside. Once again, without detriment to her application, the applicant disclosed her sexual orientation in her court papers. The court ordered the return of the child and awarded punitive costs against the respondents on an attorney and client scale.

29. Unreported case no 2700/99 CPD in this case the Applicant was involved in a motor vehicle accident. His passenger was his partner which limited the partner's claim on the Multilateral Motor Vehicle Fund. This made the Applicant liable for the remainder of his partner's claim and accordingly the Applicant relied on his own insurer, the respondent. The Respondent repudiated the claim alleging it was not liable for claims in respect of family member. The court upheld the repudiation by finding that the Applicant's partner was a member of his family.

30. Unreported case no CCT 35/99 which dealt with immigration permits for foreign spouses.

31. Ibid para 31. Internal footnotes omitted.

32. See also Satchwell v The President of the Republic of South Africa 2002 (10) BCLR 1006 (CC) in which the court recognised employment benefits for same-sex couples, in this case judges of the High Court.

33. There have been a number of statutory changes as well; see *National Coalition* (note 1 above) note 43.

34 2000 (1) BCLR 39 (CC)

35. For a fuller explanation of ripeness see para 22 of the *National Coalition* judgment (note 1 above).

36. Ibid. para 25 and note 23.

37. Ibid. para 25.

38. Ibid. para 26.

39. Ibid. para 50.

40. Ibid. para 53.

41. Ibid. para 57.

42. Ibid. para 57.

43. Ibid. paras 58 to 60.

44. Ibid. para 86.

45. Thus far the most significant gains made have largely been at the insistence of the Coalition for Gay and Lesbian Equality who have wither lobbied or litigated (or assisted in litigation) to change the law. See P Gerber 'Case Comment: South Africa: Constitutional Protection for homosexuals–A brave initiative, but is it working?' (2000) 9 *Australasian Gay and Lesbian Law* Journal 37.

46. This is contrary to the argument by Cameron (note 37 above) that '[G]enuine recognition of non-discrimination on the ground of sexual orientation would entail granting some recognition to permanent domestic partnerships. This need not take the

form of extending heterosexual marriage, which both by name and tradition may well be unnecessary and inappropriate' (471, internal footnotes omitted). It should be noted that the article was written in 1992, prior to any certainty that non-discrimination on the ground of sexual orientation would be constitutionally protected. Furthermore the issue of same-sex marriage had not been debated in South Africa and particularly as at the time the right seemed to be an unattainable one. Since the enactment of both the interim and final Constitutions gay and lesbian jurisprudence has changed to such an extent that Cameron's comments must now only be seen in their historical context and as not relevant to the current debate. The anti-marriage debate has not been developed in South Africa either by activists or academics; see generally: C Lind 'Sexual orientation, family law and the transitional Constitution' (1995) 112 South *African Law Journal* 481; T L Mosikatsana 'The definitional exclusion of gays and lesbians from family status' 1996 (12) *South African Journal on Human Rights* 549; L Wolhuter 'Equality and the concept of difference: same-sex marriages in the light of the final Constitution' (1997) 114 *South African Law Journal* 389 (although she raises the debate more seriously than any other South African writer, she concludes that in the light of the equality provision, the right to marry cannot be constitutionally disallowed) and A Pantazis 'An argument for the legal recognition of gay and lesbian marriage' (1997) 114 *South African Law Journal* 556).

47. It is important to note that in coming to the conclusion that the term 'spouse' did not include gay and lesbian couples, the court explicitly confined itself to the Act: 'Under all these circumstances is not possible to construe the word "spouse" in section 25(5) as including the foreign same-sex partner of a permanent and lawful resident of the Republic' (*National Coalition* (note 1 above) para 26).

48. National Coalition (note 1 above) para 60.

49. See M P Boberg 'The registered partnership for same-sex couples in Denmark' (1996) 8 *Child and Family Law Quarterly* 147 and M Roth 'The Norwegian Act on registered partnership for homosexual couples' (1996-97) 35 *University of Louisville Journal of Family Law* 467.

50. Act 91: Act Relating to Civil Unions, to come into effect on 1 July. The statute was a direct result of Vermont's Supreme Court's decision in Baker v State (www.lambdalegal.org/sections/library/decisions/vermont December 1999) which held that the state had a 'constitutional obligation to extend to plaintiffs the common benefit, protection, and security that Vermont law provides opposite-sex married couples' (39).

51. Ibid. S 1(7).
52. Ibid. S 1(8).
53. Ibid. S 3.
54. Ibid. S 1(1).
55. Ibid. S 3.
56. Ibid. S 1(11).

57. If substantive equality is what was being sought it would have been much easier to have admitted gays and lesbians to the institution of marriage rather than creating a look-alike institution.

58. The cogency of these claims have been extensively commented on by other writers and it is not my intention here to reconsider these arguments. See generally B Grant 'Comments and cases on same-sex marriage' (1996) 12 *SAJHR* 568.

59. Note above para 38. Internal footnotes omitted.

60. *Dawood v Minister of Home Affairs* 2000 (8) BCLR 837 (CC)

61. Ibid. para 37.
62. The law has recently recognised marriages concluded in terms of customary law (Recognition of Customary Marriages Act 120 of 1998) but marriages concluded by religious officers of the Christian and Jewish faiths have no legal force. The South African Law Commission has recently (Project 118 Domestic Partnerships, June 2003) raised the possibility of removing the civil function of religious officers thus removing the religious emphasis in marriage.

Sexuality and Human Rights: An Asian Perspective

Erick Laurent, PhD

Gifu Keizai University, Japan

SUMMARY. In Asia, the lesbian and gay rights movements are clearly dominated by activists, who tend to think in terms of a binary opposition (homo- vs hetero-) and clear-cut categories. Based on "Western patterns," the approach is practical, the arguments based on minority rights. "Coming out" is often perceived as a "white model" bringing more problems than real freedom. On the contrary, "Asian values" put the emphasis on family and social harmony, often in contradiction to what is pictured as "lesbian and gay rights." Homophobia follows very subtle ways in Asian countries. Asian gays have to negotiate their freedom, lifestyle and identities in an atmosphere of heterosexism, and not the endemic violent homophobia prevalent in many western countries. In Asia, one's identity relates to one's position in the group and sexuality plays a relatively insignificant role in its cultural construction. That Asian gays

---

Erick Laurent has a doctorate in Anthropology (Ecole des Hautes Etudes en Sciences Sociales, Paris) and in Zoology (University of Kyoto), specialized in Japanese culture and society, and is Professor of Cultural Anthropology, with a seminar in Gay and Lesbian Studies, at Gifu Keizai University in Ogaki, Japan. His present themes of research include "male homosexuality in contemporary Japan," "gay ways of life in rural Japan" in an anthropological perspective, and based on fieldwork in different places in the country. Correspondence may be addressed: 8-73 Inuzuka-chô, Shûgakuin, Sakyô-ku, Kyoto 606-8083, Japan (E-mail: ericklaurent@yahoo.co.jp).

[Haworth co-indexing entry note]: "Sexuality and Human Rights: An Asian Perspective." Laurent, Erick. Co-published simultaneously in *Journal of Homosexuality* (Harrington Park Press, an imprint of The Haworth Press, Inc.) Vol. 48, No. 3/4, 2005, pp. 163-225; and: *Sexuality and Human Rights: A Global Overview* (ed: Helmut Graupner, and Phillip Tahmindjis) Harrington Park Press, an imprint of The Haworth Press, Inc., 2005, pp. 163-225. Single or multiple copies of this article are available for a fee from The Haworth Document Delivery Service [1-800-HAWORTH, 9:00 a.m. - 5:00 p.m. (EST). E-mail address: docdelivery@haworthpress.com].

http://www.haworthpress.com/web/JH
© 2005 by The Haworth Press, Inc. All rights reserved.
Digital Object Identifier: 10.1300/J082v48n03_09

often marry and have children shows the elasticity their sexual identity encompasses. Fluidity of sexuality does not really match the Western approach in terms of essentialist categories that have a right to exist. Most Asian societies can be thought of as "tolerant" as long as homosexuality remains invisible. Procreative sexuality can be seen as a social duty, and heterosexual marriage is often not considered incompatible with a "homosexual life." The development of the Internet has even facilitated the encounters while allowing secrecy. Unfortunately, the traditional figures of transgender and transvestites have often been separated from the gay liberation movement. *[Article copies available for a fee from The Haworth Document Delivery Service: 1-800-HAWORTH. E-mail address: <docdelivery@haworthpress.com> Website: <http://www.HaworthPress.com> © 2005 by The Haworth Press, Inc. All rights reserved.]*

KEYWORDS. Human rights, sexual rights, homosexuality, Asia, Asia-Western relations, marriage, sex-education, homophobia, religion, transgender, shamanism

INTRODUCTION

In order to be fully understood, the complex relation between homosexuality and human rights in Asia must be integrated into a broader reflection about the universality of human rights on the one hand, and into cultural and social aspects specific to the Asian cultures considered, on the other hand. In this sense, traditional ideas, and their evolution, about sexuality in general and same-sex relationships and practices in particular, must be considered. As a matter of fact, these conceptions affect, at different levels, lesbian-gay-bisexual-transgender[1] issues, their human rights not being the least of them.

In order to do so, and before giving a panorama of LGBT rights in different Asian countries, generalities related to human rights and Asia will be considered. First, it seems important to discuss the universality of human rights in general, as well as to try to evaluate Western historical influences in Asia, Western impact on Asian modernities.[2] Indeed, homosexuality bears a cultural "coloration": its definition, broadness, social integration and acceptance depend on cultural factors. Secondly, while emphasizing the diversity of Asian cultures and societies, another important question that has to be considered is the existence–or not–of "Asian identities" or of an "Asian model" as far as LGBT issues are concerned, and which could be thought of as in opposition–or not–to "Western identities" or a "Western model." Referring to the much debated question in anthropological spheres of the globalization of culture, one could ask: is there any (pan-)Asian "queer subculture," or else an Asian type/model of a "queer subculture"? At the same time, the relationship between traditional Asian practices of same-sex relations and the present movement of gay liberation, has to be investigated.

HUMAN RIGHTS: A "WESTERN MODEL" IN ASIA?

Are Human Rights Universal?

There is a large body of literature, mainly from "Third World" scholars, that tends to put into question the universality of human rights, as defined through "Western criteria."[3] Lesbian and gay rights cannot be excluded from such a debate.

The definition and the conception of human rights bear a western bias, whether one likes it or not, having been written under American influence, via mainly western concepts. It can be pictured as the outcome of political debates and bargaining, and was thus necessarily based on specific cultural assumptions that still influence discourses about human rights today. Many rights listed in the Universal Declaration of Human Rights are specific rather than general, emerging from modern (Western) ideas: for example, freedom of marriage, right to social security benefits, right to elect political representatives (which means as a prerequisite the existence of political parties, free mass media, general literacy and so on). Not all rights are trans-historical nor trans-cultural. In this sense, human rights do bear a historicity and a topicality: they have a cultural background. In other words, human rights are culture-dependent. This may be one of the reasons why human rights (and lesbian and gay rights) found no real popular acceptance in Asia. As Chang puts it: "While western liberalism does have its followers in Asia, fewer Asians would defend (...) the rights of homosexuals (...)."[4]

This does not mean, of course, that Asian countries deny the universality or the ethical importance of human rights, but they stress the idea of diversity as much as the concept of universality. Stress on diversity can certainly not justify gross violation of human rights, but their universality can be harmful if used to mask the diversity of the Asian realities. One could rather consider that Asian countries and cultures are mostly just emerging from centuries of colonization and/or cultural influences. Truly "Asian" thinking concerning these issues has not yet had the opportunity to fully develop.

In 1993, the "Bangkok Declaration" stated that "while human rights are universal by nature, they must be considered in the context of a dynamic and evolving process of international norm-setting, bearing in mind the significance of national and regional particularities and various historical, cultural and religious backgrounds."

This bears, naturally, important consequences as far as the rights of homosexuals are concerned. Without following the anti-homosexual critics in Asia (voiced among others by Mahathir Mohammed in Malaysia and Lee Kuan Yew in Singapore), one cannot help being concerned with the ways "the West" influenced, nay shaped, social, legal, and cultural aspects of the LGBT liberation movements in different parts of Asia from the 1980s on. This is a very tricky way to put it, for nobody could deny the numerous positive concrete aspects that such ("western-like") campaigns and movements have brought to Asian homosexual communities, but at the same time nobody could deny the negative points either.

The relation to society in non-Western cultures is made of obligations and responsibilities. The language of "right" is a cultural construct imported from "the West." There is always a gap between the right and a set of beliefs, values and social relations that constitute a framework to negotiate one's position in society and culture. Such a set is non-reducible to mere "rights." Nevertheless, for LGBT issues, one needs to speak a sort of "language of power" to be accepted in the age of globalization. It seems nearly impossible, but could this not be done while trying to respect the constellation of beliefs? This is to me the important challenge that the locals have to take up in order to find "Asian ways."

Western Influences in Asia

Since the end of the 1990s, voices have emerged, mainly from anthropologists, to denounce the "imposition" of Western ideas and categories concerning LGBT matters on the peoples and cultures of non-Occidental societies.[5] Western influence can be directly witnessed in the "pride parades," festivals, and mainly in the structure, activities and symbols of LGBT organizations with agendas similar to those found in the West.[6] However, such an influence may not have reached individuals' lives. Asian specificities play a major role in drawing a line, and establishing differences with (and perhaps dissociation from) Western modes.

Besides, the very existence of a "Western model" is contested.[7] Ways of life, political opinions, socioeconomic situations of homosexuals in Europe and the United States show a broad diversity.

The so-called western influences do not necessarily always come directly from "the West." Most gay activists in Asia have been influenced by Western thinking very concretely, through overseas studies. It seems that it is often during these stays that they came out of the closet. For example: Dede Oetomo[8] (Indonesia), Chung To (Hong Kong), Shamshasha (Hong Kong). Likewise, Asian activist organizations themselves did not used to speak negatively about western ideas, influence, or a Western model. Times are changing though. For example, the Indonesian activist Dede Oetomo seems to me rather suspicious about "the West," in the sense that he considers it very important to keep the indigenous traditions concerning "homosexuality," as he said in July 1996 at the Vancouver International Aids Conference. Khan,[9] while recognizing the progress made, is sceptical about the ways an "English speaking urban elite" lead LGBT activities in India and sees the imposition of Western categories on Asia as partly neo-colonialist: "What we, as diasporic Indian 'lesbian' and 'gay' men, often do is to try to fit Indian sexual and cultural histories as well as contemporary behaviour and identities into a Western sexual discourse."[10] In my opinion, this is not necessarily incompatible. The concrete hybrid results, on a pragmatic, theoretical as well as legal level, that one could anticipate from such a mixture of sources are now emerging.[11]

GAY ASIAN IDENTITIES?

Asian Diversity

It is far beyond the scope of this paper to enter into the debate between the economic and political explanations of new forms of homosexuality (that tend to universalism) and the anthropological theories (that tend towards cultural specifics).[12]

What seems important to consider is each country's views towards homosexuality within its own cultural context (languages, religions, etc.) as well as the historical particularities of the Western influence, which usually is of tremendous importance in shaping these views.[13] Asian diversity is by far larger than what one deals with in Europe or North America. But in all Asian cultures considered, gender and sex differences have been marginalized in one way or another, allowing traditional spaces for expression, more or less hidden according to the culture.

Religion has, in general, a stronger influence on beliefs and behaviour than in Western countries. It is impossible however to determine for Asia as a whole whether religious factors favor tolerance towards homosexuality, or slow down the emergence of human rights issues and individual freedom.[14] Each case must be handled and analyzed separately. Here follow some considerations to fight generally accepted ideas and clichés.

- It is usually considered that Confucianism, which culturally influenced a wide area in eastern Asia, is a barrier to human rights. It is, however, difficult to understand why it did not, at the same time, constrain rapid industrial growth in Korea, for example.[15]
- Whereas Buddhist scriptures are rather silent about issues of same-sex relations[16] and whereas practices are rather tolerated by societies (at least in India, China, Thailand and Japan),[17] some homosexual members of the clergy state that homophobia does exist in Buddhism, as well as misogyny, mainly because it appears to be male-centered.[18] However, this may be interpreted as more the reflection of society than merely of religious background.
- Though Islam has a reputation of intolerance towards homosexuality, the reality might be somewhat different.[19] The Qur'an has been interpreted as condemning homosexuality, but no real punishment is stated for same-sex practices, as opposed to heterosexual relations. They do not seem to represent an abomination offensive to Allah. Though no uniform legal position towards same-sex relations can be found in Islamic countries, where societies are very diverse, most regard sodomy as illegal. Islamic societies show a certain "tolerance" towards same-sex relations, provided no claims for acceptance of a homosexual way of life are made, and provided no competition with family responsibilities is at stake. Recently, groups of Muslim queers have emerged, struggling for acceptance and tolerance among Muslims.[20] The first Muslim LGBT conference was held in Boston in 1998, the second in New York in 1999, to reflect on the complexities facing many queer Muslims.[21]

Asian Traditions of Homoeroticism

When one now tries to look at the situation in Asia before the Western presence, which still has some influence today, two facts appear clearly. First, most Asian countries and regions had, and often still have, a tradition of tolerance towards traditional same-sex feelings and practices, culturally determined and accepted by society. There is little overt anti-gay hostility, like one might find in "the West." Secondly, the traditional place of transgender people in society is much more important than in western countries, being recognized by society and bearing a precisely defined place in the culture. Transgender persons appear relatively freely and often on TV shows, at festivals, as guest lecturers, and so on.

There were traditions in most Asian cultures before the Western presence that could be interpreted as "queer-like." or gender non-conformity, for instance in the entertainment world, or bearing a medical or religious function. In certain cultures, "gay" is even seen as a new category, not replacing the traditional ones, but existing beside them. Moral condemnations of homosexuality did not occur through Asian traditional discourses. With the exceptions of Catholicism in the Philippines and Islam, religions in Asia have no theoretical objections to same-sex relations and love. Most European travelers, from the 16th century on, have left records stating "institutionalized pedophilia," "abominable crimes," etc. Many Asian men would engage in sexual encounters with men without being defined as gay.[22] They sometimes do not even refer to sexual relations with men as "sex," but just as "play," sex occurring only with women.[23] This can be related to these traditions of homoerotic relationships and practices. The separation between gay and straight encounters is not as clear cut as in "the West," the moral stigma not as violent, provided the social formalities are respected and gay encounters remain (an open) secret. These traditions do not need to be romanticized, but what can certainly be said is that they have been erased or diminished under Western influences (upon medical, and sometimes religious reasons) from the end of the 19th century. In this sense, homophobia can be interpreted indeed as a by-product of Western cultural expansion.

The general picture of the situation of gays and lesbians in Asia seems to look like the situation in "the West" some years ago: organizations are small and have little power; they are gender-segregated; their publications are few; public discourse about homosexuals and their rights is very limited; the media are far from being helpful, often unaware of homosexuals' legal and social problems and sometimes hostile. Even if Western influence shaped the general outline of LGBT worlds in Asia,[24] there are nevertheless cultural specificities which have not yet been sufficiently investigated. The emergence of an "Asian pattern" could be on its way, trying to make the most of, and at the same time coping with and reactualizing, the traditional ways of dealing with same-sex relations.

METHODOLOGY

Some problems concerning research sources need to be mentioned. Scholarly documents on homosexuality and homosexual communities in Asia are almost nonexistent. Some doctoral theses are certainly being written now (mainly in Australia, the United States and Japan), or will be in the next few years, but information is unfortunately not always easily accessible, even on the Internet. LGBT organizations exist in almost every Asian country–sometimes officially recognized, sometimes secret–but the problem is they do not share much! Many of them still live in a paranoid-like atmosphere of suspicion regarding the sharing of information. I had a rate of response of about 2 to 3% from those local organizations. Moreover, most of the material is not available in western languages, making the access the more difficult.

Many organizations specializing in human rights do not take into account the rights of LGBT in the scope of their activities. Most, such as the Asian Human Rights Commission and Human Rights Watch, do not even mention it. It seems difficult to push human rights linked to sexual orientation in regions where people have few political rights, have no food, where there is war, and so on. This does not excuse the lack of concern, but it partially explains it. Likewise, and this may not only be limited to Asia, even for the United Nations, the concept of "minorities" essentially refers to "national, ethnic and religious" minorities. For example, in the document published in 2002, "Racism, racial discrimination, xenophobia, and all forms of discrimination" (E/CN.4/2002/21), sexual minorities or discrimination on the basis of sexual orientation is never mentioned.[25] Also, Asia is often ignored in research on human rights by LGBT organizations and international NGOs. For instance, in their 1999 "Antidiscrimination Legislation–a worldwide summary," ILGHRC does not present the situations in Asian countries and regions. And most of the documents posted on the Net lack basic information at an acceptable academic standard (dates of journals, papers, full names of authors, etc).

THE SITUATION COUNTRY BY COUNTRY

One can find in Asia a wide range of different legal situations. Laws in most of the countries do not address directly the question of homosexuality. There has been recently some improvement on the law, but not really in practice. The legal status of same-sex relations ranges from no legal discrimination (in countries like Japan, Indonesia, the Philippines, Thailand, Cambodia, and Vietnam)–even though homosexuality is sometimes repressed (as in China and Taiwan)–to legal punishment (Nepal, Bhutan, Laos, India, Singapore), to more than 10 years in jail (Sri Lanka, Brunei, Malaysia, Bangladesh). Nowhere in Asia is homophobia considered a crime.

In nearly all Asian countries sexuality tends to be a private matter. There are gay and lesbian movements, gay and lesbian magazines (most of them of the commercial gay "beefcake" or "effete" type), and gay and lesbian bars (most of them hidden) in almost all Asian countries. Local academics have written articles and books about LGBT issues in India, Indonesia, Singapore, Korea, Japan, etc. Most of the time, academic publications are (still) written by foreigners. There are a lot of gay Asian sites on the Web, mainly from Japan, Korea, the Philippines, India, etc. Most of them seem to be commercial or gallery sites.

Amnesty International, after having recognized individuals imprisoned on the basis of their sexual orientation in 1991, opened branches in the Philippines in 2001 and in Thailand in 2002, both with LGBT sections. The first gay parade in Asia was held in June 1994, in Manila, commemorating the 25th anniversary of the Stonewall Riots. It has become an annual event. From 1996, some gay stores (book stores, clothing, etc.) gradually began to open in several cities in Asia (Hong Kong, Bangkok, Taipei, Manila, Tôkyô).

In South-East Asia and China at least, drug injection and heterosexual sex (mainly through prostitution) are seen as the main cause of AIDS.[26] It is not often associated with homosexuality. In Singapore, in 2000, homosexual sexual transmission accounts for only 5% of the transmission of AIDS, heterosexual sex accounting for 86% (Ministry of Health, 22.11.2000). In Indonesia, most of the cases result from heterosexual contact. In the Philippines, only 5% of the transmission occurs through homosexual intercourse, 40% through heterosexual activities (mainly prostitution) and 55% via drugs.[27] Consequently, even where homosexuality is not socially accepted, some groups have been able to work through their involvement with AIDS, and thus occupy a certain social space.

India

Socio-Cultural Background

Hinduism recognizes the existence of "third sex" persons, showing a rich culture of alternative sexuality, without condemning homosexual behaviour. In the *Kama Sutra* "men who prefer men" are referred to as "the third nature," without moral condemnation. This text also clearly indicates the presence of egalitarian (some scholars' translations state "marriage") same-sex relationships between (urban) males in pre-modern India.[28] In classical Indian literature, "third sex" persons are generally associated with prostitution and dance, and have a low social status. From the 12th to 17th centuries, when Muslims came to dominate most parts of India, iconography, carvings and poetry were often explicitly homoerotic.[29]

Homophobia, introduced in the nineteenth century, draws on a Victorian version of Judeo-Christian discourse.

There are several types of "third gender" people in Indian traditions who still are culturally relevant. The *hijras*–transvestite, transgender, passive homosexuals, "third gender" who are sometimes castrated[30] as a religious sacrifice–are often beggars (they are forbidden to take regular jobs), sometimes sex workers, and also earn their living by providing entertainment at weddings. They come from all parts of India and all religious and ethnic backgrounds. Many Indians believe they have occult powers, fearing them. Some *hijras* take advantage of this to extort money. The unofficial estimations of their population vary from 0.5 to 5 million. With British rule, *hijras* lost their right to property and adoption. They live in communal households, bearing strict rules and organized according to seniority.[31]

There are also uncastrated effeminate males–*jankhas* or *zenanas*–receptive homosexuals who cross-dress and may perform as singers and dancers. The *jogta* are "male temple prostitutes," whose tradition in Hinduism is prevalent in western India. They are offered as young boys to the deity Renuka, and often exploited by priests for several types of work at the temples. A *jogta* always dresses up as a woman and wears married women's accessories. Unlike the *hijras*, they can marry women and lead a family life.

The *shivshakti*, mainly found in Southern India, are uncastrated men who were married as boys to a specific god or goddess, sold because of poverty or given as an offering. They dress and behave like women. They worship the *shivlinga*, the symbol of male and female genitals, perform religious rituals, and are also used for sexual purposes.

Display of affection between men is socially accepted, as well as sharing the same bed for adolescent school friends, provided an alternative gender identity is not adopted. "Passive" homosexual encounters are not related to a loss of manhood. Masculinity is rather asserted through marriage and fatherhood. Marriage means offspring. Without a son, one cannot be released from the chain of reincarnation.[32]

Legal Situation

"Carnal intercourse against the order of nature with any man, woman or animal" is criminalized under section 377 of the Indian Penal Code. While this applies to men, it has also been used to prosecute women[33] as well. The Penal Code considers, as an "explanation," that penetration is sufficient to constitute carnal intercourse, being an attempt *de jure* to criminalize sodomy, but *de facto* also stigmatizing homosexuality. It has also been invoked to condemn male-male fellatio and intercrural sex. However, section 377 does not expressly mention homosexuality per se.[34] People risk, under section 377, up to 10 years in prison. Introduced by the Indian Law Commission into the Indian Penal Code in October 1860, section 377 has also been used for blackmail and extortion. There have been only thirty cases in the High Court or the Supreme Court related to section 377. The current usage is by the police to sexually harass and blackmail gay men and intimidate women. Most cases involve the rape of children by an adult. Among the cases involving adults, the issue of consent has been taken into account only once, in a married couple.[35]

In April 1994, a high rate of AIDS, as well as a common practice of "homosexual activities," were discovered among prisoners. After the refusal of authorities to distribute condoms in prisons, a petition was filed in the High Court of Dehli, against the state and local administrations, requesting section 377 be deemed unconstitutional, illegal and void. The case is still pending. Moreover, in December 2001, activists from the Naz Foundation began a court case challenging the "anti-homosexual criminal law." In June 2002, the government was examining the legal, ethical and social aspects of decriminalizing homosexual acts among consenting adults.

The treatment of sexual minorities in India was denounced on April 11, 2002, by the United Nations Commission on Human rights, after Indian lawyer and gay activist Aditya Bondyopadhyay made a speech at an NGO briefing of the Commission. Nevertheless, a marriage between a *hijra* and a "man" has been recognized by Chennai High Court.[36]

The Situation of LGBT

Persons who engage in homosexual behaviour are excluded from the military or are liable to up to 7 years of detention.[37] State-supported oppression and persecution of sexual minorities have been reported. Several "affairs" have put issues concerning LGBT and their rights on the front pages of newspapers. In December 1998, violent demonstrations occurred against the screening of Deepa Mehta's movie *Fire* depicting lesbian love, orchestrated by the Hindu fundamentalist group Shev Sena. This incident urged the creation of the collective Campaign for Lesbian Rights in 1999. As well, Sahayog is an organization working since 1992 on AIDS education in Uttar Pradesh. They published in September 1999 "Aids and Us," a pamphlet in which sexual acts are explicitly described. By April 20 the following year, their offices were attacked by a mob, and 11 staff members arrested, 5 for "breach of peace" (under sections 107, 116, 151 of the Penal Code–but released on April 25), and 6 for "obscene publications" and "public mischief" (under the sections 292, 293, 505). On May 4, they were handcuffed and paraded through the market, and on May 9, the National Security Act was invoked, usually intended to deal with terrorists and smugglers. The Sahayog office was still closed by September 2001.[38] In Lucknow (Uttar Pradesh), on July 7, 2001, the police raided and sealed the offices of Naz Foundation and the Bharosa Trust, two NGOs working on AIDS interventions with "men who have sex with men," and arrested four workers, charging them with conspiring to commit "unnatural sexual acts" under section 377, as well as with selling obscene books under section 292. Sections 2 and 3 of the Indecent Representation of Women Act (1986) and section 60 of the Copyright Act (1957) were also invoked because safer-sex educational materials found on their premises were considered to be pornography. They were beaten, and stayed in captivity for 45 days before being granted bail by the High Court. Activists and attorneys who attempted to intervene were threatened by the Lucknow police. The offices of the two NGOs were sealed until mid-September 2001. In addition, police recently began to raid cruising areas (e.g., in Hyderabad) and arrested homosexual men, or forced them to provide them with sexual favors, sometimes turning to gang rape.[39]

Chandini, a 22-year-old *hijra* died in mysterious circumstances on December 1, 2002. According to her husband, she set herself on fire when he discovered her *hijra* identity and threatened to reveal it to his parents. According to a fact-finding team, there is evidence that the husband knew the identity of his wife at the time of marriage. Some months after their marriage, she fled to her previous community and her guru because of her husband's violence and constant demands for money. The local police refused to register the complaint of Chandini's guru, saying they do not recognize the *hijra* community or its relationships. The police concluded that Chandini had committed suicide.

Today there are organizations, helplines, newsletters, health resources, social spaces and drop-in centers for LGBT in most major cities in India. On the other hand, bars, discos and clubs where sexual minorities might socially interact are being suppressed by the state. "Dating services" recently appeared on the Net with the goal of helping lesbians and gays find a marriage of convenience.

Compared to other Asian countries, the rate of HIV-positive and AIDS infected persons in the population of "men who have sex with men" is very high, estimated by the Humsafar Trust to be 1 in 5. The fact that a large number of men who do not self-identify as "gay" or homosexual have sex with men does not help in engaging preventive and educative action. According to a 1992 survey, 12% of unmarried men and 8% of married men reported that they had their first sexual experience with a man.[40]

According to a 1983 survey,[41] 38% of the female students interviewed reported that they had their first sexual experience with a woman. Still, lesbians often face oppression and violence, including within their family when they express their sexuality, for example, when they refuse to marry. Sangini helpline for lesbians was created in 1997, under the umbrella of the Naz Foundation, Aanchal helpline in 1999, and then Sakhi, the first lesbian collective, in Delhi. The lesbian community is not as united as the gay community and their movement is very fragile.

India's first-ever public "walk" of gays and lesbians took place in July 1999 in Calcutta. Since then, a series of public gatherings has occurred. For example, in July 2001 in Bangalore, the "Coalition for Sexual Minority Rights" organized a public meeting entitled "Breaking the Silence," providing a forum for LGBT, which more than 200 people attended.

Sri Lanka

Socio-Cultural Background

Despite its largely Buddhist background, Sri Lanka seems to be quite a conservative and prudish society. An editorial in the state-run *Sunday Observer* stated that until colonization, same-sex relations were considered so natural they never were a matter of controversy. It follows: "the challenge is to recognize our own Sri Lankan sexual nature (. . .) to normalize our island society (. . .)."[42]

Legal Situation

Section 365a of the Penal Code, introduced by British colonial rulers, criminalizes same-sex sexual activities. The existence of lesbianism was not acknowledged by the 1883 Penal Code, but lesbian acts were added to the formerly male-only statute in 1995. Homosexual acts are punishable up to 12 years imprisonment.[43]

The Situation of LGBT

There have been no prosecutions under section 365a since 1950. The law is mainly used by the police to blackmail homosexuals, sometimes forcing them to have sex.[44]

The gay rights group "Companions on a Journey" (and its president Sherman de Rose, a former Catholic brother) filed a complaint with the Sri Lanka Press Council after *The Insland* published a letter in August 1999, condemning lesbians and calling on police to "let loose convicted rapists" among them as a punishment. The complaint was dismissed with costs on June 2, 2000, by the Council, whose five members (journalists and lawyers) were motivated in their ruling by the perception that "lesbianism itself is an act of sadism and salacious," it is "illegal, immoral and obscene," and that lesbians are "spreading social menace in society." They also invoked the protection of the family, which "basically consists of a man and a woman."[45] The case has been taken to a higher court by de Rose.

There are no clubs and bars where gay people can meet freely[46] in Sri Lanka. The first-ever gay dance party was organized by "Sri Lankan Gay Friends" and "Companions on a Journey" in January 2000, in a hotel on the western coast of the country. A survey by Silva et al. revealed that 50% of the interviewed male university students in Sri Lanka have had their first sexual experience with a man.[47]

"Companions on a Journey," funded by the Dutch government, was created in 1995. Members of the staff were threatened and attacked when they first called a press conference to announce their existence. People stoned the offices and 3 members, including the president, were assaulted. They now boast 1400 members and branches all over the country. They also run a drop-in center in Colombo. Thanks to a wide network of associations dealing with human rights issues and activists, they press for the decriminalization of homosexuality. "Women's Support Group" was founded in 1999 as an autonomous body within "Companions on a Journey," working at developing a community of support for lesbians and bisexual women, as well as at promoting their rights. In

June 1999, the second National Gay Conference organized by Companions on a Journey attracted 60 gay men, who did not hide. In December the same year, the first Lesbian Convention was held in Colombo.

Nepal

Socio-Cultural Background

Hinduism is the official religion of Nepal, but Buddhism has an important influence on everyday life and beliefs. Public display of affection between men seems perfectly acceptable, whereas heterosexual display of affection is frowned upon. Nevertheless, same-sex relationships do not seem to be accepted by the general population, bringing discrimination and potential violence towards LGBT people.[48]

Legal Situation

According to IGLHRC, homosexual acts are criminalized for men and women, and given life imprisonment; but only for men according to ILGA, the case of women not being mentioned (a legal situation similar to India). According to the United Nations Human Rights System,[49] on the contrary, homosexuality is not mentioned in the law.

The Situation of LGBT

Torture, arbitrary detention, and disappearances are widely mentioned as pertaining to the treatment of LGBT in Nepal. Foreigners can be expelled for committing homosexual acts (ILGA, IGLHRC). In July 1998, 2 women (24 and 16 years old) were married in the Kawalparasi district. After being reported by their parents, they were first arrested but then released on the grounds that there are no laws against same-sex marriage in Nepal. IGLHRC forwarded an action alert on a specific case in May 2000, relating to two young lesbians (18 and 17 years old), asking for their protection against potential mob violence. A "Nepal Queer Society" was founded in Kathmandu in 1993, but they have virtually no contact outside the country.

Bangladesh

Socio-Cultural Background

Bangladesh is predominantly a Muslim society. Male prostitutes are available in towns, most of them homeless or coming from a working class background, although the social range of their clients seems quite wide. In rural areas, sex between men is generally considered something young people do for fun; and it seems quite common even after marriage, bearing no implications on sexual identity.[50] As elsewhere in Asia, family is a very important structural unit of society. Social pressure to marry is very strong.

Legal Situation

Homosexual acts are criminalized for men and women (up to 10 years of detention) under article 377 of the Penal Code, as well as by the Islamic *sharia*.

The Situation of LGBT

Very little information is available. In September 1999, police clamped down on homosexuals in Dhaka, arresting fifteen men, describing them as "perverts" on the charge sheet. They were accused of "public nuisance," fined, and all released.[51]

The Bandhu Social Welfare Society was founded in October 1996, with technical assistance from the Naz Foundation of India. The acceptance of LGBT in Bangladesh seems to be much more difficult than in Bengali society across the border in India. Issues regarding homosexuality are usually denied, or at best ignored, by the media.

Mongolia

Socio-Cultural Background

Mongolian society seems very conservative, especially regarding sexual matters, and homosexuality bears a very negative image. No information about it can be found in libraries or book shops. The existence of transgender people, however, seems to be attested. They are called "*maning*," which seems to be a true Mongolian word; gays are usually called "*gomo*" which is derived from Russian. Some people publicly live as *maning* and seem to be more or less accepted by society.[52]

Legal Situation

Homosexuality is not mentioned in the law, but the Penal Code prohibits, under section 113, "immoral gratification of sexual desires," which is used to prosecute LGBT people.[53]

Tavilan (literally "destiny"), the first Mongolian human rights association for LGBT people, was formed in April 1999 (with 22 members), in response to police harassment. They opened a small office in downtown Ulaan Bataar, and are active at trying to protect and promote the rights of gays and lesbians in Mongolia and to develop connections outside the country.[54] The first ever hotline for LGBT people in Mongolia was created in November 2000, thanks to financial assistance from the National Aids Foundation, and with the cooperation of Tavilan.[55]

China

Socio-Cultural Background

Historically, during the later part of the Zhou Dynasty (722-221 B.C.), homosexuality appeared as a component of the sex life of the rulers in many states. Male and female homosexual relations were unexceptional and did not require justification. During the Han Dynasty (206 B.C.-9 A.D.), bisexual or exclusively homosexual emperors ruled China for 150 years. Imperial male favorites are mentioned and discussed in official records. In post-Han China, homosexuality spread in other classes, and male prostitution flourished, celebrated but also denigrated by poets.[56] By the Ming dynasty (1368-1644), homosexuality had attained a high degree of representation in the arts and society in general.[57] In Fujian province (South-East China coast), a form of marriage between men developed that could last for many years and was usually terminated for procreational purposes. In Ancient China, such same-sex relations were very rarely egalitarian. Sexual domination reflected social domination. The Qing Dynasty (1644-1911) did not fundamentally change the high profile of homosexuality, male actor-prostitutes dominating the stages and male brothels flourishing. Nevertheless, the Neo-Confucian influence extended to any form of sexuality outside marriage. For example, Emperor Kang Xi promulgated a law in 1690 against consensual homosexuality as part of a series of laws designed to strengthen the family. A very rich specialized vocabulary refers to same-sex relations and behaviour, coming mainly from poetry.

Under Western influence, and the uncritical acceptance of Western science and medicine that viewed homosexuality as pathological, China shifted from a relative tolerance to open hostility towards homosexuality within a few generations. In 1949, homosexuality was declared by the Communists a sign of bourgeois decadence. Gay- and lesbian-friendly bars were closed. Oppression intensified during the Cultural Revolution (1966-76), and homosexuals were punished by re-education in labor camps. Thousands of gays and lesbians were publicly humiliated, tortured, exiled to the countryside, given electroshock therapy, and sometimes executed.[58]

Religion exerts much less substantial influence in China than in most other Asian or Western countries. Buddhism never really played a negative role regarding homosexuality. The familial and social pressure to marry appears to be very strong, in accordance of the importance given to the family and having heirs. As a 19-year-old Shenzhen gay bar's host puts it, in order to explain his plan to marry in the near future: "Marriage is a part of one's life." It seems more important than "liberation" to a lot of Chinese gay men.[59]

The term mostly used to refer to LGBT people, especially in Hong Kong and Taiwan, is *tongzhi*, a traditional Chinese term meaning "friend" or "partner," adopted since the late 1980s. It seems to be markedly used to resist Western labels like "gay" and "lesbian."[60]

Legal Situation

It seems that on two occasions in the past, same-sex behaviour has been the target of legislation. In the early 10th century, under the influence of Confucian moralists, male prostitutes would receive 100 strokes of a bamboo rod and pay a fine, which can however be considered lenient regarding other legal penalties at that time. This law quickly became a dead letter. In 1690, a law prohibiting consensual homosexuality was decreed but was rarely enforced.

At present, there is no law against homosexuality per se, but homosexuals are sometimes prosecuted under the "hooliganism" law (article 106 of the Criminal Law), that is, "sodomizing children, forced sodomy of adolescents, the use of violence or force, multiple partner acts of sodomy,"[61] which was a part of the first criminal legislation enacted in 1979.[62] The law is unclear and applied in different ways according to the cases. Until the 1980s, homosexuals faced up to 10 years, and sometimes life, imprisonment but the situation eased after the mid-80s.

Chengdu, the capital of Sichuan, is the first city in China to adopt legislation against HIV-positive people, preventing them from marrying, and ordering police to test "high risk groups" (prostitutes and drug users). Such people are banned from a number of professions, such as kindergarten teacher and surgeon. The ban on using public swimming pools and public baths was lifted after a press campaign. China requires foreign applicants for long-term residence to test free of HIV.[63]

The Situation of LGBT

In 1999, in a verdict condemning author Fang Gang who outed a manager of a dance hall, Beijing's Xuanwu District Court stated that homosexuality is an "abnormal sexual behaviour and is not acceptable to the public." It seems to be the first time that a mainland court ruled on the nature of homosexuality.[64]

Several activists and researchers have suffered harassment by police and authorities. In 1985, Da Dan of the Nanjin Railways Medical Institute committed suicide, after he was asked to come to the police because of his research on homosexuality. Activist Wan Yanhai was detained nearly one month in 2000 by the police under the suspicion of "leaking state secrets." He was released after confessing to the charge.

In Beijing, on May 14, 1993, the first "homosexual salon" was shut down by authorities, arguing it was spreading erroneous points of view by advocating homosexuality. Massive police crackdowns are also reported to have happened between August and December 1994, in several places where gay people meet in Beijing. As part of a campaign against prostitution, drug and vice (July-September 2000), police raided a gay health spa in the southern city of Guandzhou, arresting 37 men, the biggest detention against gays. They were not arrested for homosexuality, but because the spa charged them for sexual services. Generally speaking, police raids are more financially than politically motivated.[65]

In December 1996, 200 people from all over the country gathered in Hong Kong for a "*Tongzhi* Conference." After discussing a number of *tongzhi*-related issues, the participants concluded that it was not necessary to imitate Anglo-Saxon model of LGBT liberation movement. Chinese LGBT tend, nevertheless, to romanticize the western world for its supposed freedom and lack of homophobia. They published a manifesto,[66] stressing the Chinese tradition of tolerance towards same-sex love and the advantages of exchanges among *tongzhi*.

Although there are still only a few bars in China where homosexuals can meet, the situation of LGBT people was eased in the late 1970s, with the ascent of Deng Xiaoping to power. It became easier to publish articles and organize seminars, as well as to receive foreign publications. Scholars, like psychologists, began to write about homosexuality in a positive way.[67] Through the 1980s and 1990s, Internet and media coverage played a significant role in building a gay community and in making its existence known. There are more than 300 gay Web sites in China, although negative consequences sometimes arise, in the form of a public condemnation.

Gary Wu, one of China's first gay activists, traveled to 15 cities around the country in 1994 for a survey of gay life in order to make a TV show, with the support of a Taiwanese television company. It has been aired by a Hong Kong TV station. He brought his documentary "Comrades" about gay life in China to the San Francisco Gay and Lesbian Film Festival in 1996.[68]

Because of the importance of the family ties and marriage, there seems to be a gulf between rural and urban gays in China.[69] Many LGBT people migrate to cities like Shenzhen, close to Hong Kong, because life seems freer there, and where some bars have recently opened. But even in big cities, the norm seems to be to get married and play straight at work. Keeping up appearances and continuing family life are regarded as much more important than self-expression. Gay Web sites may function as a kind of virtual therapy for rural homosexuals.

"Men's World," a discussion group for gay men, was founded in Beijing in November 1992, followed by other groups and hotlines in other cities. It was banned by the government in May 1993 because of extensive media coverage of their distribution of condoms in parks. Many organizations work from abroad. China Rainbow was founded in the USA in 1996. The "Chinese Society for the Study of Sexual Minorities" was founded in the USA as well, in 1997, by a group of scholars and professionals. Its focus is information dissemination, mainly via Internet, in order to counter prejudice against sexual minorities. International Chinese Comrades Organization, a non-profit political group, was founded in the USA in 1997, to provide information to Chinese gays.

Lesbians are much less visible than gay men. The first lesbian feature film, *Fish and Elephant* (2001) by director Li Yu, won a prize at the Berlin Film Festival, and was shown at more than 70 film festivals around the world, but was screened only once in China. The first gay and lesbian festival, where it was programmed, was shut down.[70] In April 2001, the Chinese Psychiatric Association removed homosexuality from the list of mental disorders, and re-categorized it under "identity crisis."[71]

Hong Kong

Legal Situation

As a British territory, Hong Kong adopted many British laws, including the criminalization of sodomy. Since Hong Kong returned to China in 1997, after 156 years of British colonial rule, the Government expressed its will to tackle discrimination issues through public education rather than legislation. Laws to tackle discrimination based on sexual orientation meet strong local opposition.

The law regarding buggery (anal intercourse) was first introduced to Hong Kong by the British government in 1861. Although the Sexual Offense Act was passed in 1967 by the British Parliament, decriminalizing buggery and gross indecency between adult males in private, no such law was introduced in Hong Kong. Until 1991, section 49 of the Offenses Against the Person Ordinance punished buggery with a maximum sentence of life imprisonment. Hong Kong became the only place in Asia to legalize homosexual acts in private between consenting adults in 1991 under the Criminal Amendment Bill.[72] The age of consent is 16 for heterosexual and same-sex female sexual intercourse, and 21 for sex between males.

The Situation of LGBT

The United Nations voiced concerns about the failure of Hong Kong SAR to prohibit discrimination on the basis of sexual orientation and age in 2001[73] and activist groups are strongly lobbying for the government to pass an anti-discrimination law.[74]

The first gay group at Hong Kong University, *Tongzhi Culture Society*, although recognized by the student union in February 1999, has seen its posters ripped off and its magazines dumped in rubbish bins.[75]

After the Equal Opportunities Commission was set up, it received four complaints in 1998, three in 1999 and fourteen in 2000 about homosexual issues. Five gay rights activists, led by Tommy Chen, filed a complaint with the Equal Opportunities Commission in July 2002, arguing the law violates Hong Kong's civil rights laws by discriminating against gay men.[76]

Pink Triangle was the first underground gay newsletter, founded in 1980 by Samshasha (pseudonym). He also published the first gay liberation book in China, *Twenty-Five Questions About Homosexuality*, in 1981, and wrote in 1984 the most extensive account so far on LGBT issues in China, *The History of Homosexuality in China* [in Chinese].[77] Since the decriminalization of male homosexual acts in 1991, Hong Kong's *Tongzhi* Movement progressed and the tolerance of the general public has increased. The number of gay-oriented bars, discos, cafes, saunas, magazines and bookshops increased too, even considered "trendy" among young people. However, despite improvement, gay and lesbian bashing continues to occur.

In December 1996, 200 people from all over the country gathered in Hong Kong for a *"Tongzhi* Conference." The second was held in February 1998. The first Hong Kong Gay Pride, in which more than 20 gay and lesbian groups participated, was organized on June 18, 1999.[78]

    The *Chi Heng Foundation* was founded in 1998 by Chung To, aimed at eliminating discrimination on the ground of sexual orientation and promoting AIDS prevention. *Queer Sisters* set up a counseling hotline for women in April 1996. The group *Satsanga* organizes workshops in schools, promoting awareness about sexual orientation and AIDS-related problems. In 1993, "Contacts," the first gay publication in Hong Kong, was founded by a British expatriate, providing news and information about gay life in the city.

    At present, Hong Kong has about 20 *tongzhi* organizations, and many exclusively *tonghzi* bars, discos, karaoke lounges, etc. The Hong Kong Queer Film Festival has been held every year since 1998. Recently, gay bookshops have even been opening in trendy locations, on ground level in busy streets. Hong Kong's four gay bookstores promote their wares with display advertisements in weekly magazines. Some sports clubs (volleyball, tennis, etc.) for LGBT have recently emerged, as well as a radio station "Gay Station."[79]

Taiwan

Socio-Cultural Background

    Like mainland China and Hong Kong, the pressure to marry is very strong in Taiwanese society, its goal being procreation and the constitution of a family. Taiwan society exhibits a hybridized form of Confucianism, Taoism and Buddhism. Gay sex is not a real problem for most, as long as it does not interfere with marriage.[80]

Legal Situation

    The Martial Law imposed by the Chiang Kai-shek regime in 1949, and lifted in 1987, was strictly anti-sex. Gays were constantly arrested in cruising areas, and bars were often raided by the police. Transgressions of sex-gender codes were not tolerated, and people not wearing appropriate outfits were demonized and sometimes arrested.[81]

    Homosexuality is legal but repressed. Legal age of consent for homosexual, and heterosexual, acts is 16 years. There has never been a sodomy law in Taiwan, due to the Japanese colonialist legacy,[82] nor systematic persecution of homosexuals. Until a 1999 amendment that includes same-sex intercourse without consent as one type of rape, rape only applied to acts between members of the opposite sex.

On the other hand, there still exists no anti-discrimination law for LGBT people.[83] The Taiwan Association for Human Rights speaks of a "fairly powerless group... largely unrecognized. Without legal status it is difficult for homosexuals to demand and fight for the rights to live freely."

While in May 2002 Taiwan said that it will drop the ban on homosexuals in the Military Police, the death-penalty may be required when homosexual acts occur during service in the army.[84]

In June 2001, the Ministry of Justice produced a new draft of the basic human rights law. Article 6 stipulates that gays and lesbians shall be allowed to have families (although not a legal marriage) and legally adopt children.[85]

The Situation of LGBT

Police raids are frequent in gay meeting places, such as parks or bars. Although same-sex marriage is not legal, the blessing of five homosexual couples (8 women and 2 men) was arranged in October 2000. In November 1996, a marriage between a gay Taiwanese writer and his American partner was held amid media fanfare, but the marriage was not officially registered.[86]

According to queer Asians, Taiwan seems to be one of the most gay-friendly countries in Asia, along with Japan and Thailand. Today Taiwan has the most open gay scene in the Chinese world. It has a monthly glossy magazine *G&L*, several radio talk shows, a lot of gay books, the beginnings of political organizations and more than 250 Taiwanese gay and lesbian sites on the Net.[87] The first lesbian bar in Taiwan opened in 1985 in Taipei.

The first Chinese-speaking lesbian organization in Asia, "Women Chih Chian" was established in February 1990 in Taiwan. In 1993, "Gay Chat," focusing on AIDS and safer sex, was founded at Taiwan University. In 2000, "Taiwan Gay Hotline" was the first national gay organization to register with the Ministry of Interior Affairs, after it had first been rejected in 1999, on the ground that "it is not proper to advocate gay relationships the formation of a gay community center and the provision of gay peer counseling and assistance could possibly have ill effects" [sic]. In 2000, the "Taiwan Gay and Lesbian Human Rights Association," founded the same year by Jan Jin-yen, was the first to be recognized by the Bureau of Social Affairs of the Kaohsiung City Government.[88]

In 1995, "Gay Sunshine," Taiwan's first publisher specializing in gay themes, was established.[89] *G&L*, founded in 1996, was the first Chinese-language commercial magazine for homosexuals in the world, aimed at helping society take gay issues seriously. In 1993, the first "Homosexual Film Festival" was planned in Taiwan, by Edward Lam, a Hong Kong drama and film artist. In 2001, the 4th annual Chinese Gay and Lesbian Conference was held in Taiwan, organized by the Taiwan Gay and Lesbians Human Rights Association.

The first Taiwan Gay Parade festival was held on June 29, 1997. The city of Taipei hosted a "Movement of Gay Citizens" in September 2000, with a "Rainbow Outdoor Fair" and a "Taipei Gay International Forum" including foreign gay activists. It also listed the "Gay Citizens Movement" in its annual budget plan. Gay activists were received by President Chen in September 2000; he then recognized the rights to safety, education, equality in the workplace for LGBT.

Taiwan's parliamentary election in December 2001, had for the first time two openly gay candidates, although they were not backed by any party. One of them, James Jan, is a long-standing campaigner for gay rights.[90]

Burma

Socio-Cultural Background

Although Burma is predominantly a Buddhist society, it is considered very hostile to homosexuality. Traditional transgender, called *acault*, cross-dressing and adopting cross-gender behaviour, are seen as being a variation of female. Man having sex with them regard these acts as heterosexual-like. *Acaults* play a role in society as shamans, seers and dancers in ceremonies. They are believed to be possessed by and "spiritually married" to a spirit who imparts femininity on them.[91]

Legal Situation

Under section 377 of the colonial-era Penal Code, "unnatural offences" are prohibited (for men) and may bring 10 years imprisonment as well as a fine. Under section 33A of the Law for the Student Army, any man or woman engaged in same-sex relations in the military is liable to one year in prison and dismissal.

One of the largest organizations of Burmese democracy activists in exile (the All Burma Students' Democratic Front) voted, in April 2001, to decriminalize consensual same-sex relations, in the legal code of what is seen as a virtual parallel government.

Thailand

Socio-Cultural Background

As in many other Asian countries, it is important in Thailand that a person has a spouse and a family, and behaves and dresses "properly" (like a "real" man/woman) in public. However, Thai society is generally tolerant of both transgenderism and homosexuality. Generally speaking, transsexuals are loved and admired by Thai people, esthetically judged for their beauty and performance. They are also often the target of sexual violence on the part of relatives or teachers.[92]

Traditionally, Thai discourse does not distinguish between gender and sex, using the sole term *phet* to refer to biological sex, gender and sexuality. The category *kathoey*, traditionally referring to hermaphrodites, transvestites, transsexuals, homosexual men, is now restricted to cross-dressing men and male-to-female transsexuals. Their number is estimated between 10,000 and 300,000. This feminine male who has sex with men is clearly articulated socially and the smallest village seems to have at least one. There is also a strong tradition of transgender shamanism in Thailand, still surviving in some rural areas. They were also used as sexual partners for young bachelors, because traditionally young women had to stay untouched until marriage.[93]

The 1960s saw the emergence of gay identified men. "Gay" has been borrowed from the West, but a distinction has been made between insertive "gay kings" and receptive "gay queens," and sometimes "gay quing" to cover the notion of sexual versatility.[94] This does not mean "gay" has the same "gay vs straight" binary meaning as in English, but is rather used to avoid the label *kathoey* and its feminine association.

Legal Situation

In the early 1900s, King Chulalongkorn criminalized male and female homosexuality as being "against nature," following European legal systems of the time. This never once led to a prosecution, and the law was abolished in 1956.[95]

The legal age of consent for homosexual and heterosexual acts was switched from 13 to 15 in 1987, and to 18 for relations involving prostitutes in 1996. Persons convicted of sex with a minor face immediate arrest and penalties as harsh as life imprisonment. On the other hand, there exists no anti-discrimination law, and the changed gender status of transsexual is not legally recognized. In official situations (school, job interviews, etc.), they are often asked to dress like men, and respond to their male names.[96] The censorship law, unchanged from the 1930s, is very strictly applied, for example, to movies.[97]

The Situation of LGBT

In Buddhism, the ban on the ordination of *kathoey* is still in force. Male transvestites and homosexuals (*pandaka*) are considered full of defiling passions, dominated by their libido, and not suitable for ordination. This should not be interpreted as homophobic *per se*, but rather as against all sexual activities.[98]

In December 1996, the Rajabat Institute Council banned gays, in its 36 vocational colleges nationwide, from receiving teaching training leading to degrees in kindergarten and primary school teaching. The announcement was endorsed by the Minister of Education, on the grounds that persons "of wrong sexual orientation" could not provide good role models for children. However, Rajabat was forced to back down in 1997, after a campaign from human rights groups and *Anjaree* succeeded in attracting international support.[99] In June 1999, the government Public Relation Department issued a directive limiting the appearances of transgender actors on television programs. Thirty actors and activists, led by the lesbian group *Anjaree*, protested against the order, which lasted only a few years.[100]

The election of the "Thai Love Thai" (*Thai Rak Thai*) party in February 2001 saw an unprecedented crackdown on gay bars in Bangkok, which lasted 6 weeks. At one point, 6 bars in central Patpong area were closed. The police action was preceded by a television show that created a scandal, apparently showing in a very crude manner the gay bar scene of Bangkok. By mid-2002, nearly every gay venue in the kingdom had been raided by the police, who left the heterosexual sex trade relatively untouched.[101]

Even if Thailand appears quite tolerant towards homosexuality, Chinese-Thai and Islamic-Thai are victims of their ethnic cultural prejudices. Homosexuality and cross-gender behaviour is tolerated by society at large, but not really accepted as appropriate, nor free from discrimination. Sanctions against homosexuality exist in the form of condemnatory discourses (in academia, the press, job interviews, etc.). The tolerance of Thai society towards homoeroticism seems to extend only to physical acts, same-sex relationships being frowned upon as disturbing the consensual heteronormativity.[102] While *kathoey* are fairly tolerated by the general population, gay men are rather viewed as perverted by the West because, by not pretending to be women, they break the feminine-masculine binarism considered as *the* accepted form of eroticism in Thailand.[103]

The emergence of gay-identified men and the presence of a gay commercial scene in Bangkok, for example, happened mainly through a cultural movement, not really supported by gay-orientated political movements or an activist network, as happened in most Western countries. The relative tolerance of Thai society and culture did not push homosexuals to mobilize in political or activist ways and Thailand lacks activist organizations and a community network. Generally, gay Thai consider there is no need for gay political organizations, for they are "not oppressed" by society:[104] "homosexuality is not illegal and homophobia is not an issue."[105] The Thai gay community barely exists, except as a commercial entity in certain cities. Its activities mainly revolve around bars, saunas and restaurants. Very few gay men come out outside gay circles. Nowadays Bangkok has the biggest gay scene in South-east Asia, with more than 100 commercial venues, and 23 Thai-language magazines oriented toward a gay readership. Gay tourism appears much more developed and organized than in any other Asian country. A self-called "world's first all-gay village," "Flower Town" with 800 luxury homes, was built in 1994 in the mountains in central Thailand. However, the project failed to attract enough buyers and had to be abandoned.[106]

Lesbians are usually called *tom-dee* (for "tomboy" and "lady"), respectively corresponding to "butch" and "femme." Thai lesbians usually consider the term "lesbian" derogatory, associated with pornographic movies. They face considerably more social resistance than gay men. There are very few lesbian-orientated venues, especially in suburban and rural areas.[107] *Anjaree*, literally "someone who follows a different path," the only Thai lesbian organization, was founded in 1986, and has over 500 members. Their first national conference was held in 1998. It receives funding from NGOs, the Public Health Ministry and the general public. They publish *Anjareesan*, a small magazine.

Parinya Kiatbhusaba, a transgender Muay Thai kickboxer, appeared in the media in 1998. She touched people's hearts when, at 16, she refused to disrobe fully[108] during a pre-bout weight-in, on the occasion of her first big fight in Bangkok, which she won. She was then allowed to wear underwear. Parinya successfully underwent a sex-change operation in 1999 and continued boxing in women's bouts.[109]

The first Bangkok Gay Festival parade was held in 1999, and became an annual event. Bangkok's first International Film Festival was held in 1998. There are several beauty contests for transvestites in Thailand, some of them even occurring in Buddhist temples, the most famous being "Miss Tiffany" and "Miss Alcazar," broadcast nationwide.[110]

Laos

Socio-Cultural Background

Generally speaking, Laos is governed by a repressive government which is not sympathetic to gay life. Moreover, family and marriage are culturally very important, as elsewhere in Asia.[111] Third gender, transvestites, the *gatoey*, were traditionally accepted by society. Not very visible, they sometimes work as prostitutes, "used" by straight men who play the 'king' (top) role. The occurrence of masculine gay men, who do not cross-dress, seems to be a problem. Sex between men was considered to be "peasant manners" by French colonialists, strongly influencing Lao upper and middle classes.

Legal Situation

Information on the legal status of homosexuality is contradictory. According to ILGA, it is illegal for males. The Swedish embassy reported arrests of gays in 1992 by police. According to Eastgarden, homosexuality is illegal, and gays were deported to re-education camps at least until the end of the 1980s. Baird[112] reports "severe discrimination in criminal law, but falling short of illegality."

The Situation of LGBT

The gay scene is mostly nocturnal and very discreet. There are no gay venues. Homosexuals meet in trendy places among other customers.

Cambodia

Socio-Cultural Background

People are expected to get married and have children, as in many other Asian countries. However, sex acts between same-sex partners are usually accepted, and are not defined as "homosexuality" *per se*, but frequently viewed as a troubled karma, resulting in avoidance by friends and family.[113] Traditionally transgender people, "*katoi*," share the same kind of social acceptance as transgender people in neighbouring countries such as Laos and Thailand.

Legal Situation

Same-sex relationships are legal for both men and women. Age of consent is 16, for both same-sex and heterosexual acts. There is one known case of officially approved marriage between two women, on March 12, 1995, in the village of Kro Bao Ach Kok, Kandal province. The authorities are said to have found the matter a bit strange, but decided to allow it because one of the women had already three children from a previous marriage. The event did not draw negative reactions, only a great curiosity, to the point that 250 persons assisted in the Buddhist ceremony, including high officials from the province.

The Situation of LGBT

Homoerotic behaviour seems generally quite acceptable. There is no overtly gay scene and no exclusively gay bars or publications. One finds two types of "out" homosexual expressions: taxi-boys and *katoi*. Taxi-boys, in rickshaws, a lot of them straights, can be rented outside any venue catering to foreigners, money being their main motivation. *Katoi*, flamboyant, socially tolerated, excelling in artistic domains, sometimes play the role of prostitutes for straight men, for a woman is expected to be virgin when she marries. A straight man may even enter into a relationship with a drag queen for a year or more. Such arrangements are kept secret, and end with the wedding of the straight man, as a result of familial and social pressure.[114]

In 1999, the first gay bar "The Tamarind" was opened in Phnom Penh by a gay businessman. Government officials even attended the launch party.[115]

Vietnam

Socio-Cultural Background

As in most Asian cultures, marriage is seen as an essential part of society, particularly in order to produce children. Masculinity is confirmed by marriage and parenthood, rather than explicit heterosexual behaviour. Therefore, affection between men, physical contact, and even sharing a bed are socially acceptable, and not usually connoted with sexuality.[116]

Traditionally, transgender persons[117] (mainly male-to-female), are used to undertake shamanistic performances. Transvestites, as mentioned by French witnesses during the colonialist period, work as prostitutes, singers and entertainers, mainly in Ho Chi Minh City.[118]

Legal Situation

Homosexuality has never been illegal in Vietnam. The ancient legal codes, from the 15th century took into account heterosexual rape, adultery and incest, but left homosexuality unmentioned. Moreover, the French did not explicitly institute a prohibition against sodomy or pederasty in their colonies. In general, little attention from authorities is given to same-sex practices, but strong penalties for female prostitution exist; male prostitution seems completely ignored. However, crimes such as "undermining public morality" can be used to prosecute homosexual conduct. On the few occasions homosexual acts have been punished, it was under "adultery" (disregarding the sexes of the partners) or "rape" (when sex has been nonconsensual).[119]

Reuters reported the first gay wedding on April 7, 1997, between two men in Ho Chi Minh City. They celebrated in a hotel with 100 guests, provoking a lot of protest from residents. The authorities said that no laws exist to allow them to marry. On March 7, 1998, two Vietnamese lesbians were married in the province of Vinh Long; registration with the local People's Committee was denied.[120] After these two couples tied the knot, Vietnam's national assembly banned same-sex marriage in June 1998.

Situation of LGBT

According to Marnais,[121] during the Vietnam War (in the late '60s) there were three lesbian bars and eighteen gay bars in Saigon. There were also homosexual nightclubs, steam baths and coffee shops. Lesbian marriage was then not uncommon and tolerated by society. Nowadays, male prostitution seems widespread in urban centers, and well-established venues for homosexuals are untouched by the authorities. Vietnam has no strictly gay venues, no "gay social or community network" other than furtive cruising spots. Most gays are closeted, mainly because of cultural obligations (towards the family, regarding marriage) and the heterocentered society. Recently the rapid development of Internet helped built a virtual gay community unknown to most of the rest of the population.[122]

After a press release in 2002, Vietnam's state-run media declared homosexuality a "social evil," along with female prostitution and drug use. It proposed law to allow the arrest of gay couples, linking their "eccentric behaviour" with drug use, prostitution and AIDS. The group "Information, Education, Communication" is Vietnam's first AIDS-prevention group, founded in 1996. The group "Nguyen Friendship Society" was founded in 1997 by 50 volunteers, specifically aimed at gay and bisexual issues, and mainly working at AIDS prevention in Ho Chi Minh city.

A novel written in 2000 by journalist Bui Ahn Tan, *A World Without Women*, won one of Vietnam's 2002 "For the National Security and Peaceful Life" literary prizes, awarded by the Police Department, the Ministry for Public Security and the Vietnam Writer's Association. The subject of the book is a gay love story, usually taboo.[123]

Malaysia

Socio-Cultural Background

Islam is the official religion of Malaysia, adopted by most Malays (60% of the 23 million people of the country). Other ethnic groups comprise mostly Chinese and Indians. Islamic religion and culture seem to have a very strong influence on the way transsexuals and transgender people see themselves,[124] especially in the way they perceive sex change operations.[125] Islam traditionally divides gender into 4 groups: male, female, *khunsa* (hermaphrodites) and *mukhannis* or *mukhannas* (males whose behaviour is similar to that of females). Islam permits *khunsa* to opt for one gender through an operation, but does not allow *mukhannis* or *mukhannas* to behave like females or undergo sex change operations. Being gay and Muslim means to have to live in the closet, to live a double life, and to marry for convenience. For example, Abdul Kadir Che Kob, head of education and research at the Islamic Affairs Department, considers "homosexuality a crime worse than murder" and homosexuals "shameless people."[126] The authorities in general label gayness as a Western phenomenon representing a polluting foreign influence that should be opposed, denying both rights and the history of traditional same-sex relationship in the culture.[127]

Male transsexuals in Malaysia are usually called *mak nyah*,[128] whether they have undergone a sex change operation or not. The term was coined in 1987 by male transsexuals themselves. Female transsexuals are sometimes known as *pak nyah* or *abang*.[129] *Mak nyah* are often labeled sexual deviants and shunned by society. Male homosexuals are referred to as *pondan* or bapok.[130]

Legal Situation

There are 2 types of laws in Malaysia: Syriah (Islamic) Law and Civil Law. Under Islamic Law, same sex sexual intercourse is illegal. Syriah Law is only applied to Muslims, but police may arrest any gay person, Muslim or not, in a public space like a cruising spot.[131] In 1983, the Conference of Rulers in Malaysia imposed a *fatwa* prohibiting sex change operations for all Muslims except hermaphrodites and also prohibiting cross-dressing.[132] Transgender people are sometimes caught by the police or Islamic authorities for cross-dressing, and charged with "indecent behaviour" under section 21 of the Minor Offenses Act (1955), in which the precise meaning of "indecent behaviour" is not defined. When caught, they are often stripped of their woman's clothing in front of other people, sometimes forced to wear men's clothes, teased or sexually abused.[133]

Homosexual acts are criminalized under the sections 377a and 377b of the Penal Code. More precisely, under these articles, anyone engaged in sodomy or fellatio, straight or gay, man or woman, can be penalized. Sodomy has been a criminal offence since colonial times. A maximum of 20 years in prison and a whipping can be imposed for "carnal intercourse against the order of nature." In fact, section 377b has not often been used in the past, being restricted almost entirely to cases involving non-consensual sex.[134]

The Situation of LGBT

The Islamic Affairs Department operates a kind of morality police, with fifty enforcement officers across the country who have the power to arrest Muslim people, after complaints have been made. Usually, several gays are arrested each month. Over 100 men were arrested in 1999 for "attempting to commit homosexual acts." In Selangor state, "the Islamic Bada vigilante groups," founded in 1994 and praised by the religious affair minister, assisted in arresting 7000 persons for "unislamic activities" (mainly for being homosexuals). Besides being charged, people arrested had to attend religious classes and receive counseling.

Adbul Hadi Awang, leader of the "Pan-Malaysian Islamic Party," a fundamentalist party that controls 28 of the 32 seats in Terengganu state, foresees Islamic laws being applied to non-Muslim Malaysians as well. Under a bill (the so-called "Hudud Code") approved in July 2002 by the Terrangu state, sodomy and adultery, among other sins, are punishable by death by stoning. The state government in Kelantan state, also controlled by the fundamentalist party, passed similar laws in 1993, but they have never been enforced because of objections by the federal government.[135]

One of the main recent controversies concerning human rights and homosexuality is Anwar Ibrahim's highly political arrest and trial. Deputy Prime Minister, he was arrested in September 1998 and convicted of homosexuality and sodomy, among other charges. Prime Minister Mahatir said: "I cannot accept a man who is a sodomist to become a leader in this country."[136] During the trial, one could read every day about homosexuality in the papers, in a country where one does not talk about sex in public, let alone about homosexuality. Anwar Ibrahim denied being homosexual. He was tortured while under Internal Security Act[137] detention. Mahatir stated that democracy would lead to homosexuality. Amnesty International "believes the accusations were a politically motivated response to Anwar's calls for political reform."[138] Homosexuality was used as a political and cultural means to get rid of an opponent who was too liberal. The use of homosexuality to humiliate a political opponent is indicative of cultural views towards homosexuality. Before this case, there had been no centralized record of sodomy cases. There were only a few instances concerning consenting adults, where sentences were never more than three years. Human rights groups remained largely silent about this political and cultural negative use of homosexuality.

In 1996 two women in a lesbian relationship were arrested in Kelantan state and humiliated. They were discovered to be "married" in the guise of a "heterosexual"-like relationship. One of them was charged with impersonating a man and for possessing a false identity card, and sentenced to two years in prison.[139] In 1998, 45 transvestites were arrested in Kedah province while participating in a beauty pageant and charged with cross-dressing.[140] In 1999, 23 Muslim men who had taken part in a Drag Beauty Contest in the state of Kedah were found guilty of wearing women's clothing and acting like women, and were fined. The non-Muslim men were not tried.[141] In November 2001,

Prime Minister Mahatir warned Britain that any gay British Minister taking their male partner to Malaysia would be expelled, referring to "differences in values" between the two countries. He was making reference to Ben Bradshaw, the openly gay Foreign Office minister. Britain issued a rebuke the same night.[142]

Considering the legal burdens, one finds a surprisingly active gay community in Malaysia, with several gay bars, discos, saunas and cruising areas in Kuala Lumpur and other cities, the first having been there since the 1980s.[143] Most gays and lesbians still have a hidden life, mainly stay in cities, and get married, but feel socially isolated because of the general negative perception of homosexuality.[144]

Organized lesbian communities have always been a small group, predominantly from Chinese and middle-class backgrounds, not very visible.

The "Pink Triangle" association was formed in 1987, focusing on AIDS education and prevention. They work together with the national Department of Health and are recognized by the government, without bearing any official connection, being funded by international agencies. Pink Triangle is not identified as a "gay group" because it remains illegal to "promote" homosexuality in Malaysia.[145] Marina Mahatir, daughter of the Prime Minister, is the head of the Malaysian AIDS Council. She vilified the activities of the anti-gay group Pasrah and the homophobic tone of certain press articles.[146]

As often is the case in Asia, the Internet has developed recently as one of the main means of communication for the "gay community."

Singapore

Socio-Cultural Background

Nearly 80% Chinese, Singapore, independent since 1965, is ethnically very diverse. Traditional Confucian ethics as well as the importance of the family dominate: heterosexual monogamous marriage, the bearing of descendants, subjection to family values and religious rituals remain the main features of Singaporean society. Homosexuality suffers from "immense social stigmatization," Singapore being very prudish. Human rights seem to be subordinate to economic parameters, linking economic growth and power to strong social cohesion. Social order must not be disrupted by subversive activities. Any kind of sexuality that does not conform to the dominant ideology is silenced and made invisible. Gayness was labeled by the authorities in the 1990s as a

Western phenomenon, a polluting foreign influence that should be opposed. The authorities used homosexuality as a focus of difference between "the West" and Asia.[147] At a UN Conference in 1993, the representative of Singapore stated that "Singaporeans (...) do not agree (...) that homosexual relationships are just a matter of lifestyle choice. Most of us will also maintain that the right to marry is confined to the opposite sex." Nevertheless, violent homophobia in the form of gay bashing does not exist significantly.

Legal Situation

Singapore has punitive laws against homosexuals, from the British colonial heritage (enacted in 1872), imposing penalties up to life imprisonment for "carnal intercourse against the order of nature." This covers sodomy and oral sex (not exclusively homosexual), under sections 377 (unnatural offenses) and 377a (outrages on decency) of the Penal Code. Section 377a is very specific, prohibiting "any male person (...) in public or private" from engaging in "any acts of gross indecency with another male person," imposing a maximum of two years imprisonment. Lesbian sexual relations are not mentioned, but this does not leave lesbians free from social oppression. Certain lesbian sexual acts can indeed be punished under section 20 of the Miscellaneous Offenses (Public Order and Nuisance) Act, in reference to "riotous, disorderly or indecent behaviour" in a public setting. A fine of up to $1000 or imprisonment of up to a month are the penalties, but so far no case has been tried.[148]

The legal status of oral sex seems to have posed a problem. The Court of Appeal ruled on February 21, 1997, that "oral sex is a crime unless it is followed by penile-vaginal sex. The coitus of the male and female organs is natural. Unnatural acts are permitted only as foreplay."[149]

Post-operative transsexuals have been permitted, since January 1996, to marry persons of the opposite sex. LGBT have no protection against discrimination on ground of their sexuality. Self-declared gay men are not admitted in the army, and they are relegated to administrative or logistics work while serving the two-and-a-half year compulsory military service.

Laws enforcing censorship are numerous in Singapore, particularly applying to homosexual materials. In 1992, the Censorship Review Committee of the Ministry of Information and the Arts called for a relaxation for heterosexual materials, but stated that "in the light of the sensitivity of homosexuality as an issue, materials encouraging homosexuality should continue to be disallowed." Consequently, visual representations of homosexual acts, as well as materials portraying homosexuality as a legitimate lifestyle, are banned.[150]

The Situation of LGBT

Police frequently use decoys to trap people soliciting for sex in public places, who can be arrested under Section 354 of the Penal Code which carries a maximum jail sentence of two years, a fine, caning or a combination of these. If touching did not occur, Section 19 ("soliciting in a public space") of the Miscellaneous Offenses Act can be used, carrying a fine not exceeding $1000 or a jail sentence of up to six months.[151]

In May 1993, the disco Rascals in the Pan-Pacific Hotel, which was "gay only on Sundays," was raided but the people arrested were not charged. In 1993, twelve men were arrested at Tangong Rhu during an anti-gay operation. They received two to six month jail sentences, and three strokes of the cane. On 23 July 2001, three undercover police officers arrested two men having sex in a cubicle at One Seven gym and spa. The accused were held overnight without access to lawyers in a police station, and charged the following day under section 377a of the Penal Code, but the charges were amended to section 20 of the Miscellaneous Offenses Act.

Singapore's first gay bar, Le Bistro, opened at the end of the 1960s, quickly followed by two others, at a time when dancing was not allowed between persons of the same sex. In the 1980s, a sense of community started to take shape, paralleling significant political and socio-economic changes in Singapore as a whole. A gay disco, Niche, opened in 1983 and persons of the same sex could dance together.

Nowadays, many gays are still closeted in Singapore. Visibility of sexual behaviour or identity can lead to several types of risk and discrimination, from public humiliation to imprisonment to caning to losing employment, etc. The gay scene has been changing mainly since 1998. There are now five gay saunas, several bars, clubs and other venues in the city, mainly in Chinatown.[152]

People Like Us (PLU), the first group dealing specifically with homosexual issues, was founded in 1993, involving gays, lesbians and bisexuals. They held monthly forums in public buildings from 1994. Their Sunday sessions (from 1993 to 1996) attracted several hundred people, among them some government undercover agents. PLU has been trying unsuccessfully to register legally since 1995, first as a company with the Registry of Companies and Businesses, then as a society with the Registrar of Societies. The group has since had to disband under the threat of severe penalties but continues to exist informally, mainly through its home page and newslists on the Internet.[153]

Lesbians are severely marginalized, even if there exists some ambiguity about the illegality of lesbian sex. Lesbian activism is far less developed than gay male activism. The first pride party was held on August 8, 2001.

Recently, the Internet allowed information diffusion on a great scale, mainly through newslists or mailing lists. Although the Singapore Broadcasting Authority issued in 1996 strict guidelines for Internet contents ("Internet Code of Practice"), forbidding "perversion" like homosexuality or its propagation, little control is devoted to personal homepages hosted on foreign servers.[154] Sites like *Yawning Bread* are activist without being confrontational in the sense that they do not aggressively attack Singaporean society.

Indonesia

Socio-Cultural Background

Indonesia, independent since 1949, has a high degree of ethnic and cultural diversity, with more than 300 ethnic groups and 50 languages. Rivalry and resentment sprang up in the post-Suharto era after 1998, which witnessed a fragmentation of values. One of the characteristics of this period was more political and civil freedom (or openness). Indonesia's human rights record has not usually been regarded as satisfactory by NGOs such as Amnesty International and Asiawatch. The response was the establishment in 1993 of a National Commission on Human Rights, while keeping nonetheless a cultural relativist discourse. The approach to human rights has been circumscribed by the desire of the State to maintain social harmony. The importance of the country as one big family leads Indonesia to emphasise duties rather than rights in order to preserve its integrity. This minimizes the rights of the individual and constitutes the global lens through which homosexual rights must be understood: human rights are nascent, fragile and contested.[155]

Many of Indonesia's cultures boast traditions of transgenderism and socially recognized sexual behaviour between males. Male transsexuals or transvestites are usually known as *banci* or *waria*. Open about their identities, they appear on television, in theatres and so on. One can expect *waria* to be anywhere: in salons, applying makeup for weddings, in tailor shops, or looking for men at night in town squares. They dress, speak and behave like women, sometimes undergoing bodily modifications. Only a few of them undergo sex-change operations.[156] The term *waria* was coined in the 1970s as an amalgam of *wanita* (woman) and *pria* (man), and has become a generic word to designate a person who displays non-normative sexual behaviour. *Waria* traditionally come from "poor and illiterate" milieus. They survive in particular professions related to cosmetic beauty, or as bar hosts, entertainers, fortune tellers, and sex workers, and are sometimes victims of social discrimination. Partly for these reasons they used not to get along very well with the "gay" population.

The Makassarese of South Sulawesi have a tradition of *bissu*: men who dress like women, or women like men, and who have sexual relations only with persons of the same gender. All rituals at the Court have to be presided by a *bissu (waria)*. Among the Makassarese, at least through the 1940s, in the traveling troupes of entertainers, *masri* dancers aged 9 to 12 dressed like women and performed in front of a audience largely composed of adult men. According to European travelers, the purpose of the dance was "sexual incitement," and the dancers received money from men in the audience. In Java, certain boys used to take girls' roles (*bedaja* and *serimpi*) in some dance troupes in the 19th century. The *ludruk*, a modern form of entertainment depicting scenes of everyday life, always features a clown and a transvestite singer, often homosexual, who sometimes wears women's clothes off stage.[157]

A central figure of the Ponorogo area, in East Java, the *warok*, an adult male spirit medium, plays an ambiguous role on the margins of social and political life. His authority depends on his martial arts ability, his magic and religious knowledge. Ever since their origin (probably in the 15th century, from Buddhist tradition), they were forbidden to have sexual intercourse with women in order to achieve spiritual strength (the loss of sperm was believed to deplete their supernatural power). Therefore, they used to take as sexual partners one or several young androgynous boys, the *gemblak*, usually aged between 8 and 16, who would also perform domestic chores for them. The tradition is an institution, with strict rules. *Warok* used to go to the *gemblak*'s parents house to "propose," using a ritualized form of speech. The parents were paid in cows and would gain social prestige as well as protection from the transaction. The majority of *gemblak* stayed with their warok until their late teens and then marry a woman. *Warok* themselves would marry at around 40 years of age. Their aim in marrying was to fulfill the ideal of Javanese marriage and procreation. *Warok* and *gemblak* would not call themselves "homosexuals." Offstage, the boy is "used" by unmarried men for intercrural intercourse. Fewer and fewer boys want to become *gemblak*, and if so, nearly always for economic reasons. Nowadays, *warok* strongly deny having sexual intercourse with the *gemblak*. The official view regards this relationship as morally offensive, representing a kind of "socialized homosexuality." The taking of *gemblak* was outlawed by the government in 1983.[158]

The family policy of the Indonesian authorities, the social pressure to marry, as well as religious concerns (89% of Indonesians are Muslim) leave no real place for gay and lesbian lifestyles. However, the gay and lesbian movement, one of the oldest and largest in Southeast Asia, became more open through the 1990s, but only with the urban English-speaking elite. The terms "gay" and "lesbian" began to be used in the 1980s, but for most people, *waria* is still synonymous with "homosexual" or "gay."

Open discrimination and violent homophobia are rare, except in religious extremist circles. Discrimination and marginalization are subtle, in education, at work, in the family, among friends, etc.[159]

Legal Situation

The Indonesian Criminal Code was revised when the Dutch Indies was a French colony, under Napoleon. So, homosexual acts have actually never had to be decriminalized. Although there is no legal prohibition, there is a moral prohibition. Homosexuality indeed seems to be considered a religious (Muslim) and moral problem rather than a legal one in Indonesia. The legal age of consent for homosexual acts is 18, but 17 for heterosexuals. Indonesia's official medical guidelines stopped classifying homosexuality as abnormal in 1983.[160]

The Situation of LGBT

During the 1980s and 1990s the media gave homosexuality an increasing profile, often linked with AIDS. The gay scene is not very diverse, but widespread. In Jakarta, gay bars and discos are numerous and nearly always full. The Bali gay scene is rather calm, consisting more of a commercial business venue for tourists than a real (local) community.[161] There are three gay magazines published across Indonesia and a national telephone counseling hotline. There are no sex shops in Indonesia (even heterosexually oriented). One was opened in 2000 in Surabaya, but was quickly closed by the police on the basis that they are "contrary to Indonesian culture and morality."[162]

The first transgender (*waria*) organization was established in Jakarta in 1969. The numerous waria organizations, quite common at a local level, are often associated with political parties. The first Indonesian gay and lesbian organization, *Lambda Indonesia*, was created in March 1982 to provide a forum for gays and lesbians. *Lambda Indonesia* disbanded in 1986, and in mid-1987 *Gaya Nusantara* was founded, which became an umbrella association for a gay and lesbian network throughout the archipelago (it has groups in 16 cities). There are now more than 30 LGBT organizations all around the country. *Gaya Nusantara* means literally "archipelago style," but it is a play on words and also refers to "gay archipelago." They publish a periodical *GAYa Nusantara*, in order to disseminate information about gays and lesbians. *Gaya Nusantara* recognizes the traditional forms of homosexuality as well as embracing the global gay culture, being *de facto* a nexus for Indonesian homosexualities.[163]

In 1993, the first Indonesian Lesbian and Gay conference was held in Yogyakarta (Java), a second was held in Bandung in 1995, and a third in Denpasar (Bali) in 1997. The first Gay Parade was held in Surabaya in June 1999 and the first Gay & Lesbian Film Festival was held in the Utan Kayu Theater in Jakarta, in July 1999.

Lesbians are a rather closed community, more hidden than gay men. In male-dominated cultures, to allow women to behave in a cross-gender manner would be regarded as jeopardizing the gender system by blurring the definition of masculinity and femininity.[164]

Philippines

Socio-Cultural Background

The Philippines went through 300 years of Spanish colonization and half a century of US colonial rule. The Roman Catholic Church is quite powerful (83% of the population is Catholic), but people usually practise a synthesis of Catholicism and pre-colonial animism, which influences sexual culture.[165] Before the Spanish, each "tribe" had its powerful shaman-like figure, the *bayaguin, bayoguin, bayog, baylan* (indigenous words for "priestess"), or *asog* (in the southern islands). As helpers of the chiefs, they lived and dressed like women, weaving and sewing. The *bayog* were burnt or crucified by Spanish conquerors, less for their sexual behaviour than for their pagan functions.[166]

Bakla, female-identified men or cross-dressing effeminate men, as well as *tomboy*, male-identified females, have long been a recognized part of cultural and even family life in the Philippines. *Tomboys* are also called, by derivation, *tibok* or *tibo*. *Bakla* have a high public visibility, cross-dress in everyday life, and usually work in beauty parlors or in the entertainment industry, as domestic helpers, market vendors, or sex workers. They usually have sex with "real men," not other *bakla*. *Tomboys* also have stereotyped occupational niches, as security guards, bus drivers, etc. Social acceptance of *bakla* and *tomboy* is on condition that they do not to leave these niches. They seem to be stigmatized by society, especially in the Muslim southern part of the country, and are often harassed or ridiculed in public.

The terms gay and lesbian came into use in the 1970s, and are now part of the Taglish, a mixture of Tagalog and English. Usually, these terms are interchanged with *bakla* and *tomboy*.[167]

Legal Situation

There are no laws against consensual same-sex relations between adults, but same-sex sexual acts in a public can fall under Article 20 of the Penal Code as a "grave scandal." Sometimes laws against "public immorality" are also used to harass LGBT people. The legal age of consent for sexual acts is 12 for both homo- and heterosexual acts. Marriage is only recognized between a man and a woman according to the Family Code, although a bill (HB 1503) has been introduced to amend this.[168]

In December 2002, an anti-discrimination bill (HB 2784) was approved by the Committee on Civil, Political and Human Rights at the House of Representatives, addressing discriminatory practices in seven areas: hiring, promotion and dismissal of workers; admission to educational institutions; use of establishments, facilities and services open to the public; access to medical and health services; access to public services; application for professional licenses issued by the government; and application for a license, clearance, certification or any other document issued by government authorities.

The Situation of LGBT

In 1988, the government launched a campaign against prostitution, both heterosexual and homosexual, during which many gay bars were raided and closed down. In September 1994, two lesbian employees of a human rights organization, the Balay Rehabilitation Center, lost their jobs on the ground that their sexual affair was disruptive to the work of the Center. This affair prompted the creation of some lesbian groups. In

January 2001, the Philippine Commission on Human Rights dismissed a complaint by the NGO Gahum-phils, concerning a male-to-female transvestite, who was twice barred from entering a dance club in Cebu for wearing woman's clothes.

The emerging gay scene was an amplification of the *bakla* world. It seems to be well developed in urban centers: mainly bars, drag shows and clandestine male brothels. There is no "gay community" in the sense of a homogeneous united group, however. *Bakla* and "gay" do not really mix, except inside activist groups sometimes. *Bakla* have for a long time been organized in neighborhood associations (beauty pageants, processions, local festivals, etc.). Beauty contests for *bakla* are very popular, often involving local authorities.[169]

In the late 1960s, the Manila gay scene was associated with the "rich and beautiful," the elite who had studied in the United States or Europe.[170] In the 1970s, the prevalent idea was that there was no need to fight for gay rights in the Philippines because *bakla* were well accepted. In the 1980s, middle-class gay men, who did not cross-dress and who sought sex with other gay men, were creating a difference with *bakla* and their world. Then, gay and lesbian organizations began to spring in the 1990s. By the mid-1990s, newspapers such as the *Evening Paper* started a weekend section called *Gayzette*, including reviews of recent American gay fiction, gay columns, etc.[171]

In 1991, a group of gay men founded The Library Foundation, a NGO which sponsors activities in building awareness of AIDS and providing information on safe sex. In Quezon City, ten gay men founded Katlo ("the third [sex]" in Tagalog), a "community for a gender-sensitive society." In the universities, the first gay students group, *UP Babaylan*, was founded in August 1992. The Sapho Society was formed in May 1999 at the University of the Philippines. At the Polytechnic University of the Philippines, another group was established in 1993, ProGay (Progressive Organization for Gays), a militant nationalist organization. The private Far Eastern University has two large gay organizations: BANANA (literally "*Bakla* united toward nationalism"), and SHE (Society of the Homosexual Encounter), which organizes gay beauty pageants. In the 1990s, lesbians formed active organizations like CLIC (Can't Live In the Closet), Lesbond or Link. Despite these groups, lesbians are largely invisible in Philippine society.[172] An umbrella organization, LAGABLAB (the Lesbian and Gay Legislative Advocacy Network), was created in 1999 by gay and lesbian organizations, in order to coordinate lobbying in Congress.

The first National Lesbian Rights Conference took place in December 1996; the first national gay and lesbian conference was held in 1997 on the campus of the University of the Philippines, in which fourteen organizations participated.

The first courses in gay literature were initiated by the University of the Philippines and the De La Salle University. An academic gay literature started in 1996, with the publication of *Philippine Gay Culture: The Last 30 Years*, by N. Garcia, followed by many other publications. The first LGBT newspaper, *ManilaOut*, was launched in April 1999, but soon suspended its activities and then resumed them in June 2001.[173]

The first gay parade in Asia was held in June 1994, in Manila, commemorating the 25th anniversary of the Stonewall Riots, drawing 50 participants and almost as many journalists. It has become an annual event since 1996. The first "Pink Film Festival" was held in July 1999.

South Korea

Socio-Cultural Background

The presence is attested, in pre-Buddhist Korea, of cross-dressing shamans called *paksoo*. Very handsome young men, bearing shamanistic functions, the *hwarang*, entertained at Court until about AD 350. They were then transformed into an elite military corps, where pederasty is said to have been common. More generally, at least from the 13th century, same-sex relations between men were very common among the ruling class. Another homosexual group known from the 13th century was the *namsadang*, members of theatre troupes traveling around the country.[174]

Buddhism and Confucianism, imported from China, influenced Korean attitudes towards homosexuality. Buddhism shows a great tolerance towards homosexuality, while preaching sexual moderation. Confucianism, its emphasis on social order and family, viewed male same-sex relations as a threat, and tended to ignore female same-sex relations. These two currents of thinking led Koreans to be tolerant regarding homosexuality as long as it does not interfere with marriage, family and procreation. Words like "gay" (*ge-i*) and "lesbian" (*le-su-bi-an*) seem to be widely used in Korea today. The direct translation of "homosexual," *doog-song-ae*, appears to belong rather to medical terminology.[175]

Awareness and visibility have been increasing since the 1990s. Nevertheless, homosexuality is still very much underground. Koreans are expected to marry by their late 20s, and it is not unusual to meet married men leading a dual life in gay bars at night, or with a secret gay lover. However, there is an enormous tolerance for homosociality: same-sex friends living together before marriage, the fact of holding hands and rubbing each other in the street, of brushing a male friend's buttock or genitals when parting. Nothing sexual will be interpreted.

The first sex-reassignment operation occurred in 1989. As of late 2000, 50 cases have been reported. A person wishing to undergo the operation has to meet 12 criteria (such as "accurate psychiatric diagnosis," "no success from long term psychiatric treatment," "family approval," "no criminal record") and obtain two recommendations from psychiatrists.[176]

The Legal Situation

There are no laws against same-sex relations between consenting adults, apparently due to the Japanese colonialist legacy.[177] The age of consent is thirteen for both homo- and heterosexual acts.

The "National Human Rights Law," proclaimed in April 2001, declares that "any discrimination on the basis of sexual-preference is not allowed." However, it is impossible for post-operative transsexuals to have their gender legally changed. The legal system looks at sex-reassignment surgery as mere plastic surgery, and not as gender transition. In 2000, Korea passed a Youth Protection Law, prohibiting the distribution of materials that contain incest, animal sex, sadism/masochism, homosexuality, etc.

The Application of the Law

The first Seoul Queer Film and Video Festival was cancelled in September 1997, because of "governmental homophobia." The Festival then planned to move to Yonsei University's theatre, but local government officials declared the screening illegal. Yonsei University withdrew its support, under pressure from the alumni. The Magnus Hirschfeld Center for Human Rights requested UNESCO to look into the case, alleging human rights violations.

In April 2001, the Korean Information and Ethics Committee (ICEC), an independent body with strong censorship powers, classified homosexuality under the category "obscenity and perversion." The

Web site ivancity.com, the gay site with the largest membership in Korea, was blocked in July 2001, without advance notice. The Web site www.exzone.com, South Korea's oldest gay site, run by the Lesbian and Gay Alliance Against Discrimination in Korea, was ruled "harmful to young people" by the ICEC. Fifteen lesbian and gay groups filed a lawsuit in January 2002 against the government, calling its ban on gay Net unconstitutional.

The Situation of LGBT

Since the 1970s there has been a developed social gay scene in urban centers: bars, saunas, cruising places. Korean gay couples rarely live together. In August 2000, the first gay show in Korea, *Hahahoho*, was held in a Seoul restaurant, featuring drag queens, singers and dancers. There was a half-hour question-and-answer session with the audience between the acts, so that they could satisfy their curiosity about transsexuals.[178]

In November 1991, nine foreign women living in Korea founded *Sappho*, which holds regular meetings, and is mainly constituted by a foreign and transient population.[179] In 1994, the first formal Korean gay rights organization was formed, the *Cho-Dong* Society (meaning "the colour of peace–green–is the same for everybody"). The group broke up one month later due to serious differences of opinion between gays and lesbians. The men organized a gay-men-specific group called *Chingusai* ("between friends"), and the women founded *Kiri kiri* ("togetherness") the same year. Each had more than 100 members two years later, publishing regular newsletters. In April 1995, "Come Together," the first Korean association of gay students, was founded in Yonsei University and the group *Ma-um 001* ("Heart 001") was established by students of Seoul National University, provoking enormous controversy. A third group, "People with People," was founded in September the same year in the University of Korea, with comparatively little uproar. Now, more than 30 universities in Korea have "gay clubs." In 1995, *Rodem* was founded as a five-member Internet group led by two missionaries. It is now a formal Catholic congregation, which aims are to give (religious) counseling to homosexuals, run seminars, as well as provide AIDS awareness education, etc. The Korean Homosexual Union (KHU) was established in July 2002, in order to provide a new framework for the human rights movement for sexual minorities. One of their first aims is to create international awareness about the situation of sexual minorities in South Korea.

The first gay Pride Parade occurred in 1994. In June 2002 "*Mujigae* [rainbow] 2002," a Korean Queer Festival in Seoul, was held "for all sexual minorities," sponsored by the Korea Culture and Arts Foundation. The event features lectures about sexual orientation and human rights, exhibitions, a film festival and a parade. Two gay magazines, *Buddy* and *Borizaku*, began publication in 1997 and 1998 respectively.

As in Japan, the Internet has become one of the most often used media by gays and lesbians to contact each other. Many gay-related sites have recently appeared, such as Gay Korea,[180] Queernet[181] and Dosamo.[182]

Japan

Socio-Cultural Background

From the 12th century, homosexuality is well documented in Japan,[183] especially through the diaries kept by Court people, which also relate numerous cases of cross-dressing. Generally, same-sex relations are to be found in three areas: Buddhist monasteries, the military and the theatre world. Female-to-male transgender practices, cross-dressing and women's same-sex relations are also attested historically in Japan, especially in the Buddhist sphere.

Young ephebes (*chigo*, from about 10 to 16 years old) were kept in Buddhist temples for domestic purposes, as well as sexual partners for the monks. Homoerotic relationships were grounded in the familiar structure of monastic life. In literature from the 14th century onwards, the numerous *Chigo Monogatari* ("Tales of the acolytes") tell the story of these relationships. The military, which had close ties with Buddhist monasteries, *de facto* ruled Japan from the 12th century to 1868. One of the principles of the system called *nanshoku* ("love/sex between men"), is a hierarchical aged-structure same-sex relationship between warlords (*daimyô* and *shogun*) and young ephebes.

From the 16th century, male prostitution arose in urban centers, catering for warlords and the local bourgeoisie. The figure of the male prostitute acquired at that time a great importance, as seen in literature (e.g., Ihara Saikaku's works). Then prostitution became associated with the *kabuki* theatre, where a homoerotic atmosphere was not uncommon. The Tokugawa regime (1603-1867) can be considered the golden age of homoeroticism, at least in the military and theatre. Commercial sex was kept in special districts of cities, away from centers. From the latter half of the 18th century, owing to Confucian influence among others, theatre and prostitution were gradually considered to be immoral. *Nanshoku* also appeared to lose its attraction because of suicides, love triangle incidents, and over-infatuation of *shoguns*, which made the government repeatedly discourage homosexuality.[184]

The first Jesuit missionaries who arrived in Japan in the mid-16th century were really horrified by the freedom with which homosexual acts were perpetrated in the temples by monks and in the military world. They tried to fight against these practices, without success.[185] After the "opening" of Japan during the Meiji era (1868-1911), tolerance towards same-sex relations changed radically, in an attempt to adapt to the "Western model." The government declared consensual same-sex relations illegal in May 1873, only to retract this ten years later. From the end of the 19th century, books and numerous articles appeared in specialized journals (mainly medical and psychological) depicting homosexuality as an illness. Compulsory heterosexuality, marriage and procreation could characterize Japanese sexual life in the 20th century. Same-sex relations were not spoken of. Fundamentally, the negative view of homosexuality in Japan still refers to a genetic disorder, psychological problems and perverted behaviour.[186] Therefore, an underground homosexual subculture (bars, saunas, cruising areas, etc.) began to be organized, as can be seen, for example, in the writings of Yukio Mishima.[187]

In present Japan, transvestites often appear on television, partly based on the rich tradition of transvestism in the theatre and entertainment spheres. They are not often directly connected to homosexuality as such. They are called "new half," in reference to the people called "half" in Japan, that is persons of several ethnic descents (in this case half-woman and half-man). It seems rather easy to live as a gay person in Japan, as on the one hand one finds little overt homophobia; however, on the other hand, few gays actually come out, there is little information and few policies concerning AIDS and its prevention, the bars and other meeting places are very hidden, and many gays still marry in order to hide. The media coverage of homosexual-related events or facts in Japan occurs very rarely, and nearly always in an ironic or "funny" way. In the media, gays often appear ridiculed (effeminate, unfit, etc.) and marginalized.[188] The usual modes of relationship in a Japanese family easily allow a double life, especially at night when its members often go out separately, the wife with her female friends and the husband with his male friends.

The vocabulary to refer to gay persons is very rich in Japan, spreading between psycho-medical terms, like *dôseiaisha*, and more metaphorical ones, such as *okama*, literally "pot, cauldron" (a reference to buttocks), or ethnological references to sexual anal intercourse, or *homo* or gei, from the English words, or the more specialised *kuiâ*. The vocabulary used to refer to lesbians is more restricted: *rezu*, an abbreviated form of the English word, or less often *onabe* (literally "pan"), in connection with the pot metaphor.

The Legal Situation

There is no reference to homosexuality in any legal text in Japan. Legally speaking, "sexual conduct" is defined as intercourse between a man and a woman. Same-sex sexual relations are called "*seikô ruiji kôi*", which can be translated as "behaviour similar to sexual conduct." From a legal viewpoint, homosexuals do not exist, but this does not mean an absence of discrimination. The legal age of consent for homosexual and heterosexual acts is 13, but all prefectures have their own laws, such as the "Youth Protection Law," that can prohibit sexual intercourse between an adult and a youth aged 16, 17 or 18. The Council for Human Rights Protection (within the Ministry of Justice) included in its May 2001 report the issue of discrimination on the basis of sexual orientation. The new Japanese Human Rights Commission is scheduled to enter into operation in 2003 or 2004. The government of Tokyo decided to reinstate the term "homosexuals" in its human rights guideline. The term had been removed in June 2000 on the ground that Tôkyô citizens do not fully understand homosexuals, a decision sharply criticized by international human rights groups, as well as by Japanese citizens.

Sex change operations have been legal in Japan since 1998. However, names cannot usually be changed on the family register. Transsexuals are also banned from marrying persons of the opposite sex, because it would be considered same-sex union.

In July 1995, the Japanese Society of Psychiatry and Neurology removed homosexuality from the list of mental disorders. Open homosexuals are banned from Japanese's Self-Defense Forces.

In March 1994, OCCUR won a suit filed against the Tôkyô Metropolitan Government because it refused to let OCCUR's members use a Youth House, on the basis of potential trouble with other young people staying at the facility. The Tôkyô Government appealed, and the Tôkyô High Court ruled in favor of OCCUR in September 1997, on the ground, notably, that "young people are perfectly capable of understanding homosexuality," and "that it is possible and necessary to provide educational guidance in the event that confusion or tension result from the presence of homosexuals in a public facility."

The Situation of LGBT

Japanese homosexuals are generally hidden and silent. This is particularly true for lesbians, who have few venues or organizations to rely on, and who do not seem to possess the same historical background as Japanese gays.

"Categorization," or typology, seems to be one of the major characteristics of the Japanese homosexual world, of which bars are the most visible part. One has to belong to a "type" (*-sen*) and be interested in a "type." The "logic of the types" is created and reinforced by the bars, the press, and self-presentation on the Net, for example. Tôkyô has more gay bars than New York, Amsterdam and San Francisco combined. Bars in big cities offer very high diversity and narrow specialization, the most extreme example being Nichôme, Tôkyô's most popular and gay exclusive area. A Japanese gay bar is quite a different concept to what can be found in "the West." Generally closed to non-informed people, rather than an exclusive place to pick up men, it is more a small convivial place where friends go and meet each other, or to gather information.

The activist sphere is small but visible. Some groups are active in favor of homosexual rights in general, but one cannot find in Japan more specialized groups like those in Europe or in the United States. In 1984, "JILGA" (Japanese International Gay and Lesbian Association), the first gay organization in Japan, was formed. The most famous activist organization, OCCUR, has 350 volunteers throughout the country, and was founded in 1986 with the aim of helping homosexuals through the publication of informative documents, the translation of (mainly American) books. Japanese gays in general appear not to be very politicized. This can be related to the culture of secrecy that surrounds homosexuality, but also to the obvious lack of confidence towards militant groups, or simply to the mere ignorance of their existence.

There are a few lesbian bars, although the 1990s saw a development of the lesbian scene and rights movement, for example with *Regumi Studio* in Tôkyô, a lesbian organization which was founded in 1992, and the nationwide *Kokusai Bian Renmei* ("International Lesbian United"). An example of transgender practices is the Takarazuka all-female Revue (founded in 1913) which is immensely popular all over the country.

Publishing is one area where gay life is particularly rich in Japan. From the 1980s, a huge number of foreign books related to homosexuality have been translated. And from the 1990s onwards, the number of Japanese books on the same subject has been mushrooming. Certain comics, often written by women and directed at young women, appeared in the 1970s, and are exclusively based on the theme of the love between young ephebes, with which most of Japanese gay men tend not to identify. This genre has been called *yaoi*, literally "no climax, no point, no meaning," the emphasis being placed on sex scenes.[189] There are seven monthly publications, one of their main aims being personal advertisements. The importance of gay magazines in Japan must be stressed, first as a provider of information in general about the communities, parties and events, but also to indicate the current state of the legal system concerning homosexuals, or other social issues. What is less obvious and hardly known is their role as the most often used media for (young) Japanese gays outside urban centers, in order to be able to contact other homosexuals; or simply just to be aware that there exist other people "like them" on the planet.

The first Gay Parade in Japan was held in August 1994, drawing 1500 persons. Sapporo saw the first Lesbian March in 1996, and Tôkyô a Dyke March in 1997. There will be no Parade in 2003 in Tôkyô, owing to the lack of organizers. The annual Gay & Lesbian International Tôkyô Film Festival, nearly an institution in itself, attracts many people of all sexual orientations.

Gay Web sites are very developed in Japan, especially since the 1990s. For example, Gay Web,[190] Gay Japan,[191] Tôkyô Metropolitan Gay Forum,[192] Gavie,[193] Men's Net Japan,[194] Rainbow Net Japan.[195] They provide a lot of information, but mainly allow people to meet and are now the most often chosen way by young gays and lesbians to find information or friends.[196]

CONCLUSION

Asian countries are slowly (but surely?) finding their own means of expression for dealing with LGBT issues.

In Asia, the lesbian and gay rights movements are clearly dominated by activists. There are few theoreticians or academics (and few university courses on lesbian and gay studies, except in Japan, Indonesia, the Philippines), and therefore few "social constructionists," as well as virtually no interest in "queer theory." Activists tend to think in terms of a binary opposition (homo- vs. hetero-) and clear-cut categories (gay, lesbian . . .). Their approach is practical, their arguments based on minority rights. They tend to try to promote visibility, legitimacy and equality, which are in the main "western" patterns that have often been adopted and used in order to resist social heteronormativity and homophobia. This was, and still is, of tremendous importance.

However, anybody familiar with local realities (through field work, etc.) would understand that "coming out" in Asia, at an individual level, is frequently considered to be unnecessary. "Coming out" is often perceived as a "white model" bringing more problems than real freedom. For example, in Japan a lot of closeted homosexuals have stated that potential problems are: troubles with family, with neighbors, at work, and so on. In China,[197] Thailand[198] and India,[199] the very same reasons are given. So-called "Asian values" put the emphasis on family and social harmony, which often stand in contradiction to what is usually pictured as "lesbian and gay rights" or "visibility" in "the West." Western (mainly Anglo-Saxon) patterns tend to draw a clear-cut separation between homosexuality and (blood) family.[200]

Individuality refers in Asia less to a combination of psychological traits than to the importance of social relations which construct and define it. One's identity relates predominantly to one's position in the extended family. Moreover, sexuality may play a relatively insignificant role in the construction of individual identity in Asian cultures in general. That Asian gays often marry and have children shows the enormous elasticity that their sexual identity encompasses. Moreover, being penetrated or having sex with a man does not at all jeopardize one's masculinity in most Asian countries. Masculinity is defined through other socio-cultural means or actions. Fluidity of sexuality in Asia does not really match the Western approach in terms of homo/hetero as essentialist categories which have a right to exist. In order to have a right, the category must be defined precisely, the frontiers set firmly. Homosexuality is perceived as a "problem" in the West only because of the implication of individual freedom and a sort of binary logic.[201]

Most of Asian societies can be thought of as "tolerant" (for lack of a better word) as long as homosexuality remains invisible. The important thing to do is to maintain (biological) family ties and social harmony, whatever it takes, which can be achieved in most cases only through secrecy, a double life, or pretending not to know ("willful blindness" as Sanders puts it). As Khan says: "procreative sexuality can be seen as a social compulsion,"[202] a duty. Heterosexual marriage is often not considered incompatible with a "homosexual life": going out to gay bars at night, participating in gay events (there is always a place in gay pride where pictures are forbidden), picking up men in saunas or parks, etc. The development of the Internet has even facilitated the encounters, while allowing secrecy. This is the main reason why the concept of "lesbian and gay rights" does not encompass in Asia the same meanings as in Western countries. We do not find post-Stonewall Anglo-American models of gay identity. Unfortunately, in many Asian countries (Philippines, Indonesia, Korea, Japan, etc.), diverse socio-economic historical reasons have separated the (western-like) gays and their liberation movement with the traditional figures of transgender and transvestites.

Asian countries are slowly finding their own expressions of LGBT Asian activism, gradually freed from Western parameters. In contrast to what happens in "the West," one of the main strategies of Chinese homosexuals to cope with the predominance of family in the society is silence regarding sexual orientation, and a smooth but intense acceptance of one's lover as "best friend," through strategically bringing him/her home for dinner, and then to sleep over. Gradually, the partner becomes like a (half-)brother or sister, through the use of kin categories.[203] They come out but avoiding overt discussion of homosexuality. What is then accepted by family and friends is not homosexuality *per se*, but a very concrete relationship between two persons they know. Asian ways of (gay) activism are more moderate, less rebellious, somewhat more "Confucian."

Parallel with this, homophobia is much more subtle and implied in Asian countries than in Europe or America. Asian gays have to negotiate their freedom, lifestyle and identities in an atmosphere of heterosexism, and not the endemic violent homophobia prevalent in many western countries.

Finally, let me draw, with Baden Offord,[204] a consequence of this. Gay and lesbian rights are not at that stage in Asia where they can be fully recognized as individual human rights. "While Asian values remain at odds with Western notions of individualism. . . , [and] human rights . . . , there is little reason to believe that homosexual rights will be regarded as anything but a part of the . . . western lifestyle."[205] "The theorist has to be careful not to assume that the homosexual experience is the same everywhere and that the same type of activism is required. . . . If this is not taken into account, the gay or lesbian theorist or human rights scholar may well be imposing an acultural stance on the Asian homosexual. . . [A]ny discussion about homosexual rights can only be meaningful if the deconstruction of homosexual identity is taken into account. . . . The evolution of homosexual rights in Asia may borrow from Western models of lesbian and gay activism and identity, but their development will take place amidst a landscape of local complexity."[206]

NOTES

1. From now on, the abbreviated form LGBT will be used.

2. It is not always legitimate and often heuristically counter-productive simply to contrast "Asia" with "the West," but as long as the subject is human rights, which take very concrete forms and emanate from Western concepts, this path will be chosen.

3. To give but a few examples: Abdullahi A. An-Na'im. 1992. Human Rights in Cross-Cultural Perspectives: A Quest for Consensus. Philadelphia, University of Pennsylvania Press. 479p. Bell, Daniel A. 2000. East meets West. Human Rights and Democracy in East Asia. Princeton, Princeton University Press. 369p. Chang, Joseph. 1995. "The Asia Challenge to Universal Human Rights," in Tang, James (ed.). Human Rights and International Relations in the Asia Pacific. London, Pinter. pp. 25-38. Kaul, Jawahar Lal. 1995. "Human Rights in Developping Countries: Some Policy and Legal Considerations," in Singh, Seghal (ed.). Human Rights in India. New Delhi, Deep and Deep. pp. 621-632. Neary, Ian. 1996. "In search of Human Rights in Japan," in Goodman, Roger; Neary, I. (eds). Case Studies on Human Rights in Japan. pp. 1-26. Shamshasha's interview in Mc Lelland, Marc. 2000. "Interview with Samshasha, Hong Kong's First Gay Rights Activist and Author." Intersections 4. *http://wwwsshe.murdoch.edu.au/intersections/issue4/interview_mclelland.html*. Renteln, Alison. 1990. International Human Rights: Universalism vs Relativism. Newbury Park, Sage. 205p.

4. Op. cit. (p. 35). See also the letter of protest by a Malaysian reader, published by the New Straits Times (16.06.1993) concerning the presence of LGBT rights within Malaysian human rights agenda, which does not seem to be an isolated case.

5. See mainly: Chou, Wah-Shan. 2001. "Homosexuality and the Cultural politics of tongzhi in Chinese Societies," in Sullivan, Gerard; P. A. Jackson (eds). Gay and Lesbian Asia: Culture, Identity, Community. pp. 27-46. Cohen, Lawrence. 2002. "What Mrs Besahara Saw: Reflections on the Gay Goonda," in Vanita, Ruth (ed.). Queering India. New York, Routledge. pp. 149-160. Jackson, Peter A. 2001. "Pre-Gay, Post-Queer: Thai Perspectives on Proliferating Gender/Sex Diversity in Asia," in Sullivan, Gerard; P. A. Jackson (eds). Gay and Lesbian Asia: Culture, Identity, Community. pp. 1-25. Khan, Shivananda. 2001. "Culture, Sexualities, Identities: Men Who Have Sex With Men in India," in Sullivan, Gerard; P. A. Jackson (eds). Gay and Lesbian Asia: Culture, Identity, Community. pp. 99-115. Nanda, Serena. 2001. Book review of [Love in a Different Climate: Men Who Have Sex With Men in India, by Jeremy Seabrook. London, Verso, 1999. 184p]. Journal of the History of Sexuality. 10.1, pp.143-146. Sanders, Douglas. 2002. "Gays Without Borders?", personally communicated through e-mail.

6. In the case of the Naz Foundation in India, the group was founded in London before splitting 4 years after into 2 groups, one of them being in India.

7. Jackson, 2001 (o. cit.). Storer, Graeme. 1999. "Performing Sexual Identity: Naming and Resisting 'Gayness' in Modern Thailand." Intersections 2. *http://wwwshe.murdoch.edu.au/intersections/issue2/Storer.html*.

8. "My family is westernized bourgeois (...) I did postgraduate work in the United States, and that influenced me to come out in the early 1980s in the way western gay academics would" (Hickson, Jill. 10.02.1999. "The struggle for gay and lesbian rights in Indonesia." Green Left Weekly).

9. 2001, p.104 (op. cit.).

10. At p.105

11. For examples of "hybridization" in (self-)representation through films, see Berry, Chris. 2001. "Asian Values, Family Values: Film, Video, and Lesbian and Gay Identities," in Sullivan, Gerard; P. A. Jackson (eds). Gay and Lesbian Asia: Culture, Identity, Community. pp. 211-231.

12. See for the details of such an analysis: Sullivan, Gerard. 2001. "Variations on a Common Theme? Gay and Lesbian Identity and Community in Asia," in Sullivan, Gerard; P. A. Jackson (eds). Gay and Lesbian Asia: Culture, Identity, Community. pp. 253-269.

13. For example, Indonesia has never had criminal prohibitions whereas Malaysia has a colonial era prohibition, because continental Europe civil law system did not criminalize homosexual acts (based on Napoleonic Code), whereas English common law did (Sanders, 2002; op. cit.).

14. See also Haggerty, George E (ed.). 2000. Gay Histories and Cultures. New York, Garland. 986p. Also the rich and practical document written by "People Like Us," a gay activist group from Singapore: *http://www.geocities.com/WestHollywood/3878/faith.htm.*

15. Shaw, W (ed.). 1991. Human Rights in Korea. Cambridge (Mass.), East Asian Legal Studies. 350p.

16. One of the main concern of Buddhism is to set barriers to sexual activities rather than distinguish its various forms. Whenever homosexuality is condemned, it is as an instance of sexuality among others, that is a human tendancy towards desire (Cabezon, Jose Ignacio. 2000. "Buddhism," in Haggerty, George E (ed.). Gay Histories and Cultures. New York, Garland. pp. 146-8).

17. After the Scriptures, "sexual misconduct" is to be avoided. Interpretations, however, usually do not include same-sex relations into its sphere of meanings. Heterosexuality and homosexuality are equivalent in the face of Buddhist's general anti-sex attitudes. Cf. Faure, Bernard. 1994. Sexualités bouddhiques. Entre désirs et réalités. Aix-en-Provence, Le Mail. 236p. Jackson, Peter A. 1995. "Thai Buddhist accounts of male homosexuality and AIDS in the 1980s." The Australian Journal of Anthropology. 6 (3). pp.140-53.

18. Cf. Rev. Vajra. nd. "A struggle with Buddhist homophobia." *http://www.geocities.com/WestHollywood/3878/bu-01.htm.* Julian Chan cited in Choong, Tet Sieu. 08.07.1998. "Revolution by stages. Things are getting better for Asia's homosexuals–but acceptance is still a long way off." Asiaweek. Besides, the Dalai Lama's position on same-sex relations is not free from ambiguities (see, for example, "Faith and Sexuality" op. cit.).

19. Murray, Stephen; Roscoe, Will (eds). 1997. Islamic Homosexualities. New York, New York University Press. 331p. Schmitt, Arno; Sofer, Jehoeda. 1992. Sexuality and Erocticism Among Males in Moslem Societies. New York, The Haworth Press. 201p. Wafer, Jim. "Muhammad and Male Homosexuality", in Murray, Stephen; Roscoe, Will (eds). 1997. Islamic Homosexualities. pp. 87-96.

20. Queer Jihad (*http://www.queerjihad.web.com*). Al Fatiha, founded in November 1997 by a 19 year old gay muslim through the Internet, it has now more than 300 members all around the world (*http://www.al-fatiha.net*). Iman (*http://www.queernet.org/lists/iman.html*). Muslim Gay Men (*http://groups.yahoo.com/group/muslimgaymen*). Queer Muslims (*http://www.angelfire.com/Ca2/queermuslims*). Gay Muslims (*http://www.queernet.org/lists/gay-muslims.html*).

21. For a personal testimony from one of the participants in the Boston conference, see: *http://www.geocities.com/bi_mal_2000/reconciling_god.html.*

22. After a survey published in Aids Analysis Asia, 72% of truck drivers in Northern Pakistan admitted that they had sex with males, while 76% stated that they had sex with female sex workers (in Khan, 2001; op. cit.).

23. Seabrook, Jeremy. 1999. Love in a Different Climate: Men Who Have Sex with Men in India. London, Verso. 184p.

24. Altman consider there exists an "international gay/lesbian identity," "global gay subcultures," within which some individuals, in Asia for example, identify with Western gays (Altman, Dennis. 2001. Global Sex. Chicago, University of Chicago Press). Indian gay activist Ashok Row Kavi states, "We are truly international and we are a truly planetary minority." These are not very convincing. One can also consider that the globalization of gay culture is only superficial (AI).

25. One document, though, refers explicitly to "torture and discrimination against sexual minorities" (A/56/156 "Question of torture and other cruel, inhuman or degrading treatment or punishment" paragraph C. [pp.6-7, 13], 03.07.2001). Though the presence of "discriminatory law" is mentioned, no precise information is given. Mention is also made of the lack of "relevant statistics" (p.6).

26. For example: Associated Press. 10.03.2002. "China Announces Jump in AIDS Cases." Interview with E. Beyrer, director of the John Hopkins Aids International Training and Research Group, in Asia Source, nd. *http://www.asiasource.org/news/special_reports/beyrerinterview.cfm.* Choi, Hyung Ki; Ryu, J.K.; Rha, K.H.; Lee, W.H. 2001. "South Korea." International Encyclopedia of Sexuality. New York, Continuum. vol.4. Naco, 2002 (*http://www.naco.nic.in/vsnaco/indianscene/overv.htm*). Pangkahila, Wimpie; Elkholy, Ramsey. 2001. "Indonesia." International Encyclopedia of Sexuality. New York, Continuum. vol.4.United Nations Human Rights System. 1999. Ottawa, Human Rights International. Vol.3 (Asia).163p. WHO Western Pacific Regional Office, Advisory Council of Aids [as of Dec. 2001].

27. Leyson, J.F. 2001. "Indonesia." International Encyclopedia of Sexuality. New York, Continuum. vol. 4.

28. Roy, Sandip. 2000a. "Hinduism," in Haggerty, George E (ed.). Gay Histories and Cultures. New York, Garland. pp. 511. 2000b. "Kama Sutra," in ibidem, pp. 438-9. Sweet, Michael J. 2000. "India," in ibidem, pp. 466-8. Sweet, Michael J.; Zwilling, Leonard. 1996. "Like a City Ablaze: The Third Sex and the Creation of Sexuality in Jain Religious Literature," Journal of the History of Sexuality, 6 (3), pp.359-384.

29. Several examples of female and male same-sex love in the literature (mainly poems) of different cultural traditions (bengali, perso-urdu, etc.) in India are given by Ruth Vanita (2002. "Introduction," in Vanita, R. (ed.). Queering India. New York, Routledge. pp. 1-11); and mainly Vanita and Saleem Kidwai (2001. Same-Sex Love in India: Readings from Literature and History. New York, Saint Martin's Press). See also Khan, 2001 (op. cit.)

30. After a survey by the Humsafar Trust, 85% of the hijras are not castrated. Though emasculation is illegal in India today, it still occurs in secret (Winter, Sam. 2002. "An Overview of TG in Asia." [Honk Kong University]. *http://web.hku.hk/~sjwinter/TransgenderASIA/papers_an_overview*).

31. Bondyopadhyay, Aditya. 2002. "State-Supported Oppression and Persecution of Sexual Minorities," United Commission on Human Rights (08.04) [IGLHRC Internet site]. Nanda, Serena. 2000. "Hijras of India," in Haggerty, George E (ed.). Gay Histories and Cultures. New York, Garland. pp. 437. Sweet, 2000 (op. cit.).

32. Asthana, Sheena; Oostvogels, Robert. 2001. "The construction of male 'homosexuality' in India: implications for HIV transmission and prevention," Social Science

and Medicine, 52, pp. 707-721. Nath, Jayapi K.; Nayar, V.R. 1997. "India." International Encyclopedia of Sexuality. New York, Continuum. vol. 2.

33. Although no charges have actually been brought against lesbians so far (Bhaskaran, Suparna. 2002. "The Politics of Penetration: Section 377 of the Indian Penal Code," in Vanita, Ruth (ed.). Queering India. New York, Routledge. pp. 15-29).

34. In fact, heterosexual couples engaged in anal sexual intercourse can also be indicted (Sherry, Joseph. 1998. "The Law and Homosexuality in India." CEHAT. International Conference on Preventing Violence, Caring for Survivors: Role of Health Professionnals and Services in Violence. Mumbai, YMCA. pp.150-4).

35. Sherry, 1998; Bhaskaran, 2002 (op. cit.).

36. No date given.

37. Caron, Sandra L. 1998. Cross-Cultural Perspectives on Human Sexuality. Boston, Allyn and Bacon. 201p.

38. Rajalakshmi, T. K. 2001. "Targeting NGOs," Frontline, 18 (18).

39. Bondyopadhyay, 2002 (op. cit.).

40. Sarava et al., cited in Nath and Nayar, 1997 (op. cit.).

41. Redy at al.; cited in Nath and Nayar, 1997 (op. cit.).

42. Price, Susannah. 17.08.1999. "Women Gather Support For Fight To Legalise Lesbianism." South China Morning Post.

43. Gay Law Net. IGLHRC. AI, 2001 (op. cit.). Planet Out, 05.06.2000. "Sri Lankan's Media Complaint Backfires"; 08.07.2000. "Raid in China Arrests 37 Gays"; 07.09.2000. "Sri Lankans Seek Sodomy Repeal." http://www.planetout.com/pno/news/.

44. Price, Susannah. 15.10.1998. "Gays Hopeful Law Will Be Changed." South China Morning Post.

45. The full text of the Council decision can be read in Planet Out, 2000 (op. cit.).

46. The international gay guide Spartacus (2002-2003) mentions some gay-friendly bars and cafes, referenced as "not gay."

47. Silva, K.T.; Schensul, S.L.; Schensul, J.J.; Nastasi, B.; Amarasiri de Silva, M.W.; Sivayoganathan, C.; Ratnayake, P.; Wedsinghe, P.; Lewis, J.; Eisenberg, M; Aponso, H. 1997. Youth and Sexual Risk in Sri Lanka. Washington, DC, International Center for Research on Women.

48. Malla, Sapana P. 30.11.2001. "HIV/AIDS: Laws and ethical issues." The Kathmandu Post. http://www.nepalnews.com.np/contents/englishdaily/ktmpost/2001. Otton, Garry. 1996. "Scottish Media Monitor–TIBET: Forbidden Fruit in the Forbidden Land." Scots Gay Magazine/Attitude. http://www.scottishmediamonitor.com

49. 1999, op cit.

50. Chowdhury, Afsan. nd. "The Shadow Citizen." Himal: The South Asian Magazine. http://www.south-asia.com/himal/July/shadow.htm. Ki Pukar (Newsletter of the Naz Foundation). 17.04.1996. "Sexual health workshops in Bangladesh and India for men who have sex with men." Mahmud, Arshad. 21.09.1999. "Dhaka forced to face sex taboos." South China Morning Post. Star Magazine. 15.11.1996. "Bangladesh: Revealing an Underworld Network: Male Prostitution in Ramna."

51. Mahmud, 1999 (op. cit.).

52. In Mongolia News Report 2000-02, dated 30.12.2000; information provided by Richard Smith.

53. Baird, Vanessa. 2001. No-Nonsense Guide to Sexual Diversity. Oxford, New International Publications.

54. Ulaan Bataar Post. 30.06.1999. "First Gay and Lesbian Group Opens UB Office." p.1.

55. These informations, from "Yahoo Group Gay Mongolia," dated 17.12.2000, have been posted in "Mongolia News Report 2000-02."

56. Hinsch, Bret. 2000. "China," in Haggerty, George E (ed.). Gay Histories and Cultures. New York, Garland. pp. 184-8. van Gulik, Robert. 1961. Sexual Life in Anciant China. Leiden, E.J. Brill.

57. For example, the 17th C. anonymous Records of the Cut Sleeve, a compilation of 50 notorious cases, is considered the first history of homosexuality in China and still serves as a primary guide to China's male homosexual past (van Gulick, 1961; op.cit.).

58. Chou, 2001; Hinsch, 2000 (op. cit.). Hogan, Steve; Hudson, Lee (eds.). 1998. Completely Queer–The Gay and Lesbian Encyclopedia. New York, Henri Holt. 704p.

59. Europe Journal. 16.04.2002. [Chinese Homosexuals: one step out of the closet] (Chinese-language daily newspaper published in Paris and London).

60. Chou, 2001; Mc Lelland, 2000 (op. cit.). To, pers. comm. 2002.

61. People's Supreme Court's "Legal Research Notes–Item 13," 2.11.1984 (cited in Wan, Yanhai. 2001. "Becoming a Gay Activist in Contemporary China," in Sullivan, Gerard; P. A. Jackson (eds). Gay and Lesbian Asia: Culture, Identity, Community. pp. 47-64).

62. AI; Hogan and Hudson, 1998; ILGA (op. cit.).

63. Hogan and Hudson, 1998 (op. cit.).

64. Nichols, Jack. 15.10.1999. "China's Landmark Decision on Homosexuality." Greenwich Village Gazette. Wockner, Rex. 18.10.1999. "Chinese author punished for outing." International News. 286.

65. Chinese Society for the Study of Sexual Minorities, update 1997/09-2000/10. Planet Out, 2000b; Wan, 2001 (op. cit.).

66. English translation: *http://sqzm14.ust.hk/hkgay/news/manifesto.html*

67. For example: Chou Wah-shan's book, Tongzhi: Politics of Same-Sex Eroticism in Chinese Societies, was published in 2000 in the United States.

68. Chao, Julie. 11.01.1997. "Chinese still reluctant to accept homosexuality; Crusader brings his cause to the city." San Francisco Examiner. p. A1.

69. Lusby, Jo. n.d. "Headline: Coming Out of the Closet." *http://www.geocities.com/andypandy_49/GNews/GNewsPg24html.*

70. Ansfield, Jonathan. 08.08.2002. "China's First Lesbian Film Quietly Tests Limits." Reuters.

71. AI; Gallagher, John. 24.04.2001. "Normal, China. The Chinese Psychiatric Association decides that being gay is no longer a disease." The Advocate.

72. Hogan and Hudson, 1998 (op. cit.); To, pers. comm. 2002.

73. UN, Economic and Social Council, "Concluding observations of the Committee on Economic, Social and Cultural Rights (Hong Kong)," 21.05.2001. Document E/C.12/1/Add.58.

74. A clash with police happened in May 2001 when more than 40 gay activists stormed a World Red Cross Day ceremony in Kowlon Bay, waving banners and throwing anti-discrimination leaflets (Ammon, Richard. 2001a. "Gay Hong Kong 1997-2001: New Hope for an Old Closet." *http://www.travelandtranscendence.com/g-hongkong.html*).

75. Wockner, Rex. 15.03.1999. "Chinese student group attacked." International News. 255.

76. Chan, 2001 (op. cit.). Hacker, Peter. 25.07.2202. "Hong Kong Gays Fight Sex Laws." 365Gay.com.
77. Mc Lelland, 2000 (op. cit.).
78. Ammon, 2001 (op. cit.). Wockner, Rex. 07.06.1999. "First Hong Kong Pride is June 18." International News. 267.
79. http://www.gaystation.com.hk
80. Cogswell, Kelly. 01.06.2000. "Lesbian and Gay Taiwan: A Yardstick of Democracy." The Gully. Hinsch, 2000 (op. cit.). Ping, Wang; Gofyy. nd. "Year 2000 Taiwan Gay Rights Report." Taiwan Association for Human Rights (tahr). http://www.tahr.org.tw
81. Chao, Antonia Y. 2001. "Drink, Stories, Penis and Breasts: Lesbian Tomboys in Taiwan," in Sullivan, Gerard; P. A. Jackson (eds). Gay and Lesbian Asia: Culture, Identity, Community. pp. 185-209. Cogswell, 2000 (op. Cit). Huang, Hans Tao-Ming. 2000. "Taiwan," in Haggerty, George E (ed.). Gay Histories and Cultures. New York, Garland. pp. 861-2.
82. Offord, Baden. 2003. Homosexual Rights as Human Rights: Activism in Indonesia, Singapore and Australia. Oxford, Peter Lang AG.
83. Gays and lesbians took to the streets in 1993 to protest their exclusion from the debates concerning the anti-discrimination law.
84. Spartacus International Gay Guide. 2002-03. 31st ed. Berlin, Bruno Gmünder. 1218p.
85. Chang, Shen-en. 03.07.2001. "Gays and Lesbians Should Be Able to Wed." Taipei Times.
86. Iin, Irene. 03.09.2000. "Gays and Lesbians remain invisible in Taiwan". Taipei Times. Lin, Eric. 1998. "A Week in Gay Taipei." Sinorama. http://www.sinorama.com.tw.
87. Cogswell, 2000; Hinsch, 2000; Huang, 2000 (op. cit.).
88. Wang and Gofyy, nd (op. cit.).
89. Lin, 1998 (op. cit.). http://www.gaysunshine.com
90. Markus, Francis. 30.11.2001. "Taiwan's Gay Campaigners." BBC News. http://news.bbc.co.uk
91. Coleman, E.; Colgan, P.; Gooren, L. 1992. "Male cross-gender behaviour in Myanmar (Burma): a description of the acault." Archives of Sexual Behaviour. 21 (3). pp. 313-21. Winter, 2002 (op. cit.).
92. Allyn, Eric. 2002. "Trees in the Same Forest." Floating Lotus. http://www.floatinglotus.com/enter.html?target=dug.html. Jackson, 1995 (op. cit.). Jackson, Peter A. 2000. "Bangkok," "Thailand," in Haggerty, George E (ed.). Gay Histories and Cultures. New York, Garland. pp. 95-6, pp. 871-3. Jackson, 2001 (op. cit.). Matzner, Andrew. 1998. "Thailand: Paradise Not (on human rights and homophobia)." Harvard Gay and Lesbian Review. Winter.
93. Winter, 2002 (op. cit.).
94. Jackson, 2000, 2001; Allyn, 2002 (op. cit.).
95. Jackson, 2000 (op. cit.).
96. Jackson, 2000; Winter, 2000 (op. cit.).
97. A famous example is the ban of a Singaporean film, "Bugis Street," depicting transvestites, from Bangkok's 1st International Film Festival in 1998, which was said to be pornographic.
98. Jackson, 1995 (op. cit.).
99. Allyn, 2002; Choong, 1998; Sanders, 2002; Storer, 1999 (op. cit.).

100. Allyn, 2002 (op. cit.).
101. Allyn, 2002 (op. cit). Tourneau, Pierre. 11.11.2001. "The Crackdown on Gay Bars in Bangkok: Summer, 2001." Gais sans frontieres. The social order campaign was criticized under the party itself for strategic reasons, in the entertainment and tourism business worlds for economic reasons, but it seems to have been supported by the general public.
102. Hogan and Hudson, 1998; Jackson, 2000; Matzner, 1998 (op. cit.). Tatchell, Peter. 1989. "Thailand: gayness, bar boys and sex tourism." Gay Times. *http://www.petertatchell.net/international/thailand.htm*
103. Jackson, Peter A.; Cook, Nerida M. (eds.). 1999. Gender and Sexualities in Modern Thailand. Chiang Mai, Silkworm Books. 289p.
104. Allyn, 2002; Jackson, 2000; Tatchell, 1989 (op. cit.).
105. Jackson, 1995, p. 267 (op. cit.).
106. Choong, 1998; Tatchell, 1989 (op. cit.).
107. Allyn, 2002; Jackson, 1995; 2001; Matzner, 1998 (op. cit.).
108. Full nudity, and the exposure of her "masculinity" would have meant at the same time the end of her performance as a kathoey, for these are tolerated provided they remain confined in certain roles or professions, where they perform femininity (Storer, 1999; op. cit.).
109. Allyn, 2002; Storer, 1999 (op. cit.).
110. Allyn, 2002; Winter, 2002 (op. cit.).
111. Ammon, Richard. 2000. "Finding Gay Laos." *http://www.travelandtranscendence.com/g-laos.html*
112. Baird, 2001, op cit.
113. Ammon, Richard. (1996) 2000. "Gay Life in Cambodia." *http://www.travelandtranscendence.com/cam-table-sm.html*.
114. Ammon, (1996) 2000 (op. cit.).
115. Wockner, Rex. 10.05.1999. "Gay Bar Opens in Cambodia." International News. 263.
116. Ammon, Richard. 2001. "Gay Vietnam (Hanoi): Crouching Love, Hidden Passion." *http://www.travelandtranscendence.com/g-hanoi.html*. Doussantousse, Serge; Anh, Ngoc; Tooke, L. 2002. "Men who have sex with men in Vietnam–Sexuality & Prostitution." Sex-Work (e-mail Forum). *http://archives.healthdev.net/sex-work/msg0051.html*
117. Called bong cai in the south and dong co in the north.
118. Pastoetter, Jakob. 2001. "Vietnam." International Encyclopedia of Sexuality. New York, Continuum. vol. 4.
119. Doussantousse et al., 2002 (op. cit.). [Proschan,] Frank. 2000. "On the Legality of Homosexuality in Vietnam. . . ." VN-GBLF (e-mail Forum). *http://www.utopia-asia.com/vietterm.htm*
120. Pastoetter, 2001 (op. cit.).
121. Marnais, P. 1967. Saigon after dark. New York, Mc Fadden-Bartell.
122. Ammon, 2001; Doussantousse et al., 2002 (op. cit.).
123. Arthurs, Claire. 20.08.2002. "Novel breaks Vietnam's gay sex taboo." BBC News. *http://news.bbc.co.uk/1/hi/world/asia-pacific/2205506.stm*. Cohen, Margot. 29.08.2002. "Busting a taboo." The Far Eastern Economic Review.
124. Not having a "clear-cut" gender is a problem notably for the Muslim burial rites.
125. Liebhold, David. 02.10.2000. "Coming Out in the Open." Time Magazine. 156 (13). Teh, Yi koon. 2001. "Mak Nyahs (Male Transsexuals) in Malaysia: The Influence of Culture and Religion on their Identity." The International Journal of

Transgenderism. 5(3). Yoong, Sean. 08.07.2002. "Malaysian State Legislature Passes Bill on Strict Islamic Criminal Code." Associated Press.

126. In Ramakrishnan, Mageswary. 26.09.2000. "Homosexuality is a Crime Worse than Murder.' Interview with Malaysia's Morality Police." Time Magazine.

127. Jackson, 2001 (op. cit.).

128. Mak means "mother."

129. Pak means "father," abang means "brother" or "man."

130. Teh, 2001 (op. cit). Teh, Yi koon. 2002. "Country Report: Malaysia." http://web.hku.hk/^sjwinter/TransgenderASIA/country_report_malaysia.

131. Ayu, Mel. 1999. "Was I Born to Be This Way? The Thoughts of a Muslim Gay in an Oppressed Society." GayReading. http://gayreading.com/Lifestyles/Muslim.html.

132. Non-Muslim mak nyah are not directly concerned by the ruling.

133. Teh, 2001, 2002 (op. cit.). Bamadhaj, Nadiah. Jan. 1999. "The Hot Potato: Sexuality Rights Advocacy in Malaysia." Saksia. 3. http://www.saksi.com/jan99/nadiahb.htm

134. Baba, Ismail. 2001. "Gay and Lesbian Couples in Malaysia," in Sullivan, Gerard; P. A. Jackson (eds). Gay and Lesbian Asia: Culture, Identity, Community. pp. 143-163. Rastam, Alina. nov. 1998. "Out of the Closet And Into the Courtroom." Saksi 2. http://www.saksi.com/novdec1998/alina.htm

135. Singh, Jasbant. 09.07.2002. "Malaysian Islamic Opposition Plans to Extend Islamic Law on Non-Muslims." Associated Press. Yoong, 2002 (op. cit.).

136. In Soong, Kua kia. 1999. "Malaysia: The Struggle for Human Rights in Malaysia." Asian Human Rights Commission online Newsletter. http://www.ahrchk.net/hrsolid/mainfile.php/1999vol09no01/776

137. A holdover from British colonial administration, it "gives the police unacceptably broad powers of search and detention, as well as restrictions on freedom of movement, speech, association and assembly" (Human Rights Watch. 1998. "Human Rights Watch on Malaysia: It's Not Just The Trial." http://www,hrw.org/press98/nov/maly1102.htm).

138. 2001, p.18, op cit

139. Bamadhaj, 1999 (op. cit.).

140. Winter, 2002 (op. cit.).

141. Human Rights Watch World Report, 2000 (op. cit.). Wockner, Rex. 02.08.1999. "Malaysia fines transvestites." International News. 275.

142. Watt, Nicholas. 02.11.2001. "Malaysian PM rebuked for thereat to UK gay ministers." The Guardian.

143. Liebhold, 2000 (op. cit.).

144. Baba, 2001 (op. cit.).

145. Baba, 2001 (op. cit.). Murray, Stephen; Allyn, Eric. 1997. "Two Islamic AIDS Education Organizations." in Murray, Stephen; Roscoe, Will (eds). Islamic Homosexualities. New York, New York University Press. pp. 297-301.

146. Tet Sieu, Choong; Oorjitham Santha. 13.11.1998. "A subject too hot to handle. An anti-gay movement quickly loses team." Asiaweek.

147. Offord, Baden. 2000. "Singapore," in Haggerty, George E (ed.). Gay Histories and Cultures. New York, Garland. p. 821. Offord, 2003; Jackson, 2001 (op. cit.).

148. Heng, Russel H. K 2001. "Tiptoe out of the Closet: The Before and After of the Increasingly Visible Gay Community in Singapore," in Sullivan, Gerard; P. A. Jackson (eds). Gay and Lesbian Asia: Culture, Identity, Community. pp. 81-97. Leong, L. 1997.

"Singapore," in D.J. West and R. Green. Sociolegal Control of Homosexuality. NY, Plenum, pp. 127-143. Offord, 2003 (op. cit.).

149. Leong, 1997 (op. cit.).

150. Leong, 1997 (op. cit.).

151. Leong, 1997 (op. cit.).

152. Ammon, Richard. 2002. "The 'New' Gay Singapore '02." http://www.travelandtranscendence.com/g-sing02.html. Heng, 2001. Offord, 2003 (op. cit.).

153. Heng, 2001; Leong, 1997; Offord, 2000, 2003 (op. cit.).

154. See for instance the analysis of Yawning Bread, personal homepage of a gay Singaporean Alex Au, a "site of storytelling and resistance" in Offord (2003, pp. 156-160; op. cit.).

155. Offord, 2003 (op. cit.).

156. Such a radical change would make women of them, and no more waria, no more members of an "alternative masculinity." Moreover, the men who look for sex with waria sex workers usually want to be penetrated. Lastly, the operation is worth, on average, 30 to 40 monthly income of a "lower-class worker" (Boellstorff, Tom. 2001. "Waria, National Transvestites." Paper presented at the 3d Conference of the IASSCS, Melbourne).

157. Boellstorff, Tom; Yatim, Danny. 2000. "Indonesia", in Haggerty, George E (ed.). Gay Histories and Cultures. New York, Garland. pp. 468-470. Murray, 1997 (op. cit.). Oetomo, Dédé (interviewed by Josko Petkovic). 1998. "Dédé Oetomo talks on Reyog Ponorogo". Intersections 2. http://wwwsshe.murdoch.edu.au/intersections/issue2/Oetomo.html.

158. Oetomo, 1998 (op. cit.). Wilson, Ian D. 1999. "Reog Ponogoro. Spirituality, Sexuality and Power in a Javanese Performance Tradition." Intersections 2. http://wwwsshe.murdoch.edu.au/intersections/issue2/Warok.html.

159. Boellstorff and Yatim, 2000; Oetomo, 1998; Offord, 2003 (op. cit.). Oetomo, Dédé. 1996. "Gay identities." Inside Indonesia 46. http://insideindonesia.org/edit46/dede.htm

160. Murray, 2001; Offord, 2003 (op. cit.).

161. Ammon, Richard. 1998. "Gay Indonesia." http://www.travelandtranscendence.com/g-indo.html. Ammon, Richard. 2002. "Gay Bali–Perennial and Tranquil." http://www.globalgayz.com/g-bali.html.

162. Pangkahila and Elkholy, 2001 (op. cit.).

163. Offord, 2003 (op. cit.).

164. Murray, Alison J. 2001. "Let Them Take Ecstasy: Class and Jakarta Lesbians," in Sullivan, Gerard; P. A. Jackson (eds). Gay and Lesbian Asia: Culture, Identity, Community. pp. 165-184. Offord, 2003; Pangkahila and Elkholy, 2001 (op. cit.).

165. Leyson, 2001 (op. cit.). Tan, Michael L. 2001. "Survival Through Pluralism: Emerging Gay Communities in the Philippines," in Sullivan, Gerard; P. A. Jackson (eds). Gay and Lesbian Asia: Culture, Identity, Community. pp. 117-142.

166. Brewer, Carolyn. 1998. "Baylan, Asog, Transvestism, and Sodomy: Gender, Sexuality and the Sacred in Early Colonial Philippines." Intersections 2. http://wwwsshe.murdoch.edu.au/intersections/issue2/carolyn2.html

167. Tan, 2001 (op. cit.).

168. Sasot, Alyssa. 2002. "Country Report: The Philippines." Paper presented at Marriage, Partnership and Parenting in the 21st Century (Torino, June 5-8).

169. Ammon, Richard. 1998b. "Traumatic History and Dramatic Queens in the Philippines." http://www.travelandtranscendence.com/phil.html. Tan, 2001 (op. cit.).

170. For example, Imelda Marcos was the ultimate fag hag, extending her patronage to "the arts."
171. Tan, 2001 (op. cit.).
172. Marin, Marin, Malu S. 1996. "Going Beyond the Personal." Women in Action (Manila). 1.
173. Sanders, 2002 (op. cit.).
174. Choi et al., 2001; Hogan and Hudson, 1998 (op. cit.).
175. Berry, Chris. 1998. "My Queer Korea: Identity, Space, and the 1998 Seoul Queer & Video Festival." Intersections 2. http://wwwsshe.murdoch.edu.au/intersections/issue2/Berry.html
176. Choi et al., 2001 (op. cit).
177. Offord, 2003 (op. cit.).
178. Ammon, Richard. (1997) 2001. "Gay Korea: A Paradigm is Shifting." http://www.travelandtranscendence.com/g-korea.html
179. Choi et al., 2001 (op. cit.).
180. http://www.geocities.com/WestHollywood/2510
181. http://simani.chol.com
182. http://www.hitel.net
183. Both Leupp (Gary P. (1995) 1997. Male Colors. The Construction of Homosexuality in Tokugawa Japan. Berkeley-Los Angeles-London, University of California Press. 310p.) and Jnanavira (Dharmachari. 2001. "Homosexuality in the Japanese Buddhist tradition." Western Buddhist Review. 3) admit not to know of any other culture that has kept such an intense historical record of love/sex between men.
184. Leupp, (1995) 1997 (op. cit.). Nakao, Seigo. 2000. "Kabuki," "Samurai," in Haggerty, George E (ed.). Gay Histories and Cultures. New York, Garland. pp. 509-511; 770-771.
185. Watanabe Tsuneo; Jun'ichi, Iwata. 1989. The Love of the Samurai: A Thousand Years of Japanese Homosexuality.
186. Laurent, 2001, Laurent, Erick. 2001. "Homosexualités masculines dans le Japon contemporain." In Lucas, N. & C. Sakai (eds). Japon Pluriel 4. Arles, Picquier. pp.299-310. Ibid. 2002. "Typology of Male Homosexualities in Contemporary Japan and its mediatized expressions." Paper presented at the Conference of the International Association for Media and Communication Research (IAMCR) (Barcelona).
187. Confessions of a Mask, published in 1949, for example, is the first modern Japanese novel, largely autobiographical, to deal directly with homosexuality.
188. Laurent, 2001, 2002 (op. cit.). Lundsing, Wim. 2001. Beyond Common Sense. Sexuality and Gender in Contemporary Japan. London, Kegan Paul. 411p.
189. Mc Lelland, Marc. 2001. Male Homosexuality in Modern Japan: Cultural Myths and Social Realities. Richmond, Curzon Press.
190. http://www.gayweb.ne.jp [in Japanese].
191. http://www.gayjapan.com [in Japanese].
192. http://www.geocities.co.jp/WallStreet-Stock/5937/about-tmgf.htm [in Japanese].
193. http://gavie.jp
194. http://www.mensnet.jp
195. http://www.rainbownet.jp
196. Laurent, 2001, 2002 (op. cit.).
197. Berry, 2001; Chou, 2001; Sanders, 2002; Wan, 2001 (op. cit.).
198. Choong, 1998 (op. cit.).
199. Khan, 2001; Seabrook, 1999 (op. cit.).

200. This can be clearly seen for example in movies about homosexuality. Western movies depict conflict situations between homosexuality and family, never suggesting a resolution by finding a space for "gayness" inside the family. This is not the case in Asian lesbian and gay films (Berry, 2001; op. cit.).

201. Offord, Baden; Cantrell, Leon. 2001. "Homosexual Rights as Human Rights in Indonesia and Australia," in Sullivan, Gerard; P. A. Jackson (eds). Gay and Lesbian Asia: Culture, Identity, Community. pp. 233-252.

202. 2001, p. 107 (op. cit.).

203. For several examples, see: Chou, 2001; pp. 36-39 (op. cit.).

204. Offord and Cantrell, 2001 (op. cit.).

205. At p. 246

206. At pp. 248-9

Laws and Sexual Identities: Closing or Opening the Circle?

Phillip Tahmindjis, BA, LLB, LLM, JSD

International Bar Association

SUMMARY. This essay considers, in comparative perspective, the articles in this volume to see what lessons might be learned with respect to the effectiveness of human rights norms in the struggle for GLBT rights and how these lessons might be used for successful activism. It notes that the concept of "GLBT" is itself not uniform, so that "GLBT rights" must also be contextual. It argues that successful change has been wrought when GLBT rights, however perceived, have been built onto the earlier successes of other movements, such as those for racial and gender equality. This in turn requires, and is assisted by, throwing off parochialism which prevents or hampers the building on the successes that may have occurred in other jurisdictions. Activism needs to be fitted to context, so that a "critical mass" is achieved, allowing sufficient acceptance of

---

Phillip Tahmidjis is Program Lawyer, International Bar Association, London. Dr Tahmindjis was for over 20 years an academic teaching in Australia, North America and Hong Kong, and was active in the struggle for gay law reform in his home state of Queensland. A consultant on discrimination and human rights to government agencies and private industry, he was also a member of the Queensland Anti-Discrimination Tribunal. The views expressed in this paper are his own and do not necessarily represent the views of the International Bar Association. Correspondence may be addressed: International Bar Association, 10th floor, 1 Stephen Street, London W1T 1AT, United Kingdom (E-mail: Phillip.Tahmindjis@int-bar.org).

[Haworth co-indexing entry note]: "Laws and Sexual Identities: Closing or Opening the Circle?" Tahmindjis, Phillip. Co-published simultaneously in *Journal of Homosexuality* (Harrington Park Press, an imprint of The Haworth Press, Inc.) Vol. 48, No. 3/4, 2005, pp. 227-232; and: *Sexuality and Human Rights: A Global Overview* (ed: Helmut Graupner, and Phillip Tahmindjis) Harrington Park Press, an imprint of The Haworth Press, Inc., 2005, pp. 227-232. Single or multiple copies of this article are available for a fee from The Haworth Document Delivery Service [1-800-HAWORTH, 9:00 a.m. - 5:00 p.m. (EST). E-mail address: docdelivery@haworthpress.com].

http://www.haworthpress.com/web/JH
© 2005 by The Haworth Press, Inc. All rights reserved.
Digital Object Identifier: 10.1300/J082v48n03_10

change. Once this is translated into law, a "halo" effect is produced. However, this is not the end of the problem, but the beginning of a new set of problems. *[Article copies available for a fee from The Haworth Document Delivery Service: 1-800-HAWORTH. E-mail address: <docdelivery@haworthpress.com> Website: <http://www.HaworthPress.com> © 2005 by The Haworth Press, Inc. All rights reserved.]*

KEYWORDS. Comparative approach, law reform, activism, human rights, contextuality

To consider whether human rights norms have been a help or a hindrance in the attempt to achieve just treatment for people of all sexualities, it is useful to reflect on the comparative insights that may be drawn from the analyses in this volume. In the amalgam of laws (international, regional and domestic), values, cultures and sexual identities presented, can we discern any themes, trends or symptomatic patterns which might help us in the endeavour to achieve in law a valuing of sexual diversity rather than a mere tolerance of it?

Do progressive values engender legal norms more sympathetic to the needs of the GLBT communities? Not necessarily. As Elliott and Bonauto point out, the progressive movements in the United States since the Stonewall riot nearly forty years ago have not led to a rush of pro-GLBT laws: the Supreme Court has only just struck down a sodomy law[1] and same-sex marriages are not legal. In Canada, on the other hand, the lack of overt pro-GLBT sentiment was nevertheless contemporaneous with the passing of the Charter of Rights and Freedoms twenty years ago, which has proven to be a crucial factor for GLBT activism and change. The Charter was also the basis for the recent decisions on same-sex marriage in Canada.[2] But it may ultimately depend on the political power of the people holding progressive values and the processes of exercising that power. The use of "initiatives" in the United States has undone many legislative advances. While Canada might not have had as vocal a pro-GLBT movement as in the United States, its political leaders nevertheless held values which were able to embrace and implement an equality norm and there was relatively little vociferous opposition to this.

Justice Kirby eloquently argues that changes in attitudes can and do lead to a change in laws. However, he points out that it is the *increasing* demands for equality together with a perception of the invalidity of the myths on which racial and gender discrimination were often based (moral, biological, religious) which help remove the barriers of stigmatisation. The question becomes: how is the "critical mass" reached to enable this to occur? Louw points out that in South Africa, after four decades of *apartheid*, the Constitution embraced difference. This occurred in a country where patriarchy and homophobia were (and are) endemic. Thus, GLBT rights in effect piggy-backed on the movement for racial equality. This phenomenon is also noted by Elliott and Bonauto when they describe the movement for gay rights developing from the movements for racial and gender equality.

So, do the values and processes of liberal democracies engender legal norms more sympathetic to the needs of GLBT communities? Not necessarily. Graupner details the situation in European countries where the liberal paradigm of equality has enabled some advances in, but has ultimately hobbled, the freedom to express one's sexuality (rather than merely be tolerated), as is particularly seen with respect to issues of gender identity and transsexualism (which Lord Reed also notes), and an inconsistency of approach between the organisations of the European Union.

Do legal systems which are more centralised in areas of law significant to GLBT issues (such as criminal law) better enable the creation of GLBT-sympathetic legal norms than do decentralised systems? For example, in the United States criminal law is a matter of state jurisdiction whereas in Canada it is a federal matter. Canada is considerably ahead of the US with respect to GLBT-friendly laws. Certainly, a positive change can be more easily made national in a centralised system. However, negative change can just as easily be made in such circumstances. It should also be remembered that matrimonial laws are state- or province-based in both the US and Canada. Canada is considerably ahead of the US here too. The legal and democratic structures might help, but it is the mix of values with political power which is more significant.

In Common Law systems the centripetal force of precedent might be thought to make for a convergence of court decisions and norms. There is some movement in this direction, such as the decision of the United States Supreme Court in *Lawrence v Texas*[3] which has mainstreamed constitutional arguments by declaring that there is no "gay exception" in the United States Constitution and indicates a slightly less parochial attitude of the Court in its (limited) recognition of arguments from courts of other nations, as Elliott and Bonauto point out. However, the learned authors also indicate that the chromosomal approach of the Court to transgender issues is at odds with the approach in other countries, a situation alluded to by Lord Reed as well. The centripetal pull is weak.

Lord Reed points out that, contrary to some arguments used to "sell" sex discrimination legislation, sex and gender identity are not irrelevant or unimportant, although the degree of relevance differs with respect to the area of law under consideration. Obviously, laws with respect to marriage are now central to this discourse, but whether as a result the metaphorical circle is being closed, or opened up, remains in issue. Sexual identity is crucial to the core sense of self, but its legal manifestations are largely a matter of law and public policy, and these can thus clash with the notion or norms of individual freedom. Laurent points out that a gay or lesbian "identity" is itself a Western notion to which people in most Asian countries are traditionally unfamiliar. Men having sex with other men in cultures where marriage is primarily for the social object of procreation and family stability does not engender "gay" identity but a tolerated private activity. "Coming out" is often considered to be "Western" and unnecessary. The problem from a global standpoint, therefore, is not only the potential clash of legal norms, but a clash of discourses arising out of different social and cultural systems.

In such circumstances, are universal human rights norms useful? Indeed, are they needed? The very universality of human rights is dependent on a symbiotic relationship with domestic legal norms, as my own article in this volume points out. Laurent extends this by arguing that the universality of human rights must also be integrated into cultural and social specifics. What his article also intimates, however, is that integration transmogrifies into breaking-point when sexualities conflict with the supreme value of (heterosexual) family, when homophobic violence is not a crime, when patriarchy means that lesbians are especially badly treated, and when one's true sexuality is kept an open secret to be tolerated but not really valued. In societies where identity is constructed more by one's position in society and as part of a family, sexuality has less to do with one's identity. Conversely, however, heteronormativity in such societies is being broken down by the very Western patterns of binary opposition (gay/straight; gay male/lesbian) which have been traditionally regarded as irrelevant. But, as Laurent argues, where the essentialist categories to which "rights" attach are less evident, not only is the very notion of GLBT "rights" less urgent, but a different form of activism is required. There is, therefore, a difference between East and West, or between developed and developing countries, with respect to the effective modalities for the advancement of GLBT rights. But this does not mean that international human rights norms are correspondingly of more or of less use. It means that where the impact of those symbiotic norms is primarily domestic and with weak international supervision, they must be *used* contextually in the light of domestic laws and values. They are indeed needed so that, even in jurisdictions with relatively enlightened laws applying to GLBT communities, sexual orientation is not reduced in law merely to forms of sexual intercourse and a "separate but equal" fallacy allowed to flourish.

Notions like "equality" and "privacy" can be, and have been, compromised. The Constitutional Court of South Africa has suggested that such notions should be used interactively, rather than as alternatives.[4] Otherwise, as Sachs J has said,[5] the recognition of a right to privacy may be seen as a poor second prize while in fact it protects people rather than places, allowing for self-actualisation.

These questions will remain important as the GLBT communities, and any right-thinking person, strives for solutions to emerging issues such as inter-jurisdictional recognition of rights (e.g., the recognition in a jurisdiction whose legal system does not allow for same-sex marriages of a same-sex marriage validly celebrated elsewhere) and the movement beyond tolerance and non-interference to protection. The demarcation between these rights and other rights such as the right to religious beliefs is still being played out, with the Pope stating in July 2003 that same-sex marriages were deviant and not part of "God's authentic plan," while North American courts have contemporaneously upheld the right of a gay student to take his boyfriend to the Prom at a Catholic School.[6]

What indications can be drawn from the articles in this volume as to the way ahead? What seems clear, in the welter of laws and norms rattling against each other, is that successful change has been wrought when GLBT rights, however perceived, have been built onto the earlier successes of other movements, such as those for racial and gender equality. This in turn requires, and is assisted by, throwing off parochialism which prevents or hampers the building on the successes in other jurisdictions. Activism needs to be fitted to context, so that a "critical mass" is achieved, allowing sufficient acceptance of change. Once this is translated into law, a "halo" effect is produced.

But law is not the end of the problem, but the beginning of a set of new problems. The closed circle frays and opens again as laws become out of step with changing values, but the halo effect mentioned above encourages inertia. The context in which both activism and law must work is not just related to country, culture or legal system; it is also temporal.

NOTES

1. *Lawrence & Garner v Texas* USSC 2003 (report pending)
2. *Halpern & MCCT v Canada (AG)* [2002] 60 O.R. (3d) 321, affirmed [2003] O.J. No.2268
3. USSC 2003 (report pending)
4. *National Coalition for Gay and Lesbian Equality v Minister of Justice* 1998 (12) BCLR 1517
5. *Id*, at para 115ff.
6. *Hall v Powers* [2002] OJ No. 1803

Index

Ackerman, J., 156-157
Activism influences, 227-232
Adoption of Children Act (New South Wales, Australia), 37-39
African Charter on Human and Peoples' Rights, 109-110
African Commission on Human Rights, 22
African law perspectives, 141-162. *See also* South African law perspectives
ALI (American Law Institute), 97-98
Aliens Control Act (South Africa), 154
All Burma Students' Democratic Front, 187
American Convention Human Rights, 109-110
American Law Institute (ALI), 97-98
American (United States) law perspectives, 92-98
Amnesty International, 23-24,195-196,199-200
Annual migration programme (RAM), 41-42
Asian Human Rights Commission, 170
Asian law perspectives, 141-162
   background and historical perspectives, 163-165
   country-by-country situations, 170-212
      Bangladesh, 177-178
      Burma, 186-187
      Cambodia, 190-191
      China, 179-182
      Hong Kong, 182-184
      India, 171-175
      Indonesia, 199-202
      Japan, 208-212
      Laos, 190
      Malaysia, 193-196
      Mongolia, 178-179
      Nepal, 177
      overviews and summaries, 170-171
      Philippines, 202-205
      Singapore, 196-199
      South Korea, 205-208
      Sri Lanka, 175-177
      Taiwan, 184-186
      Thailand, 187-190
      Vietnam, 191-193
   future perspectives, 212-214
   Gay Asian identities, 167-169
      diversity-related issues, 167-168
      homoeroticism traditions, 168-169
   overviews and summaries, 163-165
   reference resources, 215-225
   religious influences, 171-209. *See also* Religious influences
      Buddhism, 175-178,180-189,205-209
      Confucianism, 168,179-180, 196-197,205,214
      Hinduism, 171-178
      Islam, 168,188,194-195
      Judeo-Christian issues, 172,209
      Taoism, 184
   Western model influences, 165-167
      overviews and summaries, 166-167
      universal human rights, 165-166
Asiawatch, 199-200
Att.-Gen *v* Otahuhu Family Court, 82-85

© 2005 by The Haworth Press, Inc. All rights reserved.   *233*

Australian law perspectives, 31-48
　background and historical
　　perspectives, 31-35
　constitutional environments, 35-36
　fluidity- and change-related
　　influences, 32-46
　　discrimination enlightenment
　　　patterns, 45-46
　　federal legislation, 40-45
　　legal environments, 32-35
　　state legislation, 36-40
　future perspectives, 45-46
　overviews and summaries, 31-32
　RAM (annual migration
　　programme), 41-42
　reference resources, 46-48

Background and historical
　　perspectives. *See also under*
　　individual topics
　Asian law, 163-165
　Australian law, 31-35
　CERSGOSIG (Center of Research
　　and Legal Comparative
　　Studies on Sexual Orientation
　　and Gender Identity), 4-6
　comparative law, 228-230
　European law, 50-55,108-109
　　sexuality rights, 108-109
　　transsexual rights, 50-55
　ILGLaw (International Lesbian and
　　Gay Law Association), 1-2,6
　international law, 9-15
　North American law, 92-103
　South African law, 143-145
Baer, S., 6
Baher v Miike, 96
Baker v Vermont, 97
BANANA, 204
Bandhu Social Welfare Society, 178
Bangkok Declaration, 166
Bangkok Gay Festival, 190
Bangladesh law perspectives, 177-178
Bell, M., 6

Bellinger v Bellinger, 85-86
Bharosa Trust, 174-175
Bibliographies. *See* Reference
　　resources
Bills. *See* Laws and legislation
Bleau v Quebec, 101
Bondyopadhyay, A., 173
Borillo, D., 6
Bowers v Hardwick, 93-96,147-148
Bradshaw, B., 196
British Columbia College of Teachers
　　v Trinity Western University,
　　99-100
Buddhism influences,
　　175-178,180-189,205-209
Burmese law perspectives, 186-187
Burnswoods, J., 39

Calvinism influences, 142-143
Cambodian law perspectives, 190-191
Cameron, E., 2,146-151
Campaign for Lesbian Rights, 174
Canadian law perspectives, 98-103
Can't Live In the Closet (CLIC), 204
Case law. *See* Court cases
Catholic Church influences, 33-35
Ceccherini, E., 6
CERSGOSIG (Center of Research and
　　Legal Comparative Studies
　　on Sexual Orientation and
　　Gender Identity), 3-8
　background and historical
　　perspectives, 4-6
　future perspectives, 6-7
　legal information databanks, 5-6
　overviews and summaries, 3-4
　reference resources, 7
Change- and fluidity-related influences
　discrimination enlightenment
　　patterns, 45-46
　federal legislation, 40-45
　legal environments, 32-35
　state legislation, 36-40

Index

Charter of Fundamental Rights (European Union), 15
Charter of Rights and Freedoms, 98-99
Chen, T., 183
Chi Heng Foundation, 184
China Rainbow, 182
Chinese law perspectives, 179-182
Chinese Society for the Study of Sexual Minorities, 182
Chingusai, 207
Cho-Dong Society, 207
Chulalongkorn, K., 187-188
CLIC (Can't Live In the Closet), 204
Coalition for Sexual Minority Rights, 175
Coco, N., 6
Common Law systems, 25,229-230
Companions on a Journey, 176-177
Comparative law perspectives, 91-106,227-232
  activism influences, 227-232
  background and historical perspectives, 228-230
  Common Law systems, 229-230
  contextuality issues, 227-232
  future perspectives, 231
  liberal democracies processes, 229-230
  North American law, 91-106
  overviews and summaries, 227-228
  progressive values, 228
  reference resources, 232
  universal human rights, 230-231
Confucianism influences, 168,179-180, 196-197,205,214
Constitution Act (Canada), 98-99
Constitutional environments, 35-36
Contextuality issues, 227-232
Convention for the Protection of Human Rights and Fundamental Freedoms, 14-15
Convention on the Rights of the Child, 23-24,109-110
Convention Relating to the Status of Refugees, 10-12,22-23
Copyright Act (India), 174-175
Corbett *v* Corbett, 57-59,73-76
Cossy *v* The United Kingdom, 17,69-72
Council of Europe (Committee of Ministers), 22-23
Court cases. *See also under individual topics*
  Att.-Gen *v* Otahuhu Family Court, 82-85
  Baher *v* Miike, 96
  Baker *v* Vermont, 97
  Bellinger *v* Bellinger, 85-86
  Bleau *v* Quebec, 101
  Bowers *v* Hardwick, 93-96,147-148
  British Columbia College of Teachers *v* Trinity Western University, 99-100
  Corbett *v* Corbett, 57-59,73-76
  Cossy *v* The United Kingdom, 17,69-72
  Dawood *v* Minister of Home Affairs, 151
  Delmas Treason Trial, 148
  Dudgeon *v* United Kingdom, 14-15
  European law perspectives, 81-85,111-125
    sexuality rights, 111-125
    transsexual rights, 81-85
  Farr *v* Mutual & Federal, 150-151
  Godwin *v* The United Kingdom, 85-97
  Herzberg *v* Finland, 13-14
  Joslin et al. *v* New Zealand, 17-18,21-23
  Langan *v* St. Vincent's Hospital, 98
  Langemaat *v* Minister of Safety and Security and Others, 150-151
  Lawrence *v* Texas, 94,229-230
  M. *v* H., 99-100
  NCGLE (National Coalition for Gay and Lesbian Equality) *v* Minister of Home Affairs, 151-152
  Nicholas Toonen *v* Australia, 12-13

R v Tan, 59-60
Rees v the United Kingdom, 66-69
Roe v Wade, 94
Romer v Evans, 94-96
Sheffield and Horsham v The United Kingdom, 17,76-79
Toit v Minister of Population and Welfare Department, 151
Toonen v Australia, 12-13,19-23, 35
Van Oosterwijck v Belgium, 63-66
Van Rooyen v Van Rooyen, 144-145,150-151
written law influences, 109-110
X, Y, & Z v The United Kingdom, 17,73-76
Curse of inconsistency concept, 121-125

Databanks, 5-6
Dawood v Minister of Home Affairs, 151
De Facto Relationship Act (New South Wales, Australia), 39-40
De Rose, S., 176-177
Decriminalization issues, 145-150
Defense of Marriage Act (United States), 97
Delmas Treason Trial, 148
Discrimination enlightenment patterns, 45-46
Diversity-related issues, 167-168
Don't Ask, Don't Tell concept, 95
Dream-reality dichotomies, 12-15
Dudgeon v United Kingdom, 14-15

ECHR (European Convention on Human Rights), 15-23, 62-81,109-125
Elliott, R.D., 1-2,6,91-106
Enlightenment patterns, 45-46

Equal Opportunity Tribunal (New South Wales, Australia), 37-39
Equity in Common Law Systems, 25
European Convention on Human Rights (ECHR), 15-23, 62-81,109-125
European Court of Human Rights, 17-19,34-35
European law perspectives, 49-90, 107-139
  sexuality rights, 107-139
    background and historical perspectives, 108-109
    court cases, 111-125
    curse of inconsistency concept, 121-125
    force of public opinion concept, 118-121
    freedom from abuse or violence concept, 111-113
    freedom to engage in sexual activity concept, 113-118
    future perspectives, 125-126
    overviews and summaries, 107-108
    reference resources, 127-139
    sexual rights as human rights concept, 110-111
    written law, 109-110
  transsexual rights, 49-90
    background and historical perspectives, 50-55
    court cases, 81-85
    ECHR (European Convention on Human Rights), 62-81
    future perspectives, 85-87
    other jurisdiction perspectives, 60-62
    overviews and summaries, 49-66
    reference resources, 87-90
    United Kingdom law perspectives, 56-60

Index

Evidence Act (New South Wales, Australia), 37-39

Fabeni, S., 3-8
Family law issues, 150-153
Farr v Mutual & Federal, 150-151
Fluidity- and change-related influences, 32-46
    discrimination enlightenment patterns, 45-46
    federal legislation, 40-45
    legal environments, 32-35
    state legislation, 36-40
Force of public opinion concept, 118-121
Freedom from abuse or violence concept, 111-113
Freedom to engage in sexual activity concept, 113-118
Freeland, J., 79
French law perspectives, 60-62
Functional symbiosis, 20
Fundamental topics. *See* Overviews and summaries
Future perspectives. *See also under individual topics*
    Asian law, 212-214
    Australian law perspectives, 45-46
    CERSGOSIG (Center of Research and Legal Comparative Studies on Sexual Orientation and Gender Identity), 6-7
    comparative law, 231
    European law, 85-87, 125-126
        sexuality rights, 125-126
        transsexual rights, 85-87
    ILGLaw (International Lesbian and Gay Law Association), 2
    international law, 22-25
    South African law, 156-158

Gang, F., 181
Garcia, N., 205
Gay and Lesbian Immigration Task Force (GLITF), 41-45
Gay and Lesbian Organisation of the Witwatersrand (GLOW), 148
Gay Asian identities, 167-169
    diversity-related issues, 167-168
    homoeroticism traditions, 168-169
Gay Chat, 185
Gay Citizens Movement, 186
Gaya Nusantara, 202
Gender dysphoria syndrome, 52
Gender identity, 91-106
Genocide Convention, 22-23
GLITF (Gay and Lesbian Immigration Task Force), 41-45
Global perspectives (human rights and sexuality). *See also under individual topics*
    Asian law, 141-162
    Australian law, 31-48
    CERSGOSIG (Center of Research and Legal Comparative Studies on Sexual Orientation and Gender Identity), 3-8
    comparative law, 227-232
    European law, 49-90, 107-139
        sexuality rights, 107-139
        transsexual rights, 49-90
    ILGLaw (International Lesbian and Gay Law Association), 1-2
    international law, 9-29
    North American law, 91-106
    overviews and summaries, xvii-xviii
    South African law, 141-162
GLOW (Gay and Lesbian Organisation of the Witwatersrand), 148
Godwin v The United Kingdom, 85-97
Graupner, H., xvii-xviii, 6, 107-139

Hadi, A., 195
Herzberg v Finland, 13-14

Hinduism influences, 171-178
Historical perspectives. *See*
    Background and historical
    perspectives
Homoeroticism traditions, 168-169
Hong Kong law perspectives, 182-184
Hong Kong Queer Film Festival, 184
Human Genome Project, 33-34
Human rights and sexuality (global
    perspectives). *See also under
    individual topics*
  Asian law, 141-162
  Australian law, 31-48
  CERSGOSIG (Center of Research
    and Legal Comparative
    Studies on Sexual Orientation
    and Gender Identity), 3-8
  comparative law, 227-232
  European law, 49-90, 107-139
    sexuality rights, 107-139
    transsexual rights, 49-90
  ILGLaw (International Lesbian and
    Gay Law Association), 1-2
  international law, 9-29
  North American law, 91-106
  overviews and summaries,
    xvii-xviii
  South African law, 141-162
Human Rights/Sexual Conduct Act
    (Australia), 35-36
Human Rights Watch, 23-24
Humsafar Trust, 175
Hurford, C., 41

ICCPR (International Covenant on
    Civil and Political Rights),
    11-12, 16-23, 35, 109-110
Identity (gender), 91-106
ILGA (International Lesbian and Gay
    Association), 23-24, 177, 190
ILGHRC (International Lesbian and
    Gay Human Rights
    Commission), 23-24, 170-177

ILGLaw (International Lesbian and
    Gay Law Association), 1-2, 6
  background and historical
    perspectives, 1-2, 6
  future perspectives, 2
  overviews and summaries, 1
  reference resources, 2
Indecent Representation of Women
    Act (India), 174-175
Indian law perspectives, 171-175
Indonesian Gay and Lesbian
    Conference, 202
InformaGay, 4-5
Information databanks, 5-6
Inter-American Commission on
    Human Rights, 15
International Bar Association, 23-24
International Chinese Comrades
    Organization, 182
International Commission on Civil
    Status, 69-72
International Convention on
    Economic, Social and
    Cultural Rights, 109-110
International Covenant on Civil and
    Political Rights (ICCPR),
    11-12, 16-23, 35, 109-110
International human rights standards,
    10-12
International law perspectives, 9-29
  background and historical
    perspectives, 9-15
  current status, 20-22
  Equity in Common Law Systems,
    25
  functional symbiosis, 20
  future perspectives, 22-25
  international human rights
    standards, 10-12
  meaning-structure resolutions,
    15-20
  overviews and summaries, 9-10
  reality-dream dichotomies, 12-15
  reference resources, 25-29

International Lesbian and Gay
   Association (ILGA), 23-24,
   177,190
International Lesbian and Gay Human
   Rights Commission
   (ILGHRC), 23-24,170-177
International Lesbian and Gay Law
   Association (ILGLaw), 1-2,6
Islam influences, 168,188,194-195

Japanese Human Rights Commission,
   210
Japanese law perspectives, 208-212
Jin-yen, J., 185-186
Joslin et al. *v* New Zealand,
   17-18,21-23
Judeo-Christian influences, 33-35,
   93-94,101-103,142-143,172,
   209

KHU (Korean Homosexual Union),
   207
Kiatbhusaba, P., 189-190
Kirby, M., 31-48
Kiri Kiri, 207
Korean Homosexual Union (KHU),
   207
Korean Queer Festival, 208

Lam, E., 186
Lambda Indonesia, 202
Langan *v* St. Vincent's Hospital, 98
Langemaat, Y., 143-145
Langemaat *v* Minister of Safety and
   Security and Others, 150-151
Laotian law perspectives, 190
Lasky, Jaggard and Brown *v* United
   Kingdom, 19-20
Laurent, E., 163-225
Lavender Law Conference, 2
Law Reform Club, 148

Lawrence *v* Texas, 94,229-230
Laws and legislation. *See also under
   individual topics*
   Adoption of Children Act (New
      South Wales, Australia),
      37-39
   Aliens Control Act (South Africa),
      154
   Asian law perspectives, 141-162
   Australian law perspectives, 31-48
   CERSGOSIG (Center of Research
      and Legal Comparative
      Studies on Sexual Orientation
      and Gender Identity), 3-8
   comparative law perspectives,
      227-232
   Constitution Act (Canada), 98-99
   Copyright Act (India), 174-175
   Criminal Procedure Act (South
      Africa), 146-147
   De Facto Relationship Act (New
      South Wales, Australia),
      39-40
   Defense of Marriage Act (United
      States), 97
   Evidence Act (New South Wales,
      Australia), 37-39
   Human Rights/Sexual Conduct Act
      (Australia), 35-36
   ILGLaw (International Lesbian and
      Gay Law Association), 1-2
   Indecent Representation of Women
      Act (India), 174-175
   international law perspectives, 9-29
   Marriage Act (New Zealand), 18
   Modernization of Benefits and
      Obligations Act (Canada), 99
   National Security Act (India),
      174-175
   National Sexual Offenses Act
      (South Africa), 145-146
   Norris *v* Ireland, 14-15
   North American law perspectives,
      91-106

overviews and summaries,
xvii-xviii
Property/Relationships Amendment
Act (New South Wales,
Australia), 39-40
Rent Act (New Zealand), 34-35
Same-Sex
Relationships/Compassional
Circumstances Bill (New
South Wales, Australia),
38-39
Security Officers Act (South
Africa), 146-147
South African law perspectives,
141-162
Stamp Duties Act (New South
Wales, Australia), 37-39
Superannunciation Act (Australia),
36-37
Workers' Compensation
Legislation Amendment Act
(New South Wales,
Australia), 40
Workplace Relations Act
(Australia), 44-45
Youth Protection Law (South
Korea), 206
Legal cases. *See* Court cases
Legal environment influences, 32-35
Legal global perspectives (sexuality
and human rights). *See also
under individual topics*
Asian law, 141-162
Australian law, 31-48
CERSGOSIG (Center of Research
and Legal Comparative
Studies on Sexual Orientation
and Gender Identity), 3-8
comparative law, 227-232
European law, 49-90,107-139
sexuality rights, 107-139
transsexual rights, 49-90
ILGLaw (International Lesbian and
Gay Law Association), 1-2
international law, 9-29

North American law, 91-106
overviews and summaries,
xvii-xviii
South African law, 141-162
Legal information databanks, 5-6
Lesbian and Gay Alliance Against
Discrimination in Korea, 207
Lesbond, 204
Liberal democracies processes,
229-230
Library Foundation, 204
Link, 204
Louw, R., 141-162
Loux, E., 6

M. *v* H., 99-100
Malaysian law perspectives, 193-196
Marriage Act (New Zealand), 18
Meaning-structure resolutions, 15-20
Mehta, D., 174
Merin, Y., 6
Modernization of Benefits and
Obligations Act (Canada), 99
Modos *v* Cyprus, 14-15
Mohammed, M., 166
Mongolian law perspectives, 178-179
Myburgh, B., 143-145

National Aids Foundation, 179
National Coalition for Gay and
Lesbian Equality (NCGLE),
143-155
National Gay Conference, 177
National Lesbian Rights Conference,
205
National Security Act (India), 174-175
National Sexual Offenses Act (South
Africa), 145-146
Naz Foundation, 175,178
NCGLE (National Coalition for Gay
and Lesbian Equality),
143-155

NCGLE (National Coalition for Gay and Lesbian Equality) v Minister of Home Affairs, 151-152
Nepal law perspectives, 177
Nepal Queer Society, 177
NGOs (non-governmental organizations), 4-5,23, 173-174,189-190,199-200, 204
Nkoli, S., 148
Non-governmental organizations (NGOs), 4-5,23,173-174, 189-190,199-200,204
Norris v Ireland, 14-15
North American law perspectives, 91-106
  background and historical perspectives, 92-103
  Canada, 98-103
  comparative law, 91-106
  future perspectives, 103-104
  Judeo-Christian influences, 93-94, 101-103
  overviews and summaries, 91-92
  reference resources, 104-106
  United States, 92-98

Oetomo, D., 167
Offenses Against the Person Ordinance (Hong Kong), 183
Offord, B., 214
OLGA (Organisation of Lesbian and Gay Activists), 148-149
O'Regan, J., 157
Organisation of Lesbian and Gay Activists (OLGA), 148-149
Overviews and summaries. See also under individual topics
  Asian law perspectives, 163-165
  Australian law perspectives, 31-32
  CERSGOSIG (Center of Research and Legal Comparative Studies on Sexual Orientation and Gender Identity), 3-4
  comparative law perspectives, 227-228
  European law perspectives, 49-66, 107-108
    sexuality rights, 107-108
    transsexual rights, 49-66
  general topics, xvii-xviii
  ILGLaw (International Lesbian and Gay Law Association), 1
  international law perspectives, 9-10
  North American law perspectives, 91-92
  South African law perspectives, 141-143

People Like Us (PLU), 198-199
Philippine Commission on Human Rights, 204
Philippines law perspectives, 202-205
Pink Triangle, 196
PLU (People Like Us), 198-199
Power, P., 33-34
Progressive values, 228
Property/Relationships Amendment Act (New South Wales, Australia), 39-40

Queer Sisters, 184

R v Tan, 59-60
Rainbow Outdoor Fair, 186
Rajabat Institute Council, 188
RAM (annual migration programme), 41-42
Reality-dream dichotomies, 12-15
Reed, R., 49-90
Rees v the United Kingdom, 66-69
Reference resources. See also under individual topics

Asian law perspectives, 215-225
Australian law perspectives, 46-48
CERSGOSIG (Center of Research and Legal Comparative Studies on Sexual Orientation and Gender Identity), 7
comparative law perspectives, 232
ILGLaw (International Lesbian and Gay Law Association), 2
international law perspectives, 25-29
North American law perspectives, 104-106
South African law perspectives, 158-162
Refugees Convention, 42-43
Religious influences, 171-209
 Asian law perspectives, 171-209
 Buddhism, 175-178,180-189, 205-209
 Calvinism, 142-143
 Catholic Church, 33-35
 Confucianism, 168,179-180, 196-197,205,214
 Hinduism, 171-178
 Islam, 168,188,194-195
 Judeo-Christian, 33-35,93-94, 101-103,142-143
 Judeo-Christian issues, 172,209
 Taoism, 184
Rent Act (New Zealand), 34-35
Rodem, 207
Roe v Wade, 94
Romer v Evans, 94-96

Same sex marriage issues, 153-155
Same-Sex Relationships/Compassional Circumstances Bill (New South Wales, Australia), 38-39
San Francisco Gay and Lesbian Film Festival, 182
Scalia, A., 94-95
Schieder, P., 6

Security Officers Act (South Africa), 146-147
Seoul Queer Film and Video Festival, 206-207
Service Members Legal Defense Network, 95
Sexual rights as human rights concept, 110-111
Sexuality and human rights (global perspectives). *See also under individual topics*
 Asian law, 141-162
 Australian law, 31-48
 CERSGOSIG (Center of Research and Legal Comparative Studies on Sexual Orientation and Gender Identity), 3-8
 comparative law, 227-232
 European law, 49-90,107-139
  sexuality rights, 107-139
  transsexual rights, 49-90
 ILGLaw (International Lesbian and Gay Law Association), 1-2
 international law, 9-29
 North American law, 91-106
 overviews and summaries, xvii-xviii
 South African law, 141-162
Shaw, J.W., 38-39
SHE (Society Homosexual Encounter), 204
Sheffield and Horsham v The United Kingdom, 17,76-79
Singapore law perspectives, 196-199
Skidmore, P., 6
Society Homosexual Encounter (SHE), 204
South African law perspectives, 141-162
 background and historical perspectives, 143-145
 challenges, 143-145
 decriminalization issues, 145-150
 family law issues, 150-153
 future perspectives, 156-158

overviews and summaries, 141-143
reference resources, 158-162
same sex marriage issues, 153-155
South Korea law perspectives, 205-208
Spielberg, S., 96
Sri Lanka Press Council, 176-177
Sri Lankan Gay Friends, 176-177
Stamp Duties Act (New South Wales, Australia), 37-39
Standards-related issues, 10-12
Structure-meaning resolutions, 15-20
Summary topics. *See* Overviews and summaries
Superannunciation Act (Australia), 36-37
Symbiosis (functional), 20

Tahmindjis, P., xvii-xviii, 6,9-29,227-232
Taiwan Gay and Lesbian Human Rights Association, 185-186
Taiwan Gay Hotline, 185
Taiwan Gay Parade Festival, 186
Tan, B.A., 193
Taoism influences, 184
Tavilan, 179
Thai law perspectives, 187-190
Thai Rak Tahi party, 188
Thomassen, W., 2
To, C., 167,184
Toit *v* Minister of Population and Welfare Department, 151
Tongzhi Conference, 181,184
Tongzhi Culture Society, 183
Tongzhi Movement, 183-184
Toniollo, M.G., 6
Toonen *v* Australia, 12-13,19-23,35
Transsexual rights, 49-90
Treaty of Nice, 15
Turner, R., 39

United Kingdom law perspectives, 56-60
United Nations perspectives, 22-36,173,206-207
  Commission on Human Rights, 23-24,173
  Conference on Racism, Racial Discrimination, Xenophobia and Related Intolerance, 23-24
  Economic and Social Council, 23-24
  High Commissioner for Refugees, 22-23
  Human Rights Committee, 34-36
  UNESCO, 206-207
  World Conference on Human Rights, 23-24
United States law perspectives, 92-98
Universal Declaration of Human Rights, 10-12,98,109-110
Universal human rights, 165-166, 230-231

Van Oosterwijck *v* Belgium, 63-66
Van Rooyen *v* Van Rooyen, 144-145, 150-151
Vietnamese law perspectives, 191-193

Waaldijk, K., 6
West German law perspectives, 60-62
Western model influences, 165-167
  overviews and summaries, 166-167
  universal human rights, 165-166
Weyembergh, A., 6
Wintemute, R., 6
Wolfenden Report, 32-35,98
Wolfson, E., 97
Women Chih Chian, 185
Women's Support Group, 176-177
Workers' Compensation Legislation Amendment Act (New South Wales, Australia), 40
Workplace Relations Act (Australia), 44-45
Written law influences, 109-110
Wu, G., 182

X, Y, & Z *v* The United Kingdom,
 17, 73-76

Yew, L.K., 166
Youth Protection Law (South Korea),
 206
Ytterberg, H., 6
Yu, L., 182

Monographs "Separates" list continued

Male Intergenerational Intimacy: Historical, Socio-Psychological, and Legal Perspectives, edited by Theo G. M. Sandfort, PhD, Edward Brongersma, JD, and A. X. van Naerssen, PhD (Vol. 20, No. 1/2, 1991). *"The most important book on the subject since Tom O'Carroll's 1980 Paedophilia: The Radical Case." (The North American Man/Boy Love Association Bulletin, May 1991)*

Love Letters Between a Certain Late Nobleman and the Famous Mr. Wilson, edited by Michael S. Kimmel, PhD (Vol. 19, No. 2, 1990). *"An intriguing book about homosexuality in 18th-Century England. Many details of the period, such as meeting places, coded language, and 'camping' are all covered in the book. If you're a history buff, you'll enjoy this one." (Prime Timers)*

Homosexuality and Religion, edited by Richard Hasbany, PhD (Vol. 18, No. 3/4, 1990). *"A welcome resource that provides historical and contemporary views on many issues involving religious life and homosexuality." (Journal of Sex Education and Therapy)*

Homosexuality and the Family, edited by Frederick W. Bozett, PhD (Vol. 18, No. 1/2, 1989). *"Enlightening and answers a host of questions about the effects of homosexuality upon family members and the family as a unit." (Ambush Magazine)*

Gay and Lesbian Youth, edited by Gilbert Herdt, PhD (Vol. 17, No. 1/2/3/4, 1989). *"Provides a much-needed compilation of research dealing with homosexuality and adolescents." (GLTF Newsletter)*

Lesbians Over 60 Speak for Themselves, edited by Monika Kehoe, PhD (Vol. 16, No. 3/4, 1989). *"A pioneering book examining the social, economical, physical, sexual, and emotional lives of aging lesbians." (Feminist Bookstore News)*

The Pursuit of Sodomy: Male Homosexuality in Renaissance and Enlightenment Europe, edited by Kent Gerard, PhD, and Gert Hekma, PhD (Vol. 16, No. 1/2, 1989). *"Presenting a wealth of information in a compact form, this book should be welcomed by anyone with an interest in this period in European history or in the precursors to modern concepts of homosexuality." (The Canadian Journal of Human Sexuality)*

Psychopathology and Psychotherapy in Homosexuality, edited by Michael W. Ross, PhD (Vol. 15, No. 1/2, 1988). *"One of the more objective, scientific collections of articles concerning the mental health of gays and lesbians. . . . Extraordinarily thoughtful. . . . New thoughts about treatments. Vital viewpoints." (The Book Reader)*

Psychotherapy with Homosexual Men and Women: Integrated Identity Approaches for Clinical Practice, edited by Eli Coleman, PhD (Vol. 14, No. 1/2, 1987). *"An invaluable tool. . . . This is an extremely useful book for the clinician seeking better ways to understand gay and lesbian patients." (Hospital and Community Psychiatry)*

Interdisciplinary Research on Homosexuality in The Netherlands, edited by A. X. van Naerssen, PhD (Vol. 13, No. 2/3, 1987). *"Valuable not just for its insightful analysis of the evolution of gay rights in The Netherlands, but also for the lessons that can be extracted by our own society from the Dutch tradition of tolerance for homosexuals." (The San Francisco Chronicle)*

Historical, Literary, and Erotic Aspects of Lesbianism, edited by Monica Kehoe, PhD (Vol. 12, No. 3/4, 1986). *"Fascinating. . . . Even though this entire volume is serious scholarship penned by degreed writers, most of it is vital, accessible, and thoroughly readable even to the casual student of lesbian history." (Lambda Rising)*

Anthropology and Homosexual Behavior, edited by Evelyn Blackwood, PhD (cand.) (Vol. 11, No. 3/4, 1986). *"A fascinating account of homosexuality during various historical periods and in non-Western cultures." (SIECUS Report)*

Bisexualities: Theory and Research, edited by Fritz Klein, MD, and Timothy J. Wolf, PhD (Vol. 11, No. 1/2, 1985). *"The editors have brought together a formidable array of new data challenging old stereotypes about a very important human phenomenon. . . . A milestone in furthering our knowledge about sexual orientation." (David P. McWhirter, Co-author, The Male Couple)*

Homophobia: An Overview, edited by John P. De Cecco, PhD (Vol. 10, No. 1/2, 1984). *"Breaks ground in helping to make the study of homophobia a science." (Contemporary Psychiatry)*

Bisexual and Homosexual Identities: Critical Clinical Issues, edited by John P. De Cecco, PhD (Vol. 9, No. 4, 1985). *Leading experts provide valuable insights into sexual identity within a clinical context–broadly defined to include depth psychology, diagnostic classification, therapy, and psychomedical research on the hormonal basis of homosexuality.*

Bisexual and Homosexual Identities: Critical Theoretical Issues, edited by John P. De Cecco, PhD, and Michael G. Shively, MA (Vol. 9, No. 2/3, 1984). *"A valuable book . . . The careful scholarship, analytic rigor, and lucid exposition of virtually all of these essays make them thought-provoking and worth more than one reading." (Sex Roles, A Journal of Research)*

Homosexuality and Social Sex Roles, edited by Michael W. Ross, PhD (Vol. 9, No. 1, 1983). *"For a comprehensive review of the literature in this domain, exposure to some interesting methodological models, and a glance at 'older' theories undergoing contemporary scrutiny, I recommend this book." (Journal of Sex Education & Therapy)*

Literary Visions of Homosexuality, edited by Stuart Kellogg, PhD (Vol. 8, No. 3/4, 1985). *"An important book. Gay sensibility has never been given such a boost." (The Advocate)*

Alcoholism and Homosexuality, edited by Thomas O. Ziebold, PhD, and John E. Mongeon (Vol. 7, No. 4, 1985). *"A landmark in the fields of both alcoholism and homosexuality . . . a very lush work of high caliber." (The Journal of Sex Research)*

Homosexuality and Psychotherapy: A Practitioner's Handbook of Affirmative Models, edited by John C. Gonsiorek, PhD (Vol. 7, No. 2/3, 1985). *"A book that seeks to create affirmative psychotherapeutic models. . . . To say this book is needed by all doing therapy with gay or lesbian clients is an understatement." (The Advocate)*

Nature and Causes of Homosexuality: A Philosophic and Scientific Inquiry, edited by Noretta Koertge, PhD (Vol. 6, No. 4, 1982). *"An interesting, thought-provoking book, well worth reading as a corrective to much of the research literature on homosexuality." (Australian Journal of Sex, Marriage & Family)*

Historical Perspectives on Homosexuality, edited by Salvatore J. Licata, PhD, and Robert P. Petersen, PhD (cand.) (Vol. 6, No. 1/2, 1986). *"Scholarly and excellent. Its authority is impeccable, and its treatment of this neglected area exemplary." (Choice)*

Homosexuality and the Law, edited by Donald C. Knutson, PhD (Vol. 5, No. 1/2, 1979). *A comprehensive analysis of current legal issues and court decisions relevant to male and female homosexuality.*

BOOK ORDER FORM!

Order a copy of this book with this form or online at:
http://www.haworthpress.com/store/product.asp?sku=5493

Sexuality and Human Rights
A Global Overview

____ in softbound at $29.95 ISBN: 1-56023-555-1.
____ in hardbound at $49.95 ISBN: 1-56023-554-3.

COST OF BOOKS _____

❑ BILL ME LATER:
Bill-me option is good on US/Canada/Mexico orders only; not good to jobbers, wholesalers, or subscription agencies.

POSTAGE & HANDLING _____
US: $4.00 for first book & $1.50 for each additional book
Outside US: $5.00 for first book & $2.00 for each additional book.

❑ Signature _____

❑ Payment Enclosed: $ _____

SUBTOTAL _____
In Canada: add 7% GST. _____

❑ PLEASE CHARGE TO MY CREDIT CARD:
❑ Visa ❑ MasterCard ❑ AmEx ❑ Discover
❑ Diner's Club ❑ Eurocard ❑ JCB

STATE TAX _____
CA, IL, IN, MN, NJ, NY, OH, PA & SD residents please add appropriate local sales tax.

Account # _____

FINAL TOTAL _____
If paying in Canadian funds, convert using the current exchange rate.
UNESCO coupons welcome.

Exp Date _____

Signature _____
(Prices in US dollars and subject to change without notice.)

PLEASE PRINT ALL INFORMATION OR ATTACH YOUR BUSINESS CARD

Name		
Address		
City	State/Province	Zip/Postal Code
Country		
Tel		Fax
E-Mail		

May we use your e-mail address for confirmations and other types of information? ❑ Yes ❑ No We appreciate receiving your e-mail address. Haworth would like to e-mail special discount offers to you, as a preferred customer.
We will never share, rent, or exchange your e-mail address. We regard such actions as an invasion of your privacy.

Order from your **local bookstore** or directly from
The Haworth Press, Inc. 10 Alice Street, Binghamton, New York 13904-1580 • USA
Call our toll-free number (1-800-429-6784) / Outside US/Canada: (607) 722-5857
Fax: 1-800-895-0582 / Outside US/Canada: (607) 771-0012
E-mail your order to us: orders@haworthpress.com

For orders outside **US and Canada,** you may wish to order through your local sales representative, distributor, or bookseller.
For information, see http://haworthpress.com/distributors

(Discounts are available for individual orders in US and Canada only, not booksellers/distributors.)
Please photocopy this form for your personal use.
www.HaworthPress.com

BOF05